FUNDAMENTALS OF STORY LOGIC

SEMIOTIC CROSSROADS

General Editor

Paul Perron
University of Toronto

Associate Editors

Paolo Fabbri
Eric Landowski
Herman Parret

Editorial Board:

Volume 5

Therese Budniakiewicz

Fundamentals of Story Logic
Introduction to Greimassian Semiotics

FUNDAMENTALS OF STORY LOGIC

INTRODUCTION TO GREIMASSIAN SEMIOTICS

by

THERESE BUDNIAKIEWICZ

JOHN BENJAMINS PUBLISHING COMPANY
AMSTERDAM/PHILADELPHIA

1992

Library of Congress Cataloging-in-Publication Data

Budniakiewicz, Therese.
  Fundamentals of story logic : introduction to Greimassian semiotics / by Therese Bud-
niakiewicz.
     p.   cm. -- (Semiotic crossroads, ISSN 0922-5072; v. 5)
  Includes bibliographical references.
  1. Semiotics--France. 2. Greimas, Algirdas Julien. I. Title. II. Series.
P99.37.F8B93   1992
302.2--dc20   92-22978
ISBN 90 272 1946 X (Eur.)/1-55619-339-4 (US) (alk. paper)   CIP

John Benjamins Publishing Co. · P.O. Box 75577 · 1070 AN Amsterdam · The Netherlands
John Benjamins North America · 821 Bethlehem Pike · Philadelphia, PA 19118 · USA

Contents

La preuve de l'analyse est dans la synthèse.

(The proof of the analysis is in the synthesis.)

CLAUDE LÉVI-STRAUSS

Foreword: Fundamentals of Story Logic or Semiotics at the Crossroads

Henri Quéré

Université de Paris III - La Nouvelle Sorbonne

One way of assessing the meaning and scope of a book of this nature is to apply to it, in reflexive fashion, the very formula which it uses as one of its main lines of argument. This formula, which takes the shape of a 'practical syllogism or inference,' runs as follows:

Major premise: N wants to do O.

Minor premise: N considers that he cannot do O unless he does P.

Conclusion: Therefore, N sets himself to do P.

Viewed in this way, the author's purpose may be described by means of two interrelated questions: what does this book set out to do? and how does it get there?

In fact, being about fundamentals, the present book serves a double purpose. In a first sense, it refers to what is basic in the theory itself and, as a kind of *Grundrisse*, it lays bare a few essentials leading to further specifications. In a second sense, it involves the kind of groundwork that is needed to provide a sound basis and firm foundation for the whole theoretical construction. As such, its critical bent exerts itself positively rather than negatively and in a highly constructive way. Drawing largely on Propp's pioneering work and on Greimas' revised version of the same, the whole book is aimed at consolidating their view of the narrative and at extending it through a series of concrete applications.

This comment, in turn, suggests that the book's method and achievement have to be measured against their own self-imposed limitations. What is at stake is the kind of logic that underlies the story as such, in terms of its gradual unfolding and programmed development. Here again, the study branches off in two distinct directions, so that, instead of stories, we should perhaps speak of the story-as-form, a notion which implies both a certain type of formally conceived logical organization and the kind of effect pragmatically identified as the 'storiness' of stories.

Being about fundamentals, the book is also, in a deeper and at the same time more general sense, a book about history and logic. It is about history insofar as it sets out to retrace the various stages in the development of Greimas' theory of the narrative, from its first tentative moves down to some halted point in its evolution. It is about logic in that it focuses on the kind of necessity that binds together the various links in the chain, from the initial premises to the ensuing conclusions. This necessity is distinctly dual. On the one hand, it bears upon the internal coherence of the model itself, that is, with the way in which its later propositions naturally follow from its basic theoretical assumptions. And, on the other hand, it reflects the kind of intrinsic logic that is at work in the story itself once it is viewed in terms of the proposed model. Those are the two aspects which the book examines in succession and which we would like to discuss next.

It is well known that the attempt to ascribe a precise origin to any given theory always proves difficult, even in cases when the theory itself explicitly refers to what it sees as its starting point. In the present instance, it appears that, along with Tesnière's actantial grammar and with Propp's *Morphology of the Folktale*, Greimassian semiotics owes much to the work of such influential figures as, say, Hjelmslev or Benveniste, although perhaps Greimas himself would not be prepared to concede to it. Furthermore, in the present book, we are actually working from two starting points, since the study may be said to move backward from some halted stage in the development of the theory towards its supposed linguistic-semantic sources of inspiration. To borrow a phrase from Foucault, this kind of 'archeology of knowledge' is, in fact, something that has to be repeated over and over again, since we are dealing with a work in progress whose renewed shifts and gradual reshaping may be viewed as a form of self-organization that is only partially controlled.

Such, then, is the mutable background against which the present study is made to stand out. Basically, the question is this: how much does Greimas' own view of the narrative owe to its professed principles and motives? Or, in other words, to what extent does it follow from what logically and chronologically precedes it and also what predictions can be made on this basis? The interesting thing here is the rationalization that takes place, as it were, after the event and which shows that perhaps the theory does not quite agree with its own self-conceived image. What is at stake, in this as in other similar cases, is the degree of self-awareness achieved by a theory, an awareness that is evinced by its own claims to a specific kind of ancestry. The gist of the matter here is to show that the initial statements and the first groping gestures amount to a typically 'false' or waylaid consciousness which has to be replaced by a better, more enlightened vision of the theory's pattern of development. Most assuredly, this raises the issue of the kind of logical reconstruction that is called upon to replace the former 'mistaken' one.

In this phase which is also the initial phase, the book may be said to work simultaneously in two different ways: first by discussing and, where needed, by discarding the premises which do not lead to the required conclusions, and then by providing an alternative foundation in the shape of a *sui generis* kind of logic based on 'the practical syllogism of action' and on 'its inversion as a teleological explanation.' The 'pattern of practical reasoning' that underlies both the analysis of the role relationships and of the textual unfolding of action appears as an empirically grounded principle of derivation which is quite in line with the tradition of American thinking and which stands in sharp contrast with the more abstract «hypothetico-deductive» mode of approach favored by Greimas and his followers here in Europe and culminating in the stratified model known as the 'generative path.'

There is a kind of Jamesian flavor attached to this geographical or even, one might say, ethnocentric distinction between diversely rooted epistemological positions and frames of reference. In the present case, it seems as if the aims and termination of the story were endowed with two different meanings. Within the framework of the practical reasoning process and teleological type of explanation, the 'end' of the story is viewed as that towards which everything is made to tend through a renewed process of entailment, whereas, according to Greimas' view of the syntagmatic development, the 'end' is that from which we start in order to reach the (logical) beginning through a series of presuppositions. This raises the question whether there are several kinds of logic which are possible here and whether they may apply simultaneously or successively. In fact, it seems as if we are dealing with two kinds of logic: a logic *of* development, resting on such notions as those of intentionality, of purpose and finality that guarantee the ultimate coherence of the story and its description, and another logic—logic *as* development—of which the syntagmatic model of the 'canonical narrative schema' would stand as the outspread, fully extended theoretical counterpart.

We now come to the second part of the book which is devoted to a critical examination of narrative structure in terms of its two basic syntactic units or sets of operations, namely the 'evental or dynamic configurations corresponding to communication or to contract or, more generally, to the structure of exchange.' At this point, what should be stressed is that the whole work of reconstruction is focused on a linear, goal-oriented view of the narrative process and on a kind of progressive, forward-looking necessity that should normally lead to predictions or at least authorize a view of the story in terms of calculated moves and formally established predictability. Here again, in this deep concern for practical results and measurable steps, we can find a trace of the pragmatic turn of mind and empiricist bent, previously illustrated by the action-oriented mode of reasoning. This way of 'generating' the story is definitely—and perhaps also rightly—in line with some notions which are to be found in the field of cognitive science and artificial intelligence, such as, for instance, those of scripts and frames.

By comparison to the above, the kind of necessity that Greimas—rightly or wrongly—seems to favor is more readily of the retrogressive type, whereby the story looks backward towards its programmed inception and ensuing developments. The so-called 'Manipulation' which sets the story going (with, for instance, the contract set up between the Sender and the subject actant) is, in fact, but an inverted replica of the final 'Sanction' which is not only what provides the narrative with its logical termination, but also what gives the story its full significance. The kind of retrogressive 'presuppositional' logic represented by the fully developed narrative schema (Manipulation – Action – Sanction) also applies recursively through hypotactic relationships and other such nesting or embedding procedures. This pliability of the model is, for example, what enables us to account for the kind of narratives which fall within the scope of the contractual process (typologically, they are stories of—that is, about— manipulation) and also for such empirical phenomena as the condensation or, conversely, the amplification of narrative discourses.

Owing to the stress it lays on the logical frame and built-in necessity that underlie the syntagmatic dimension of the story, the present book might be viewed not so much as a post-Proppian, post-Greimassian reconstruction and

theoretical advance as, perhaps, a neo-Proppian «relogification» and improve-
ment of the existing proposals leading to an integrated descriptive model
deliberately and also, one might add, restrictively centered on 'narrative semiotics as a branch of descriptive poetics.' (Hence, for instance, the author's concern
with literary works of fiction and specifically here with Nathanael West's *Miss
Lonelyhearts*.) In this sense, the author's own proposals are turned as it were
backward towards a theoretical foundation that is both re-found and re-founded
and which should provide us with a methodology of textual analysis whose scope
extends to include hermeneutics and interpretation. At the same time, through
the analysis it makes of the 'contractual and communication events,' the book
is led to lay the stress on their sociological aspects and philosophical implications. In particular, it demonstrates convincingly that the basic components of
narrative structure 'involve the element of promise, trust and morality [...]
regulating interaction.' Hence, for instance, the correlated notions of the legal
subject and of the object of right. What is interesting then, is that, although it
confines itself to a first stage and limited period in the history of semiotics, the
study prophetically guesses the growing importance to be taken later in the
theory by such things as 'value' as well as 'belief and believing.' Value, in fact,
now stands as the basic axiom on which the whole theoretical construction is
made to rest and from which it stems: it permeates the original 'thymic' moves
and presides over its further articulations; it helps define the subject/object
relationship and, indeed, it accounts for the whole modal organization as it was
first sketched out by Greimas in his seminal article, "Toward a Theory of
Modalities." Furthermore, as is clearly shown here, it is firmly rooted in society
and its laws and it is closely related to what motivates and what regulates
interpersonal dealings. In a way, the discussion of value in its social and legal
context brings to light and, at the same time, brings back to mind the links
between the theory of narrative and its anthropological sources.
    A last series of remarks that we would like to make concerns itself with the
kind of rewriting to which narrative semiotics happens to be submitted here.
The question is: are there several alternative ways of retracing the theory's
historical development and of rebuilding its logical unfolding? One way of
looking at semiotics—the one that is practiced here—is to see it moving backward
towards its origins, the better to ensure that it rests on proper foundations and
that, starting from there, it develops soundly to provide all the necessary equip-
ment. Another way of looking at it is to see it moving *away* from its supposed

origins and gradually freeing itself from all that ties it up to its first tentative formulations. What is at stake, here, is the continuous process of reshaping and refashioning which the theory—or any theory, for that matter—is bound to undergo in the course of its own progressive development. This evolution process or even, at times, 'blind' rearrangement (an issue which is reminiscent of contemporary theories characterized by a certain complexity and of the kind of logic at work in the various forms of self-organization) leads us to reflect on the 'impure' nature of theoretical constructs, on their mixed or even muddled mode of existence in which we find both traces of previous states and the seeds of as yet unformulated or even unsuspected future developments. As suggested earlier, not only should the critical work of appraisal be carried out repeatedly as the theory keeps moving on, but also, at each one of its halted stages, the latter typically requires the kind of backward and forward-looking 'symptomal' deciphering that Louis Althusser once applied to Marx's early writings.

Over the course of time, what we were able to witness was truly a rearrangement of semiotic theory carried on or rather taking place along two main lines. On the one hand, the research work and the ensuing systematization were successively brought to bear on what now appears, in retrospect, as four distinctive phases which, in their present integrated form, respectively constitute the sequential, actantial, modal and, finally, aspectual components of the model. On the other hand, but also, one might say, at the same time, the whole construction was, as it were, re-oriented so as to produce the paradigmatic structure known as the 'generative path' in which the syntagmatic mode of organization and its projection into narrative discourse would be included as parts of the overall syntactic component. Besides illustrating the way in which the stages in a history and the logic of a system happen to combine, this evolution also points towards a gradual process of abstraction through which the theory may be said to have moved still further away from its strictly 'story-like' origins. As it now stands, semiotic theory aims at encompassing all kinds of meaningful phenomena (it was seen to move from the study of action to that of passion and it is now breaking new semiotic ground with the stress laid on perception and sensation), and it is this cumulative process of abstraction and generalization which explains why the present book's strict concern with story logic required a kind of turning back to a former stage when the preoccupation with the story-as-form was still prominent.

At the beginning of the book, the author states her hope that this kind of work will 'continue to promote an orientation to literary studies advanced by Greimas' and, of course, the first thing to do is to thank her for the very convincing and highly perfected way in which the present book contributes to the spreading of the «good word» in spite of all the obstacles raised by the distance in time and space and also by the challenge of bilingual thinking. Moreover, by putting the theory in perspective while carefully testing its premises, the book opens up large vistas of the utmost epistemological importance. Thus, for instance, weighty questions such as these: how do logic and history combine to produce those mutable sets and ever-changing constructions that go by the name of theories? And, speaking about fundamentals, what kind of future can we predict for a theory by examining and, as in the present case, reactivating what once was its past? What kind of renewed life may emerge from such a rebirth?

Introduction

1. The field of semiotics and the tradition of the Paris School of semiotics

The semiotic field is broad and covers a number of different intellectual traditions and several dynamic centers of activity. Two such geographical centers represent the two major and opposing traditions in semiotics: Greimassian semiotics in France and Peircean semiotics in the U.S. The locale, however, is an indication of an institutional center which sustains the activity in the city or region and charters it beyond, forming prismatic chapters in all the corners of the globe. French semiotics is done in the U.S. and in the English-speaking world just as American semiotics is done in France and in the French-speaking world.

Even though the works of C. S. Peirce provide the U.S. semioticians with a uniquely American foundation, semiotic studies in the U.S. are strongly associated with the development of French structuralism in the 1960s and 1970s and its osmosis into American intellectual life in the 1970s and early 1980s. In this imported and naturalized sense, American semiotics is not differentiated from structuralism and is often identified with it. To take one humanistic discipline as example, literary semiotics in the 1990s "refuses to give to the word 'semiotics' the precise but too narrow meaning of Paris School semiotics" and "prefers the larger extension which includes all those attempts at elucidating meaning generated by structuralism" (G. Thérien 1990:9). Semiotics is thus perceived in its diversity and in its potential to incorporate a mosaic of existing theories and practices, as varied as the list of its practitioners: R. Barthes, C. Bremond, G. Genette, A. J. Greimas, the Paris School, T. Todorov, and many others. This multiplicity of semiotic perspectives together with the assessment that any single one is "too narrow," have led to the current call for the development of a semiotic epistemology which would account for the links between semiotics and literary studies and would also synthesize the mosaic of local and international contributions to semiotics (Jules-Rosette, Thérien). With the U.S. now designated as the host country for the Fifth International Congress of Semiotics the status of semiotics in America will acquire a new meaning and the place of the Paris School of semiotics will be ascertained in an epistemological synthesis of the discipline.

The titles of three recent books all published in 1989 give two different labels to the discipline of French semiotics. The two books in this collection choose the name of *Paris School Semiotics*, thus emphasizing that as a school it has a particular vision and a specific program of research. The third book is actually a special issue of the American journal, *New Literary History*, and the implicit assumption to its title *Greimassian Semiotics*, is to emphasize the thinker and author, A. J. Greimas, who created the discipline and whose writings inspired a *school* in the wider sense—the dispersed set of all writers who, in their practice, are united by virtue of their conditional allegiance to the same master and by a general similarity of principles, methods, or styles. Greimassian semiotics refers to a *school* or tradition of semiotics but it is ambiguous inasmuch that it could also refer impersonally to the works of Greimas himself. It is an oddity of American thought that it accepted certain original thinkers and charismatic shapers of structuralism and post-structuralism, like C. Lévi-Strauss, R. Barthes, G. Genette, J. Derrida, almost as mythical figures playing mythical roles in the shaping of the intellectual scene yet it is strangely reluctant to grant that role to A. J. Greimas, merely conceding to it at the height of literary structuralism in the 1970s.

The *Paris School of semiotics* was, in its period of popular dominance, a recognizable cluster of writers and ideas with a geographical and temporal locus, namely Paris at the end of the 1970s and in the 1980s. It was identified in France and in Europe with the "Semio-linguistic Research Group," sponsored by the École des Hautes Études en Sciences Sociales in Paris and the Centre National de la Recherche Scientifique (C.N.R.S.). In this sense, it is possible to see the *Paris School of semiotics* as a "movement" since it had the combination of doctrinal and social unity that term implies and which is missing in *Greimassian semiotics*. The Paris School had an institutional center which fostered this type of research and it had an official publication channel from 1979 to 1986, *Actes Sémiotiques*, initially edited by A. Hénault and later by E. Landowski, and from 1989 on, *Nouveaux Actes Sémiotiques*, edited by J. Fontanille and E.

Landowski, although these journals had and still have limited distribution abroad. Since the mid-1980s the geography of the Paris School burst through its parochial setting and emerged at other places so that a standard geography of the subject would include all the research affiliates in Europe, in the Americas and other continents. By transcending the locality of origin, the Paris School of semiotics has become the school of Greimassian semiotics in the wider sense.

The question of which label is more inclusive or international in scope is an arbitrary one since the discipline is one and the same, but it can, in all fairness, be provisionally evaluated by the representation of the researchers in the books considered. The articles chosen as representative of the *Paris School* were articles translated into English and originally published in *Actes Sémiotiques* over a period of eight years, from 1979 to 1986, primarily by French and Francophone researchers and none from North America or other continents. *Greimassian Semiotics*, as the profile of the *New Literary History* articles shows, by its representation, is slightly more international in scope. Half of the articles are translations of work carried out by Greimas and the Semio-linguistic Research Group, dating to the period of publication of *Actes Sémiotiques*, and the other half consisting of articles outside France, American and international semioticians.

2. The Paris School of semiotics in America

The event that brought French structuralism most vividly to the attention of the English-speaking world was the publication in 1966 of a translation of Lévi-Strauss' *La pensée sauvage*. The French original appeared just four years earlier in 1962.

It is well known that the fame and authority of Greimas derive from the publication in 1966 of his first book, *Sémantique structurale*. During this decade when semiotics was beginning to establish itself, Greimas' book stood out like a culmination and pinnacle of all previous attempts to produce a broad and systematic theory of meaning. "The impression it gave," says C. Segre "was that the new science was not still awaiting construction, but that it has already been constructed" (1989:685). And indeed the book has since then become 'a classic' of *scientific structuralism* the world over, a marker to indicate a new and different kind of human science in constant search and evolution. Unlike Lévi-

Strauss' book, it took almost two decades and a team of three translators for this 'classic' to appear in 1983 in an English translation, *Structural Semantics*. The research affiliates of the Paris School of semiotics outside of France had, in fact, to be bilingual in order to participate in that research project as it was emerging and unfolding in the 1970s and 1980s.

Academic literary structuralism achieved almost canonical status in the mid-1970s in what might be called its international form in a broad, introductory book by an American critic, J. Culler's *Structuralist Poetics* which devoted one chapter to Greimas. Since that time it has been a standard part of the landscape. With the impetus of structuralism, *narrative theory* became the hero of a triumphant international development and gained swift recognition under the aegis of S. Chatman's *Story and Discourse* (1978) and R. Scholes' *Semiotics and Interpretation* (1982).

Not until recently, when the major works of Greimas and the Paris School have been translated, most English readers will probably have encountered Greimassian semiotics not at first hand but through the commentaries of critics like R. Scholes, *Structuralism in Literature* (1974), J. Culler, *Structuralist Poetics* (1975), J. Calloud, *Structural Analysis of Narrative* (1976), T. Hawkes, *Structuralism and Semiotics* (1977) which provide a discussion of the contributions certain continental writers had made to the development of structuralism as an intellectual position.

The career of semiotics in America, of the movement which was influenced by French structuralism and poststructuralism, peaked in 1975 and went into an eclipse barely five or six years later. The only indication that it did not come to an end and was thriving behind the scenes was the unique publication of the first comprehensive survey in English by R. Schleifer of the major works of Greimas, entitled *A. J. Greimas and the Nature of Meaning* (1987), and the scattered enthusiasm of young and unpublished scholars working out of the mainstream. With this sole exception, it was a phase with which English readers scarcely had a chance to catch up before other critical approaches emerged which provided a greater continuity with their own dominant and long-established tradition of New Criticism. In the most influential variant of the Yale school of deconstructive criticism and in other variants—reader-response criticism, Marxist criticism, cultural studies, the new historicism—interpretation and close reading of particular texts still maintained priority over the conventions, generic codes and the more general as well as systematic aspects of literary discourse emphasized by structuralism and semiotics. In their concentration to make science out of theorizing literature, structuralism and semiotics appeared to be irreconcilable with the traditional role of interpretation central to Anglo-American criticism and, consequently, were pushed out of sight or, at least, out of the limelight. It was a phase of such short duration that gestation was not possible and the status of semiotics became passé in the American public eye, at about the same time when the international scene of semiotics began showing signs of problems. The Third International Congress of Semiotics, which almost did not take place, was marked by the attempt to redefine both the status of semiotics itself and its relation to other disciplines. The Plenary Lecture given by J. Pelc was 'A Plea for Semiotics' and it characterized the prevailing atmosphere in those days of June 25-29, 1984. As to the relation of semiotics to other disciplines, the organizers aimed at intensifying the dialogue not only with those disciplines traditionally considered to be contiguous or overlapping, but also with the whole range of natural sciences. (For the report on the Congress see Withalm.)

For the scholars who had accepted since the 1970s the gradual passage of literary studies from the tradition of fine arts or humanities to a new tradition, that of the human sciences—a change which some, like Thérien, see as marking the sudden rupture between the old and the new and creating a profound upheaval in literature—Greimas' *Sémantique structurale* was the single most ambitious beginning of a full-scale systematic method to characterize the meaning of the text. There were two drawbacks to this systematicity, one which was peculiar to the Greimassian semiotics and the other, unexpected, which swept the field of humanities and the social sciences like a sudden hurricane. The first one might be characterized as an irony of situation since the systematicity attracted imitators who were sycophants. As unpleasant as the situation was, Segre is right to recall that "in the wake of *Sémantique structurale*, a Greimassian *vulgata* came into being. The techniques of the master would be applied over and over again without any investigation of their bases, researchers accepting them uncritically, in block" (1989:685). As P. Perron says (1989:531), this is no longer the case not only because, as he cites, of the publication of the second semiotic dictionary (1986) which highlights the achievement of the collaborative and reflective nature of the enterprise, but also because external criticism of the 1980s denounced what it called the "myths" of objectivity, scientificity, and the relevance of formal methods in studying literature and other cultural phenomena. So the sycophants and the *vulgata* no longer had the surface reason for mindless applications.

As we entered the 1980s the linguistic lens also became the focus of internal and external skepticism together with an attack on "certain certainties" and the ideal of scientificity inspiring narratology and structuralism. Since narratology is at the heart of the Paris School of semiotics, we can see how the external sign of distress made towards semiotics in general manifested itself as an opposition to a particular semiotics of which the domain is well-defined and well-focused. Yet, it can be argued that criticism develops through argument and debate between different positions and that change is created not by pluralists but by those who identify uncompromisingly with a given position. The Paris School of semiotics, like other researchers who adopt a particular methodological orientation, are the ones who set the main terms for debate even where its claims are most vigorously contested—and the claims will be contested in direct proportion to the clarity and specificity of focus set by the given position. As with the problem of disciplinary relevance to which Jules-Rosette responded with a view that it is perhaps a chimera and "'serious semioticians' should remain content with refining technical elements of theory in focused domains" (1990:6) so also with the issue of scientificity—specificity of focus is inherent in any science and is the only tool serious semioticians saw we have to arrive at "certain certainties" in the humanities or human sciences.

Internal criticism of the Paris School of semiotics in America did not come until 1988 with T. Pavel's counter-argument of a moderate position which leads, in principle, to a modification of the semiotic system without dismantling it altogether. His paper, "Formalisms in Narrative Semiotics," is a constructive critique which like other contributions of the Paris School carries on a dialogue and a debate with Greimas' work. It is a paper revised from an earlier article, published in December 1986, which was addressed to a specialized audience of French-speaking Canadian researchers and dealt at length with details of a technical polemic. The title of this article, written in French, "L'Avenir de la sémio-linguistique. . ." indicates the major preoccupation of Pavel in both articles, his concern for the healthy future of the Paris School of semiotics. When we consider the need for recontextualizing semiotics with other disciplines, Pavel's viewpoint stands out as that of the troubleshooter, addressing "the most pressing problems [it] should tackle" in order to assess "its best choice" for opening up to other disciplines (1988:593, 605). As Pavel sees it, the strength of Greimassian narrative semiotics consists of its remarkable conceptual wealth and notional richness and its dramatic predicament is that of introducing idiosyncratic albeit powerful formalisms which prevent the interested outsider from navigating the simple conceptuality. His suggestion to abandon formal claims and to sever the formal ventures from the conceptual ones, plausible as it sounds, is not an easy task as it requires treating the formalisms "as if it were a rhetorical device without much consequence and treating the more interesting concepts as hermeneutic notions" (597). Pavel's appeal to semioticians is to suggest an alternative to formal research in the humanities and social sciences: "since formal systems are not the only way to knowledge, narrative semioticians may choose to stress the most valuable aspects of their discipline through more open hermeneutic practices, the use of the heuristic models or any other softer kind of rational argumentation" (605).

Since my own work makes common cause with Pavel's position, I shall return to it in the last section of this introduction. The value of Pavel's article is that it also sheds a retrospective explanation on the career of Greimassian semiotics in the States. It makes explicit certain objections which were already there and kept silent since 1978. *Story and Discourse* (1978), for example, spoke in silence when S. Chatman did not apply, modify, nor address the narrative theory of Greimassian semiotics. So did *Semiotics and Interpretation* (1982) when Scholes, in his breezy manner, articulated the same objection as Pavel against "the use of logical and algebraic symbols and the employment of elaborate diagrams," leading him not only to "reduce this paraphernalia" but to exclude Greimassian semiotics altogether from consideration even though, in his work of 1974, he had found Greimas' work on narrative theory and on actants most interesting and worthwhile pursuing (1982:xi, 1974:11).

With the slow unfolding of the Paris School of semiotics in the States, its positive development can be ensured by fostering Franco-American collaborative research activities, linking individuals with national associations (The Semiotic Society of America, The Canadian Society of Semiotics), with research groups (The Semio-linguistic Research Group) and the research centers developing (University of California–San Diego, University of Oklahoma, University of Toronto). With the recent English translations of Greimas and the Paris School, the audience will surely widen but with the lag of two decades and a different intellectual climate, the interested newcomers will need all the more "not one, but many introductions to this 'semiotics'" to grasp the international and the universal importance of the ideas it embraces, the way Segre saw it in 1979: "if, at the beginning, semiotics might have been considered as a daring experiment, it now is a fundamental element of our culture to which it gave tools of global interpretation" (Jameson, vi; Segre qtd. by Withalm, 644). This exuberant assessment leads me to a final positive thought. Basic tools or techniques do become familiar and timeless, like knives or scissors, without losing their efficacy even when used as background to promote a more current, popular trend.

3. A historical sketch of Greimassian semiotics

In the oft-quoted "Foreword" to A. J. Greimas' *On Meaning* F. Jameson mentions that in its current state of multifarious expansion, Paris School semiotics needs to re-orient itself by retracing its own history and articulating the development of its rich conceptual field:

> Indeed, we have reached a paradoxical moment in the development of *this particular semiotics* [...]. Some twenty years after the inaugural texts of a kind of research sometimes denounced as ahistorical and universalizing [...] semiotics has now begun not merely to reflect *on its own history* but also to discover the deeper historicity of its own inner logic of development. A local concept, modified at its saturation point and at the moment of diminishing returns, in its turn proves to demand the enlargement and subsequent modification of the entire conceptual field of which it was a part. The consequence is that in Greimassian semiotics, in some intense and original way, concepts bear a date and are historical in their very essence—*not, to be sure, in crude calendar years, but on the intrinsic calendar of the unfolding of the semiotic problem field itself* (1987: vi, my emphasis).

The intrinsic history of semiotics became a matter of importance since 1983 with the publication of *Du Sens II*. In the introduction to this book Greimas was more concerned about maintaining the continuity of the semiotic project and not seeing a radical break, as suggested by the discrete number, between *Du Sens* (1970) and *Du Sens II* (1983). The English translation of this introduction appeared in 1990 under a different title, "Ten Years Afterwards," as a chapter in Greimas' *The Social Sciences: A Semiotic View*.

Two years later, on November 22, 1985, at a conference in Toronto, Greimas again addressed the intrinsic history of semiotics. This paper was published for the first time in an English translation under the title "On Meaning," in the special 1989 issue on *Greimassian Semiotics* mentioned earlier.

Both of these articles which are very similar in content are important as historical surveys of semiotics in Paris since 1956. They are short surveys of the widest scope and written in the imponderable and fluent style of entries found in literary histories. In addition to these two "early" articles, all the introductions to the recent English translations of the works by Greimas and researchers of the Paris School have touched upon the semiotic history of ideas and sketched out the intellectual horizon in which the theory was elaborated. (See, for instance, F. Jameson (1987), H. Parret (1989), P. Perron (1989), P. Fabbri and P. Perron (1990)).

The version that I will provide in this section is based on the two articles by Greimas in which he takes the stance of an interpreter reporting on the "progress brought about by individual, but also and especially by collective thought and effort" (1989: 540). It is the emphasis on the collective thought and effort of the Paris School semioticians which makes Greimas' articles widely relevant and especially appropriate to any historical sketch of semiotics. Moreover, since my work deals only with the writings of Greimas, his viewpoint on the history of semiotics is especially pertinent to the next section, on the situation and plan of this work.

The capacity to see semiotics as a historical process and to distinguish in it several states is gained from the vantage point of the end. Only "after the fact" can we look back to the beginning and "recognize several stages or several distinct states which are separated by a series of transformations situated within a continuity and which are not 'epistemological breaks'" (1989:540).

Four major stages can be seen in the *progressive conceptualization* of semiotic theory. The first stage which began in 1956 was influenced by structural linguistics and a linguistically-based structuralism from anthropology and folklore. V. Propp's *The Morphology of the Folktale* became the initial text or object study which served as a starting point for a new type of narrative analysis and as the basis for more encompassing theories. Propp's model attempted to explain the "surface structure" of narratives—the sequence of actions or syntagmatic dimension—and it could be improved through recourse to Lévi-Strauss' paradigmatic analysis of myth. When Greimas did that, he noticed four main segments that could be paired, and that two of these pairs made up a Lévi-Straussian schema. The structuration of the functions in Propp's model uncovered a logical and semantic structure behind the *linear and canonical succession*. Thus, by linking together two complementary narrative models, it became evident that the varied surface structures of stories are generated from a smaller set of deep structures that can be actualized as a temporal succession. The structuration of the functions, or the projection of paradigmatic categories on the syntagmatic development of stories, yielded a new and more complete model, *the narrative schema*.

The second stage of semiotics began in 1964 and culminated with the publication of *Sémantique structurale*. Since the structuration of Propp's functions and the actantial model make up two chapters in this book, recognized for their theoretical genius and as the *tour de force* of the book, the second stage of semiotics is often seen as the first outside of Paris and, thus collapsed, make up the early *narratological period* of Paris School semiotics. *Narratology* was at the origin of this semiotics and continues to be at the very core of it. In this early stage, however, narratology had a relatively concrete focus on the problematic of events, actants, contracts, and exchanges whereas later it moved towards a more complex and abstract modal grammar. Later, around 1970, an attempt was made to formulate better the elements of narrativity. The principle consisted in saying that what Propp called a function was not a function but a sentence, that is to say, an utterance specifying a relation between actants. Another step was taken in differentiating the types of event, making it possible to interpret action as program of doing and to construct an autonomous syntax that could determine narrative programs.

The third stage of semiotics began in the early 1970s and focused on two different angles related to discourse analysis and narratology. One angle focused on the *modalities and aspectualities* of the function as verb (want, have-to or must, know-how or can) leading not only to the exploration of what action is (thus providing a model of the organization of behavior) but also to the construction of a *modal grammar*, which in turn covered the entire cognitive dimension of discourse. It was at this time that narrativity was seen as the organizing principle of all discourse, and "the syntactic form of the organization of the world" (Greimas 1989:543).

The other angle consisted of a progressive formalization of the intuitive components of the Proppian schema so that, at the end, Propp's model was abandoned in favor of an ostensibly more rigorous syntax that functioned as a calculus. "It is not that we completely abandoned heroes and traitors," says

Greimas, "but we discovered that Propp's model could be broken down into parts, into important sequences covered over by the model. . . Without noticing it we began to work on something other than the tale" (1989:543). For example, *semio-narrative syntax* (as the conceptual structure of narrative is called) took the idea of the confrontation between two subjects from Propp's hero and villain and interpreted it as a relation founded either on a confrontation, a sort of polemic, or on the contract, postulating that all interaction is, therefore, *polemico-contractual* in nature. As the simplest and most rudimentary model of narrative, the analysis and reevaluation of the Proppian schema led to the blooming of what might be called socio-semiotics: "we discovered a *semiotics of manipulation*—how the sender manipulates the subject; then a *semiotics of action*—how competence is acquired to carry out performance; and finally a *semiotics of sanction*—that is to say, passing judgments on self, on others, and on things" (1989:543). These new semiotics which are still being worked out are also modal organizations.

Semiotics was, in a way, freed from Propp and yet its strength and success depended on the fruitfulness as well as the rather unexpected success of the Proppian model itself. Since the 1960s the Proppian model was considered as the model par excellence of the narrative and even when it was abandoned temporarily in the search for more general structures, it was reinstated as an ideological narrative schema, a universal schema to be kept side by side with the modal grammar. To free oneself from the constraints of the Proppian schema and to acquire an autonomous modal syntax was an effort which took on a "revolutionary" aspect and it gradually changed semiotic practice from top to bottom. The basic theory of the decade was published as *Sémiotique: Dictionnaire raisonné de la théorie du langage* (1979) by Greimas and Courtés and was translated into English as *Semiotics and Language: An Analytical Dictionary* (1982). It is now referred to as the first dictionary since a second volume came out in 1986, where the authors of the first volume turn editors in the second, giving the helm to forty semioticians of the Paris School.

The fourth stage, which began in the early 1980s, changed focus from narrative syntax to discursive syntax and set out to construct an *aspectual syntax*. Unlike the opposite categories of yes and no, black and white, aspectualities are tensive, valuative, and gradual ones. The salient features of temporal aspectualities can be defined by duration and becoming which are continuous and gradual processes, as opposed to the state before, when the processes began and the state after, when the processes end.

In this stage semiotics was sufficiently developed to overcome an initial methodological limitation of viewing characters only as vessels of action. Since Propp structural poetics and semiotics have avoided treating the character as a psychological essence, as a "person," or even as a well-rounded "being." This self-imposed bias was justified in the beginning when it was necessary to define the *actants* and differentiate them from psychological issues of characters, their emotions and temperaments. Semiotics began with the theory of actants and initially attributed to subjects only the ability to act. One of the research areas which opened up since 1979 was instigated by the need to grapple with the subject's ability to feel, to respond, and to evaluate. It became possible at this point to undertake an examination of the traditional *theories of passions* (Descartes, Spinoza, Leibnitz, Neitzsche, Freud) and give it a semiotic interpretation. This possibility rested on the fact, noted by E. Landowski, that the semiotics of passion would be anchored fully on "all levels . . . of the theory of narrativity: not only the semio-narrative structures proper . . . nor the discursive structures, but also the deep level abstract structures" (1979:8).

"We first noticed..." says Greimas, calling attention to the focus of narration. We: meaning the Paris seminars where Greimas functioned as the center of a whole group. We: the individual and the group, the individual reporting on the group activity. We: the group actively thinking and discussing fresh and exciting problems. In the Paris seminars, then, it was first noticed that, contrary to the implicit postulations of these classical theories, one rarely encountered *solitary* passions. They were almost never linked to a single subject, and their description always called for the establishment of an actantial structure. It was then noted that the semiotic interpretation of these passions was almost exclusively undertaken in terms of modalities. Thus, passions can be described in terms of modal syntax and at least two interdependent actants; for example, avarice = wanting to + conjunction. Parret has explored this area in his enterprising work on *Les passions* (1986) and showed how the modal organization of passions alter the subject's pragmatic performances. A crowning milestone in the "passional" phase of this semiotics was surely marked most recently, in April 1991, with the publication of a comprehensive work by Greimas and Fontanille, *Sémiotique des passions*. This far-reaching study has not only extended semiotic analysis but also has patently integrated a new area of research such that semiotics today has become not only a semiotics of action but also a *semiotics of passion*, a *pathemic semiotics*.

The semiotics of action, however, has not come and gone. It remains pivotal in the flourishing areas of socio-semiotics and the semiotics of law. B. S. Jackson in his *Semiotics and Legal Theory* (1985) paved the first foundations for legal semiotics based on the theory of A. J. Greimas and his close collaborator E. Landowski and their analysis of legal discourse. Patterns of legal behavior are described as juridical mini-narratives and are taken to be manifestations of a general narrative. In his recent book on *La société réfléchie* (1989) E. Landowski works on the premise that language is, first of all, action and a space of interaction, and through this actional focus analyzes the conditions of the exercise of power and law, evincing all the strategies of persuasion, trust, and manipulation.

The fourth stage of the 1980s also manifested the *collective* nature of the Paris School semiotics which Greimas had often stressed, as it charted many new and plural directions. In his historical survey of Greimas and the Paris School, T. Broden observes that "the flexible centralized organizational structure—when Greimas functioned as the center of a whole group—has moved closer to a plurality of nodes and voices resembling more a rhizomatous network than a pyramid" (1990:4,5). The collective nature of the semiotic enterprise is evidenced by "the mature projects elaborated by veteran Paris semioticians whose conceptual apparatus contains significant innovations vis-à-vis established semiotics, while still maintaining a strong family resemblance" (Broden 1990:4-5). Eleven broad fields of applications and disciplines and fifty-some researchers are randomly listed in H. Parret's introduction as participating in and creating the semiotic enterprise. Equally evident is that semiotics as an interdisciplinary methodology does not, in most places, exist as a separate discipline, inside of established university departments and traditional fields and this explains the fact, observed by Parret, that most Paris School semioticians have a "dual competence": in semiotics and another field, be it linguistics, philosophy, literature, law, sociology, and so on (1989:xv).

The dual competence reflects a special difficulty in countries outside of France, such as the U.S., where literature departments are built not according to topics but according to writers or groups of writers and century. The literature department is taken as one specific case to shed light on how crucial the situation can be for the future of semiotics. Universities are the social institutions for the development of a systematic approach to literature but, unfortunately, the theory of literature as well as semiotics play a secondary and minor role in many American university departments and programs; they are used as secondary tools or embellishments. This factor, more than the dizzying paradigm shifts of literary fashions, provides the key explanation as to why in the States "in spite of great strides made in literary studies, linguistic research, the philosophy of science, and the analysis of cognition, semiotics remains marginal in many humanistic and scientific disciplines" (Jules-Rosette 1990:6). By contrast, the situation in Canada, and especially Montreal, a bilingual milieu between Europe and America, reflects no such difficulty as some universities have established an undergraduate and doctoral program in semiotics as part of their official curriculum. (See Thérien 1987.) In the graduate program a 'dual competence' is required of students, a traditional discipline and semiotics, so as to foster interdisciplinary thinking and to *apply* semiotics to the other discipline.

4. Situation and plan of the work

The writing of this work began in the early 1980s but its stimulus originated somewhat earlier and grew from formative experiences in Ann Arbor, Michigan, when literary structuralism was at its height and discussions were often lively and exciting. A few years before this project, I had attempted to encompass the field of narrative semiotics in its blooming decade by subsuming a wide range of materials into an integrated survey. (See Budniakiewicz 1978.) As I look back, the survey crystallized many issues for me and pointed to the avenue I was about to embark. Given the radiance which structuralism and semiotics broadcast far and wide in the mid-1970s, I must admit that great would be my surprise, years later, to know that this paper of mine would be one of the few to appear on the American scene. (See W. Martin 1986.) I had imagined the cultural milieu of the American Midwest and of the States to be as exhilarating as Paris and the writing that it would produce to reflect the range and enthusiasm of *Actes Sémiotiques*. History tells us this is not what happened but already I am diverging to the American scene which belongs to section 2.

The area that I was about to pursue was the work of Greimas which increasingly I came to feel deserved particular attention. It had inspired some, but comparatively little consideration in literary semiotics; it was recognized for its ingenious and basic concepts (the actantial structure, the semiotic square); and yet it was wittingly or unwittingly ignored, feared for what seemed the wrong reasons (the rigor or the formalisms), or keenly misunderstood. This work was the process of investigation and the process of discovery. It is an in-depth study on the fundamentals of narrative roles and events and simultaneously a constructive critique—a dialogue, a debate, and a proposal of solutions—with the work of Greimas from the 1960s and 1970s. As outlined in the historical sketch of Greimassian semiotics, this work covers the first, second, and third stages of its development. The starting point which provided me with the methodological and operational anchor is a work from the second stage, a set of two chapters from *Structural Semantics*, chapter 10 on the actantial model and chapter 11 on the semantic analysis of V. Propp's chain of folktale functions. These two chapters have since been acknowledged by seasoned readers of the field to provide the more practical and profitable entry for newcomers to this semiotics.

In the opening paragraph on the historical development of semiotics, I made a reference to an important comment by F. Jameson to the effect that concepts get dated, not in crude calendar years, but in the intrinsic unfolding of the semiotic conceptual field. His next point, however, is more relevant to the position of my work. Jameson adds that in Greimassian semiotics the concepts of each stage have a validity of their own and the later concepts do not in any way supplant the earlier ones:

> Nor is the matter of the inner date, the inner chronological mark, merely some vague provisionality whereby later, more "rigorous" formulations take the place of earlier hypotheses. In Greimas's work *all the formulations—early and late—are interesting and in some sense "valid" in themselves*. Only their intelligibility is incomplete without a keen awareness of the "moment" of each, of the time of the problematic as a whole, of the shape and point in the life cycle of *this particular exploding galaxy* in which that technical term pulsates with its brightest life (1987:vii, my emphasis).

It is the intelligibility of the early narratological period of semiotics that I was trying to discover and the coherence of concepts in the second and third stage when the vantage point of history had not yet sharply separated them. This period is so fundamental for narratology that we need to re-examine the "exploding galaxy" of actants, events, contracts, and exchanges and put them on a firmer footing by clarifying them, aligning them, and deepening their connections in a more measured way than was possible when they were first introduced.

The intelligibility, first of all, had to be one of style. This work aims to make Greimas' style more transparent and amenable to new and seasoned readers of Greimas and to narratologists in all fields who seek to have a better understanding of the contributions brought to bear on narration by Propp, Greimas, and discourse analysis. The primary means of simplifying the style was to explain the formalisms so thoroughly as to enable the more basic and powerful concepts to spring forth clearly. Due to the tone of self-deprecating humor Greimas occasionally used when talking of the 'jargon,' it had always appeared to me that the formalisms were a by-product rather than a central goal of Greimassian semiotics. The increasing technical and formal vocabulary of the later stages of this semiotics refute my earlier perception. But I owe my clearest insight into this issue to Pavel's articles on the formalist ambitions of the school and his foresight on what would be gained from abandoning them:

> Freed from the pseudo-formal shackles, these ideas would gain to be presented in the rational but non-formal language practiced by philosophers, literary critics, ethnologists. Abandoning formal chimeras does not forecast the twilight of a humane discipline; on the contrary. The way of rational argumentation, of heuristic models, or even of hermeneutics always remain available to it [to this discipline]. Let us note, in passing, that a re-orientation of this nature would have a beneficial influence on the style of semio-linguists; since it would no longer be necessary to affect the esoteric tone which comes sometimes from the formal rigor, semio-linguistic writing would acquire a new simplicity and transparency (1986:635, my translation).

I was not following Pavel's suggestion, which was not known to me at the time of writing, but his evaluation retrospectively echoes my thoughts on the matter. My attempt to use a softer kind of rational argumentation is especially evident in the literary analyses embedded in the work and the excursus on the philosophy of contract and exchange. The relative looseness of the literary, philosophical, and legal terminology contrasts sometimes stylistically with the technical linguistic analysis required at other parts and with the ostensible rigor of the semiotic terminology. Each style was necessary to achieve its specific purpose and I chose to stress the most valuable aspects of the literary and philosophical analyses through a softer kind of rational argumentation, seeing no value to "semiotizing" them, if the latter meant clothing them in formalisms, symbols, and formulae.

The intelligibility also required working out the theoretical mediations of the transplantation and uneasy fusion of interdisciplinary terms and concepts. The pervasive knot with which the reader of Greimassian semiotics struggles is having to cope with key terms in actantial grammar and in narrative semiotics which altogether seem to lead a double, triple, or even multiple life, and understanding the transplantation of these terms which are already debated about in their own habitat of linguistics to the field of narrative semiotics where they do not acclimatize readily. In addition to the loose or unsettled meaning of some concepts which accrues in instability through transplantation, another kind of osmosis has seeped over from linguistics. We could call it a tone of final doctrine, a this-is-a-well-knit-theory attitude which caps off, like a sheet of solid ice, something that is shifting and not so well-knit underneath. W. Chafe has talked about this tone in linguistics and bemoaned the fact that "characteristically, theories of language are presented in a dogmatic manner, much as if they were religious pronouncements" (1971:346). In order to attune to the hesitation some of us feel at times with the usage of certain terms and to be alert to the perplexities activated by a young methodology in search of itself, we need to restore it to its suggestive 'maybe,' to dial it back to something tentative and illustrative. In this way perhaps we can accept the role of linguistics as a speculative model which selects, emphasizes, suppresses, and organizes features of narrative studies by implying statements about it that do not immediately and literally apply to it.

The intelligibility should not sacrifice the complexity of the subject nor distort the true conceptual style of Greimas' demonstrations. The appropriate method would have to meet his work on his own terms in the manner of a dialogue, and with the effect akin to that of a magnifying mirror. Greimas' theory in semantics and in narrative semiotics is a set of interlocking concepts where each is defined in terms of the others, an interlocking whole with no beginning and no end such that, in entering it and dislocating one idea, we have a domino effect. Such a tight orchestration of ideas and concepts gives Greimas' work an air of mastery and brilliance but its very self-containment also seals it off from any interpenetration and flexibility in discussion. The only way, in fact, to analyze Greimas' writings meaningfully is to reconstruct them and expand them. A linear critique of the method is made impossible for it would only lead to what M. H. Abrams spoke of as "a sealed echo-chamber" in which the disorderly parts would "bombinate in a void." It would also fail in meeting a major challenge of theoretical poetics: to take up the responsibility of a constructive approach to methodology by increasing the clarity and thinking through the implications of a method.

Last but not least, the intelligibility necessitated a hermeneutic activity of interpreting the meaning-bearing structures which semiotics specified. It is a misguided view to believe, as some semioticians have, that any textual analysis inspired by his method excludes hermeneutics and interpretation of meaning. As one representative critic put it, "distance is taken toward any hermeneutics; the aim is not to talk of meaning but, as semiotician, to discover the mechanism of the production of meaning." I hope to dismantle these attitudes and predispositions by demonstrating throughout my work that, indeed, we cannot understand Greimas' linguistics, the logic, and the formulas without reintroducing hermeneutics and interpretation.

The thesis of the book is developed through a thorough reconstruction and recreation of the entire theoretical foundation of Greimas' narrative semiotics and it is made concrete through literary analysis of selected passages from a single novella, *Miss Lonelyhearts*, by Nathanael West. But before getting into the interpretation of the novella, the reasons why it was chosen and how I envisioned the interpenetration of description and theory, let me first discuss the overall thread of continuity in this work and separate into two stages what I tried to interweave into a single whole.

Let us first discuss the theoretical concerns of narrative semiotics and deal with the perils and fascinations we just mentioned that lurk behind the creation or misuse of Greimas' methodology. The theoretical continuity in this work is provided by trying to answer a central question on the paths of the two-way flow:

1) We can start from actantial grammar. Then the question is how the foundation text, Propp's *Morphology of the Folktale* received its linguistic and logical reconversion;

2) Inversely, we can start from the linguistic-semantic case roles. Then the question is how to justify the hypothesis of their correspondence to textual units called actants.

Since we did not have a clear vision of the intermediate, linking terrain, the proper strategy seemed to dictate that we take each point of departure by aiming at the other. I have chosen to proceed along the second route for two reasons. The first is that the establishment of the actants, Propp's "spheres of action among dramatis personae," is clearly accounted for in the *Morphology* and constitutes less of an unknown than the linguistic-semantic case roles. Thus the *Morphology* provides a clear endpoint by which to guide ourselves through the case roles. Another and more important reason depends on the overall thrust of this work which consists of a theoretical recall and analysis, the aim of which is to specify the starting point set up by Greimas in his chapter of *Sémantique structurale*, entitled "Réflexions sur les modèles actantiels," and the successive stages of the actantial grammar. Greimas claims that the actantial model was hypothesized essentially from the syntactical structure of the sentence. If we are to find the justification of the notion of actant, one must then start seeking it in the sentence. This, we might say, is what actantial grammar forces us to ask. The need to rewalk this path and focus on the conceptual sights en route has been briefly mentioned by F. Nef in an article stressing the differences between sentential case grammar and textual and particularly narrative actantial grammar:

> The notion of actant may seem to be one of the most solidly established attainments of semiotics but, in fact, this notion is often adopted or rejected without much justification (1979:638).

Thus, when the grounds or criteria of justification have not been solidly fixed, when there is no settled opinion as to what the grounds are, *reflection* on the grounds for identifying the actants and calling them by a certain grammatical term is challenged. The urge to do this kind of conceptual investigation goes hand in hand with the sharpest awareness we must activate about the constructed metalanguage in order to meet the responsibility of a genuine critique of the method.

Since I use the actantial model, revised and newly reinterpreted, as a tool for discovering the nucleus of the text of *Miss Lonelyhearts* and for grasping the simple evental structure and the component subplots in bare form, it became imperative for descriptive procedures also to refine and deepen the notion of actant. In practice, the specific aim of narrative semiotics or its theoretical and systematic branch, cannot be isolated from the aims of description and textual interpretation. It is impossible to analyze a text without a theoretical framework, however implicit it may be, as much as it is impossible to develop a theory without the empirical material from descriptive studies. Narrative semiotics, as a branch of descriptive poetics, is a systematic study based on a set of specific questions derived from the theory of narration. In the process of guiding the textual analysis with the actantial model, the *Object* actant first and the *Sender* next raised many problems of definition and application. The novella itself stimulated questions on the protagonist's object of desire and goal-object and thus widened the amplitude of the questions derived from the actantial model. *Miss Lonelyhearts*, a classic from contemporary American fiction, is a work which centers upon a central character who is only known as "Miss Lonelyhearts," the name by which he signs his column, floundering in the quicksand of helplessness and wrestling with obstacles to an all-consuming quest, the precise nature of which is as vague as the mystical experience which the hero eventually undergoes at the end of the story. The hero is oppressed by a sense of urgency and an anguished activity which drives him along like the propeller of a steamer. But towards what? There is much force in Miss Lonelyhearts but to what end? While the goal-object is diffuse and vague, the relationship to the goal-object, as shown in deed and word, is intensely charged and invested with value. From this point of view, it is the events and the actional objective of Miss Lonelyhearts which present a primordial interest of definition and it is their tenor which we attempt to account for with the help of the actantial model.

Almost against my stubborn wish not to fly away from the text itself, questions of a theoretical nature on the *actants* asserted themselves. Due to the demands raised by the contact of text to theory, the description became subordinated to and tested within the theory making the theory concrete rather than vice versa. In order to display the build-up of the theoretical demonstration from sentence to paragraph to minimal narrative, the movement of the investigation has to be analytic and the scope of it restricted to segments of the text and the discovery of connections among these segments. The idea is to use the same event in the novella and describe that event at different levels of analytic complexity such that text and theory alternate in the role of giving a "footlight" sense to the stage of the other and in reinforcing each other. The more widespread and conventional approach of using a set of examples drawn from a variety of novels would not achieve the effect of mutual embedding that was sought after and would only serve as arbitrary decoration to the theory.

Mutual embedding and mutual grafting is how I envision the symbiosis of theory and text. However, there is also a simple theoretical reason in choosing a single novella. It is to take the next step in the lineage of Propp and Greimas by moving to the "higher" genre, one of the "isolated novellas" which Propp believed "display the same structure" functionally as the folktale. *Miss Lonely-hearts* is a relatively short fictional work though highly complex when compared to Propp's folktales and certainly more complex than the short story "Two Friends" by Maupassant which Greimas analyzed in 1976. *Miss Lonelyhearts* has been compared to a symbolist prose poem for its rich layering of meaning, its density of action, and its breathless craftsmanship. The story, bitter in its satire, brief and episodic in its treatment, ironic in its outlook, is condensed so that too much happens in too short a time. And yet a mere retelling of the story would miss the chiselled effectiveness West achieves with a great economy of words. The style, in its stark simplicity of language and sentence structure, is intensely lucid and exact. The logical mesh of the connections between key events seems very compact. The compression and complexity of the action, the linear momentum and galloping acceleration of the plot achieve an economy, clarity, and inevitability as relentless as the kind that characterizes a validly drawn argument. The global coherence, intensity of feeling, and idealistic vehemence are perfectly fused with the logic which harnesses it such that the unity of effect also has the electric inevitability of brilliantly staged drama. In fact, it was the literary and dramatic appeal of *Miss Lonelyhearts* which cast the determining factor in my selection of a particular novella.

Fundamentals of Story Logic presents primarily the development of the general theory but it still leaves the explicit global literary analysis of the novella largely unfinished. However, this analysis will be carried out in detail elsewhere, as a topic for another book made possible by the results of this study. Our ultimate intention is to present a literary analysis of the novella as a whole, making the theory an instrument which would allow the analyst to obtain from the novella its own models of organization and to exhibit the concrete logic underlying its manifestation.

Finally, I hope that this work will continue to promote an orientation to literary studies advanced by Greimas and to renew the commitment he made to build on an acquired theoretical foundation, rather than starting over again from the very beginning (as many literary scholars do, by default) and relying purely on the individual art of interpretation. As Greimas was open and willing to build on the work of Propp, Souriau and Tesnière, so are we now open and willing to build on the acquired terrain of Greimas, case grammar, the philosophy of action and contract. I believe that a meaningful advancement is only possible by a combination of bold theoretical models and specialized studies which contribute to their development. Only with this team spirit can we speak of advancing a science of literature and only then can we speak of achieving an accumulative effect. As the critique and development of Greimas' bold theoretical models which we are about to carry out are quite detailed and complex, it might be useful to have a chapter-by-chapter summary of this work.

In chapters I and II, I attempt to engage the reader in central problems of the second stage of Greimassian semiotics as quickly as possible, starting from a synoptic account of the nucleus of the sentence and the nucleus of the text and developing certain strands of the discussion on roles and events from the linguistic angle. There are two major parts to the core of this book which mirror the two major actantial categories and axes, the axis of desire (chap. III and IV) and the axis of communication (chap. V, VI, and VII). For those readers already familiar with the work of Greimas, chapter IV on the subject and object actants provides another entry to this book.

In the chapters examining the subject and object actants I prove that the actantial categories are not derived from sentence syntax but are conceptual notions stemming from the practical syllogism of action, its teleological inversion, and its opposition to (or union with) one or more practical syllogisms. The general discussion of the semantics of event and role relationships and its link to the sentential grammar (chap. II) is only one stage of a necessary path, a path made obligatory by the linguistic claim of actantial grammar. We anchor ourselves at this position long enough to fissure it and rebuild it fully so as to turn around, cut the path behind oneself and gain a new position. At this new stage (chap. III) we stop to examine the textual unfolding of action as a pattern of practical reasoning and its inversion as a teleological explanation which proves to be essential in understanding the object actant. The practical logic of action serves as a radically lucid and controlled strategy in the analysis of the subject/object actants and in demonstrating conclusively that these actants are not derived from sentence syntax (chap. IV). One of the implications and consequences from this canvassing is the following: the main focus of narrative models since Propp, especially that of Greimas, is not linguistic nor grounded by linguistic morphology even if it is inspired by it. The inferential patterns uncovered in the relation of the textual subject and object actants link it to research on narrative structures in cognitive science and to models of story comprehension based on logical semantics which differentiated itself sharply from post-Proppian research.

Chapters V, VI, and VII examine the actants sender/object/receiver that are grouped into the evental or dynamic configurations corresponding to communication and to contract or, more generally, to the structure of exchange. This exploration picks up where Greimas himself left off. In 1966 Greimas spoke of the complexity of these actants and said that it "necessitated long developments" which he never pursued. Critics were quick to point out that many difficulties arise when trying to apply the categories of sender and receiver. I consolidate more than a decade of Greimas' groundbreaking research and introduce ideas from the legal philosophy of contract and sociology of exchange (chap. VI) in order to explain and put a solid structure beneath the extremely important chapter on the "functional analysis" of the Proppian functions. This chapter, entitled "A la recherche des modèles de transformation," (initially published under the title "Le conte populaire russe. Analyse fonctionnelle," 1965) is the source of derivation and the most substantial analysis of the sender and receiver. The major thrust of the analytic review is to carry out two successive "approximations" on the normalization of the Proppian chain, to reconstruct the derivation of the sender and receiver, and to get a basic perspective on how communication and contract units come up through the analysis of the entire narrative schema. There is a need for clear exposition on the technical details and supplementing all the steps involved in recreating the chain of reasoning which led to the semantic network of functions or events. To fill this need is to meet the methodological criteria for the well-formedness and descriptive adequacy of literary theories: generality, explicitness in its operational definitions, internal coherence, consistency, and completeness. The analytic table, showing the results, is displayed in full in the *Appendix*. We titled the table "The Boolean Algebra of Narrative Events" partly after the suggestion of the research direction C. Lévi-Strauss made when he reviewed Propp's work in 1960. Lévi-Strauss suggested doing a "Boolean algebra" to account for the global underlying system and semantic coherence which surpass the simple, linear order in which the Proppian functions succeed one another. The table is highly recommended as a guiding adjunct, like a map of sorts, to the reading of the chapters dealing with communication and contract.

The purpose of the reconstruction is not only to review and illuminate a subject matter which Greimas presented densely and in parts as an enigmatic puzzle but also to revise its underpinnings and rebuild on a more suitable, clearer, and hopefully more solid foundation. In the course of the second

approximation we investigate the object of communication within the higher
episodic unit of the Test which is shown to be an object of exchange in a
normative pattern of interaction we call "contract evolution." We also consider
the global meaning of the object within the tale as a whole, its relation to initial
and final sequences of the tale, and the dramatic springs or movements traced
by the circulation of the object-value which provide the genuine nodes or hinges
of the tale.

The analysis of the sender and receiver within the complete narrative
schema and the three global structures of the simple narrative bring to light a
surprising finding utterly overlooked or glossed over in Greimas' narrative
semiotics. The contractual and communication events take place within a
domain of mutual agreement or consensus and involve the element of promise,
trust and morality, a contractual ordering of associations and their attendant
cooperation, a normative and legal conduct regulating interaction. The complete contractual sequence of the tale—a breach of contract initiating the tale
followed by four established contracts—point to an inherent normative or legal
conflict between the hero's desire and the sender or manipulating agent: between desire, on the one hand, and law, on the other. It allows us to consider
the proposition that narrativity is impossible without some notion of the *legal
subject* who can serve as the agent of a story militating against or on behalf of
a legal system. The closure of the story which consists of the Justice of the
Situation raises the hypothesis that narrative, on the whole, has to do with topics
of justice, law, legitimacy or, more generally, authority.

The VIIIth and final chapter deals with the three global interpretation of the
tale by interrelating the axis of desire and the axis of communication in different
ways. Three basic models account for the simplest representation of the meaning of a story in its totality. I discuss these three models within a broader
context of general questions on narrativity. For example, I consider the narrative as a process of change or the reversal of a situation and I look at the three
global interpretations of the tale within the basic aim of the narratologist which
is to explain what this change consists of and why it happened. The syntagmatic
and diachronic structure of the tale assigns a central place to the role of the
protagonist's action and shows what the relationship of the actantial situation
was to the act itself. In other words, the diachronic model defines what an event
is and relates the agent's or character's action to it. It defines and establishes
something that has not been done in narrative theory as clearly or rigorously

thus far: the relationship of the character's action to the vague sense of a narrative as change or narrative as a sequence of events.

All translations from the French are my own. Since most of the works of Greimas were only available in the original French at the time of research or writing, I decided to keep the original text and the translation within the body of the work. This choice also reflects a matter of taste in scholarship; I prefer seeing the original text together with the translation, when that is possible, which may also be of value to the French-English reader. The bibliography, however, has been completely updated to include all the English translations that were published over the past few years, thus giving the English readers all the scope possible to pursue their interest in Greimassian semiotics.

Nucleus of the Sentence and Nucleus of the Text: The Semantic Grammar of Propositions

A basic principle of traditional grammar parses the sentence into two immediate constituents, the *subject* about which something is said, and the *predicate*, what is being said about it. The subject and the predicate together are held to form the *nucleus* of the sentence; any additional constituents are considered optional or syntactically dispensable. L. Tesnière described and illustrated the concept of the nucleus by means of two figurative images, the nucleus as building block and the nucleus as living cell:

> Le nucléus est en dernière analyse l'entité syntaxique élémentaire, le matériau fondamental de la charpente structurale de la phrase, et en quelque sorte la cellule constitutive qui en fait un organisme vivant.
>
> (The nucleus is ultimately the elementary syntactical unit, the basic building material of the structural framework of the sentence and, in a way, the constituent cell which makes of it a living organism.)   (Tesnière, 1965:45)

To illustrate the application of these terms, let us consider the following sentence, drawn from Nathanael West's novella *Miss Lonelyhearts*

The mahogany bar shone like wet gold.

All subsequent illustrations and examples will feature direct quotations or paraphrases from this text. According to traditional grammar, the subject of the sentence is *the mahogany bar* and the predicate is *shone like wet gold*. A further assumption is made on the distribution of the noun phrases and verbal phrases in this traditional parsing. The nucleus of a simple sentence contains only one verbal phrase but may have several noun phrases, one of which can occur as part of a verbal phrase. A sentence like

Shrike dashed against Miss Lonelyhearts

has for its subject *Shrike* and for its predicate *dashed against Miss Lonelyhearts*.

Closely associated with this bipartite analysis of the sentence nuclei is the distinction between the noun and the verb, the noun phrase and the verbal phrase.

There is an alternative analysis of the sentence nuclei which is formulated in predicate calculus. Other terms used for the system are 'calculus of functions' and 'functional calculus.' According to this view the sentence is considered as a proposition. Propositions consist of terms which are of two kinds, predicates and arguments. The *predicate* is an operator with one or more arguments; it is a (semantically) relational term and usually corresponds to the verb. The *arguments* are the terms that are related and usually correspond to nouns but may, however, also be propositions. According to the number of arguments upon which a predicate operates, it will be classified as a one-place predicate, a two-place predicate, a three-place predicate. Equivalent terms are monadic, dyadic, triadic. In general, many-place or n-place predicates are polyadic. In order to avoid confusion with the use of the term 'predicate' in traditional grammar, we shall adopt the term *predicator*, introduced by C. Fillmore (1968) and taken up by J. Lyons (1977) to signal this rather different meaning of 'predicate.' According to this classification a verb like *smile*, which requires only one argument, is a one-place verb; the one 'place' going with *was smiling* is filled or taken by *Miss Lonelyhearts* to form the nucleus of the sentence *Miss Lonelyhearts was smiling (an innocent, amused smile)*. The expressions enclosed in parentheses are extranuclear adjuncts of the sentence that are syntactically omissible. Logicians would treat the verb *smile* in the same way as one-place predicators like *was canvas-colored* in *The sky was canvas-colored*. A transitive verb like *knead* is a two-place verb, one place being filled by the subject and the other by the object, as in *Miss Lonelyhearts kneaded Mary's body (like a sculptor grown angry with his clay)*. Transitive verbs are classed together with dyadic predicators such as *was less than* in *The deadline was less than a quarter of an hour away*. Verbs like *give* are three-place verbs, requiring a subject, a direct object, and an indirect object, as in *Miss Lonelyhearts gives advice to the readers (of a newspaper)*. Logically, a triadic verb is treated on an equal par with triadic relations such as *was between* in *The meadow was between the market and the hill*.

Another concept closely related to the n-place classification of predicators is the syntactic concept of the *valency of a verb* which comes from Tesnière (1965:238-58). A one-place verb can be described as having a valency of one, a two-place verb as having a valency of two, and so on. According to the predicate calculus/valency conception of the sentence structure, the predicator is an element which combines with a single noun phrase or relates two or more noun phrases to each other. The predicator is the 'pivot,' to use Lyons' word, of the sentence nucleus. Taking up our earlier example,

Shrike dashed against Miss Lonelyhearts

the valency formulation views *dashed* as the predicator which relates the two arguments *Shrike* and *Miss Lonelyhearts* to each other. Unlike the bipartite analysis represented in traditional grammar which gives an unbalanced and highly disproportionate importance to the subject, lumping the object with the verb under the predicate, the predicator-arguments analysis represented in the predicate calculus attributes an equal status to each argument, thereby highlighting the parallels between them. A suggestive metaphor of Tesnière makes of the predicator or "verbal knot" in his terminology, "an expression of a complete short play." The metaphor is very brief and I would like to quote it here, while looking far ahead into this work, as a reminder of a source of Greimas' speculation on textual actants and their derivation from the sentence:

> The verbal node [...] expresses a complete short play. Like a dramatic play, in fact,
> it includes obligatorily a process and most often actors and circumstances. Trans-
> posed from the plane of dramatic reality to that of structural syntax, the process,
> actors, and circumstances become respectively the verb, the actants, and the circum-
> stantial indicators (Tesnière, 1965:102).

To consider the subject, as one of the arguments of the predicator, on the same plane as the other arguments, is useful in another respect. It allows the analyst to represent semantic relations holding within a sentence and interconnecting the various arguments into a semantic network, namely, a structure that contains meanings of language arranged in a network. The analysis of the sentence nuclei in terms of the predicator-arguments semantic structure leads to a radical change or abandonment of many concepts from traditional grammar and to the elaboration of a linguistic model that is closely related to generative transformational linguistics. The several new models of grammar arose as an offshoot from generative semantics and have been repositioned lately as theories of "Relational Grammar," of which Fillmore's case grammar plays the role of precursor. (See P. Cole and J. Sadock, 1977.) Another term for relational grammar, and one which I shall use, is "the semantic grammar of propositions," suggested by the terminology of predicate calculus and coined by J. Grimes

(1975).

The semantic grammar of propositions functions as the *very general, highly abstract*, and *formal* framework common to what has come to be called case grammar and actantial grammar. Since 1965 Greimas has repeatedly appealed to this semantic grammar as the means to provide a theoretical basis, a more "uniform canonical formulation," as well as a more "homogeneous notation" to Propp's sequence of 'functions' and list of 'spheres of action'—the narrative predicators and arguments (Greimas, 1976a:7). From a practical standpoint, however, it is difficult to say whether the semantic grammar does anything to straighten out the numerous conceptual difficulties encountered with the Proppian function or whether, as I suspect (and regretfully so), that it simply adds an additional meaning on top of it, without disambiguating the semantic and conceptual web. Greimas himself sees the formulation of the function as a "baffling" one, due to the motley and amalgamate nature of the unit, its descriptive and summarizing variability (1976a:6-7). Two other narrativists, working in the post-Proppian research, have raised the same issue on the ambiguous complexity of the function. P. Larivaille (1974:370), in his attempt to apply Propp's schema to nine versions of an Italian folktale, forerunner of *Le Chat botté*, finds the definition of the function so confusing as to constitute one of the two "essential defects which makes the application of Propp's canonical schema laborious, indeed useless, and at times even random" ("défauts essentiels qui rendent laborieuse, voire inexistante, et parfois même aléatoire, l'application du schéma canonique de Propp"). W. Hendricks (1975) devoted a long paper to a critical examination of the use of the term 'function' in Propp, Bremond, and Greimas. The results uncover "a notoriously complex, polysemantic term, one which requires careful, explicit definition" (1975:282).

Greimas' actantial system is the only one of its kind devised to be used on texts. Contrariwise, many role or "deep case" systems have been proposed since Fillmore's landmark study, "The Case for Case" (1968). (Cf. among others W. Chafe, 1970; R. Jackendoff, 1972; D. Parisi and F. Antinucci, 1973; R. Schank and R. Abelson in R. Schank and K. Colby, 1973; J. Grimes, 1975; L. Doležel, 1976; G. Genot, 1979.) Parisi's and Antinucci's *Essentials of Grammar* adopts an expository orientation in a direct and nontechnical presentation of one version of generative semantics. It concerns itself with describing explicitly the predicator and the arguments on home grounds, intrinsic to semantics, and without having recourse to "the intellectual style, vocabulary, form of argument and the scope" of modern logic with which the model was associated until then but which, according to Fillmore, "are so strikingly different from traditional concerns in linguistic semantics" (in Parisi and Antinucci, 1976:x). Other linguists who have written on roles/cases have taken the predicator-argument framework as a self-explanatory or heuristic point of departure, centering their attention on the notion of role relationships as part of the semantic and conceptual meaning of words.

The list of roles do not match in a one-to-one correspondence with each other. Some roles are common to all studies. Other roles are diversified; that is, a role in one list is split into a number of roles in another. And conversely, some roles are synthesized; that is, several roles in one list are fused into one role in another. In addition to these, a few roles are unique. As research into roles/cases continued, the failure of an empirical shaking down of the roles, of determining their variety and number, has become a vexing problem. For Fillmore the issue is serious and requires action:

> [A] truly worrisome criticism of case theory is the observation that nobody working within the various versions of grammars with 'cases' has come up with a principled way of defining the cases, or principled procedures for determining how many cases there are (1977:70).

The latest shift in Fillmore's position to the perspectival or orientational structuring of language was suggested in order to draw the problem closer to resolution. The scope of our enquiry necessitates bypassing this particular issue. The criterion which dictated my list of roles is prompted by the aim to meet the one given by Greimas. The very brief discussion which Greimas provides of his revision of Tesnière's "linguistic actants" motivates the second criterion of selection (1966:173-4). To help round out and explain the one-page discussion, we chose the work of linguists which has some theoretical affinity and agreement to Greimas' textual semiotics in one important aspect: the concentration on the verb and verb-noun relationships. Besides Tesnière whose work Greimas uses, we found the work of Chafe (1970) and Grimes (1975) in substantial agreement with that of Greimas on the sentence level.

We shall assume this schema of the levels of narrative and textual structure (figure 1.1), postulated by structuralist poetics and narrative semiotics, and include the complemental distinctions among the various 'arguments' in the right-hand column:

narrative-textual structures	deep textual story	actants
	surface textual discourse	actors
linguistic structures	deep sentential	deep structure cases or roles
	surface sentential	verbal valence

Figure 1.1

Let us now define the basic terms needed for referring to the proposition at
each level. It is practical to have at our disposal three sets of terms: one set for
use when we are speaking about the deep structure cases, another set for use
when we are speaking about an actant, and finally, a third set that can be used
indifferently for both cases and actants. Consider the generalized set first.
Much of the nuclear meaning or content of a sentence or text is expressible by
means of propositional arguments. Each *proposition* contains a *predicator* which
relates the *arguments* in a small number of ways called semantic or conceptual
relationships. We shall use the following frame to represent it:

proposition = (predicator)(arguments)

The propositional core of a simple sentence is a statement assigning a (verb-)
predicate to one or more entities, each of these related to the predicate in a *case*
or *role* relationship. The frame is:

statement = (predicate)(cases or roles)

More specifically, the statement assigns an action to a character, an event to a
set of characters. When referring to a simple narrative, the proposition will be
called, following Greimas, the *canonical narrative énoncé* or simply *narrative
énoncé*, with the understanding that it is given in its canonical formulation. The
énoncé is said to be 'canonic' in order to distinguish it clearly from the level of
linguistic 'statement.' The narrative énoncé is defined by its immediate constituents which are *actants* related to each other in specified ways by a *function*.

The paraphrastic frame is:

narrative énoncé = (function)(actants)

Less abstractly, the énoncé attributes a 'sphere of action' where 'sphere' is provisionally understood as a network of Proppian functions, to its performing actant, such as the hero or villain, the protagonist or antagonist.

The relations between the predicator and the arguments may be called *dependencies*. Their nature was seen at the beginning to be syntactic-semantic but more recently research in cognitive science argues for their conceptual status. These dependencies, and only these, make up the formal organization of the stratification in semantic-conceptual networks. Assumptions concerning the universality of these dependencies allow us to use roles and actants as a basic *predictive* or explanatory mechanism, available to the language user. That is, if I were to say "I am going," a highly reasonable inquiry would be "where?". The questioner makes use of an unfilled argument slot to search for a given type of information that will fill the needed slot.

I would like to comment briefly on Fillmore's latest interpretation of the concept of deep structure cases as a position in semantic theory with which he associates the slogan: "Meanings are relativized to scenes." Whenever we choose a linguistic expression of any sort, we activate in our memory an entire background scene or image or situation within which the particular word or expression chosen foregrounds or brings into perspective only a particular aspect or part of that scene. This perspectivizing which selects certain situation participants into perspective is to be distinguished from role/case analysis proper. Two different hierarchies overlap:

> We recognize scenes or situations and the functions of various participants in these scenes or situations. We foreground or bring into perspective some possibly quite small portion of such a scene. Of the elements which are foregrounded, one of them gets assigned the subject role—in underlying or logical structure—and one of them if we are foregrounding two things—gets assigned the direct object role in the clause. Something like a *saliency hierarchy* determines what gets foregrounded and something like a *case hierarchy* determines how the foregrounded nominals are assigned grammatical functions (Fillmore, 1977:80).

The situational or orientational lamination of role participants in the sentence seems at first to bring it closer to the actantial model which is very strongly situational. What I have in mind is something I shall approximate as follows for the immediate purpose at hand. The actantial 'situation' of a simple narrative is an accretion of all the successive situations in a text or play, obtained by 'linking' one situation to the next and 'adding' one to the following ones by nesting each as part of the situation before. The final summation image in this accretion is made up of a textualized representation of a social system, a system of actors in situations, which are abstractions in terms of principles of relationship. The social-situational system is a system of interaction with boundaries defined by incumbency in the roles and actants constituting the system. For the system to exist, however, the differentiated actions of each actor or set of actors must be coordinated and viewed as 'action in concert.' The actant, then, is the point of contact between the system of action of the actor(s) and the total actantial situation. The actor becomes a categorial unit in the sense that he or she becomes a composite of various action units which in turn are actantial roles in the relationships in which he or she is involved. The actant is categorized relative to the others.

E. Souriau's many suggestive definitions of the 'dramatic situation' and the 'character-in-situation,' terms which make up one of the theoretical and nominal parents of the actantial model and of the actant best catch the immediate force within which the actantial model arises and the spirit through which it is analytically and pragmatically manipulated. Much of the power and impressiveness of the actantial model lies in its attempt to account more systematically, that is, more clearly and more surely, for the situation and the character of which Souriau spoke informally, free from the mediation of a highly theoretical and derivative notation—linguistic, logical, and other—but which has the infelicitous power now and then to outwit the critic using it. Consider this passage from Souriau:

> A dramatic situation is the *structural figure* drawn in a moment of action by a system of forces; the system of forces [...] embodied, undergone, or given life to by the main characters of the action. [...] These forces are dramatic functions. That is, each and every one of them exists as a function of the combined system so formed. [...] Due to these functions, each character, being bonded to the others and being simultaneously united in the action with them, through this dynamic form of the moment, receives a *dramatic meaning*—the key to their fates in the dynamism of this world in action. [...] Without these situations which gather the characters architectonically into dramatic relations, action would only be a course on the wane, fluid and inorganic, of confusedly parallel fates, like the strands of an unwound cord or like a series of disorderly atomic shocks (1950:49,55).

One marked difference obviously separates the scene which is activated in the daily use of language—a sense that seems to predominate in Fillmore—from the 'forceful' scene represented in the dramatic situation, charged with a peculiar intensity and a strategic pattern of characters that make us recognize a distinct situation long before the major conflict has been stated and to see the whole set-up of human relationships into a sharp, artistic foregrounding, fraught with the excitement that something momentous and far-reaching is about to happen.

On the other hand, it is clear that Souriau would subscribe to the statement: "Dramatic meanings are relativized to dramatic scenes" which is a recognizably light variant of Fillmore's slogan: "Meanings are relativized to scenes." This agreement raises the issue of saliency criteria for actantial theory, i.e. the judicious proposal to consider looking at the functional structure of *text* constituents in terms of orientational or situational foregrounding. The new question for the theory of actants, parallel to and motivated by, the theory of cases, would be: among the various narrative actants, how are the Subject and Object established or put into perspective? Rephrasing this for the Subject, what makes the protagonist a protagonist? Surprisingly perhaps, the new question for the theory of cases is an old one for the theory of actants and even older for prose fiction criticism. The saliency criteria for foregrounding the narrative were tackled by the 'functional analysis' of the narrative at the same time as the actantial analysis. (See Greimas, 1965, 1966.) The functional analysis consisted of paradigmatizing Propp's syntagmatic chain of thirty-one functions and uncovering the large units called Tests which set up and secure the narrative Subject. At the level of the text, the two types of narrative analysis, functional and actantial, are interdependent and complementary. Neither could proceed without bearing consequences for the other. Since, as Greimas insists, the Subject and Object actants are structurally relational and neither could exist and be defined without the other, saliency criteria which determine the Subject should forthwith determine the Object. I shall argue at great length on why this is decidedly not the case. The discussion will require looking into the definition of the actants, particularly the nuclear ones which appear as the Subject and Object, and the procedures by which they were determined.

II

The Semantics of Event and Role Relationships

1. Theoretical target

Starting from the canonical formulation of the simple narrative énoncé $F(A_1,A_2)$ where F is the function and A_1 and A_2 two separate actants, Greimas presents a typology of two elementary énoncés which characterize the narrative. A sequence of chained énoncés of these two types make up the narrative, if the narrative is viewed upon as one global énoncé

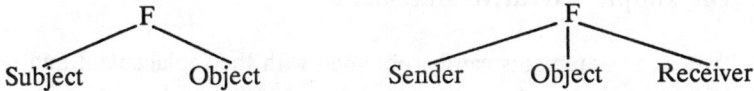

or, in his linear and unique notation

$$NE_1 = F_{doing}(S \longrightarrow O)$$

$$NE_2 = F_{communication}(Sr \longrightarrow O \longrightarrow R)$$

The units of the first canonic énoncé, NE_1, define one of the two distinct components of the narrative: the component referring to *event*. The function is semantically invested with an 'active doing' which includes all the predicates describing every variety of human action and behavior at the level of natural language with the exception of communication acts. The units of the second canonic énoncé, NE_2, define the other component of the narrative: the component referring to *contract*. The function here is semantically invested as a 'communicative doing' or simply as 'communication.' It corresponds to the description of communication acts which are mostly verbal (the transmission of information) but may also be non-verbal (the transfer of objects, the structure of exchange.)

Both the active and communicative doings are *verbs of action* and are set off from *stative verbs*. Moreover, only the former are said to be exclusively narrative.

The above sketch of the two major components of the narrative presented in Greimas 1969, 1971, and 1973a will serve as a double point of enquiry, a point of departure and a point of return. Our first task at hand will be to study the most common linguistic distinctions among verb-predicates and the semantic roles they specify. Unlike events which are highly complex and present us with too many features, verbs give us some clear-cut examples which in their predominant use show forth the typology involved in pure form. At this stage, I will try to ignore stretched and borderline schemas of verbs. However, the task of returning to Greimas' typology will provide some traction to challenge neat patterns and to admit of disagreement about the neatness of these patterns.

2. The simple narrative statement

Two basic statements can be obtained with the replacement and semantic specification of the verb-predicate into two familiar and less inclusive classes, states and events:

(a) *static* statement of the form: state(role) or state(role$_1$, role$_2$, . . .)

(b) *evental-dynamic* statement of the form: event(role) or event(role$_1$, role$_2$, . .)

We shall start with the seemingly obvious distinction between states and non-states which overlaps with the distinction between static situation and dynamic situation and we shall attempt to clarify the meaning of certain related terms, such as 'event,' 'action,' and 'process.'

One good way to approach the problem is to first try to state the most striking difference between state verbs and event verbs. As a practical rule, nonstates can be distinguished from states by the fact that they answer questions like *What happened? What's happening?*. A nonstate is a *happening*, an *event*, a *going on*.

What happened?

Shrike dashed against Miss Lonelyhearts.

Miss Lonelyhearts smiled an innocent, amused smile.

but not (for example)

Miss Lonelyhearts' forehead was high and narrow.
The sky was canvas-colored and ill-stretched.

There are other rule-of-thumb criteria which can be used to distinguish events from states. In most cases, for example, an event verb can occur freely in the progressive aspect which is normally not taken by a stative verb:

Shrike was dashing against Miss Lonelyhearts.
Miss Lonelyhearts was smiling an innocent, amused smile.

but not

Miss Lonelyhearts' forehead was being high and narrow.
The sky was being canvas-colored and ill-stretched.

The criteria are not hard-and-fast rules nor fully automated discovery procedures. They are used as flexible and practical tests which help in detecting a bit of verbal meaning.

Events are not all of the same kind. Consider the following set of exceedingly simple sentences:

(1) a. *The door opened.*
     b. *The kerosene lamp lit up.*
     c. *The lamb died.*

(2) a. *Shrike laughed.*
     b. *Miss Lonelyhearts drank.*
     c. *Miss Lonelyhearts was working on his leader.*

In the sentences of (1) we seem to be dealing with *processes* where the noun is said to have changed its state. I shall say of such sentences that the verb is specified as a *process* and that it is accompanied by a noun which is its *patient*. On the other hand, the verbs in (2) have nothing to do with a change of state. In kind, they are poles apart from processes. What they manifest instead are *actions* or *activities*, which are things that someone *does*. A widely accepted, practical test among linguists which helps make the distinction between action and process is the do-test. Formulate the question *What did N do?*, *What is (was) N doing?* where N is some noun and if the answer is acceptable, the verb is characterized as an action:

What was Miss Lonelyhearts doing?

He was working on his leader.

but not (for example)

He got sick.

Conversely, formulate the question *What happened to N?* and an appropriate answer will often express a process. An answer in terms of an action sentence will be unacceptable:

What happened to Miss Lonelyhearts?

He got sick.

but not

He was working on his leader.

Although I am using these practical tests to uncover a rough definition and I shall not say much more about processes, it is crucial to point out and sobering to think about the following fact. The differentiation between events-processes and events-actions is one of the most difficult and complex tasks faced by all theories of human behavior, theories built within the social sciences, philosophy, psychology, and logic. Likewise, the problem looms large for narratology and literary theory. No adequate and meaningful semantics can evade this task.

The proper noun in an action sentence like those of (2) does not specify something which is changing its state; rather, what it specifies is someone or something which performs an action. Such a noun can be said to be the *agent* of the verb or the *actor*.

Let us now turn to a third set of simple sentences, related to the first set, which illustrate another kind of event:

(3) a. *Shrike opened the door.*
    b. *Miss Lonelyhearts and Betty lit the kerosene lamp.*
    c. *Miss Lonelyhearts killed the lamb.*

In these sentences it appears that the verb is simultaneously both a process and an action. As a process it involves a change in the state of a noun, its patient. As an action, it expresses what someone, its agent, does. The agent is still someone who does something, but in (3) the agent does it *to* someone or something, the *patient* of a process.

What did Miss Lonelyhearts do?

He killed the lamb.

What happened to the lamb? (in the sense of: What did Miss Lonelyhearts do to the lamb?)

Miss Lonelyhearts killed it.

The answer to the lamb question was framed in the perspective of the agent. The verb 'killed' is said to be in the active voice; or, as some linguists like Tesnière would say, in the active *diathesis*. The etymological meaning of diathesis is made up of *dia*, meaning through, between, across, by, and of *thesis*, meaning arrangement, disposition, and setting; the composite gives something like 'a setting through.' The *active* diathesis sets the verb through the action. An equally acceptable answer to the lamb question which conveys the same semantic content but frames the patient directly employs the verb 'killed' in its *passive* diathesis.

What happened to the lamb?

It was killed (by Miss Lonelyhearts).

The passive diathesis sets the verb through the process which involves the change in the state of the lamb.

Finally, the answer to the question "What happened?", presupposing the knowledge of the two roles-nouns, will report both the action and the process:

What happened?

Miss Lonelyhearts killed the lamb.

In summary, an event or dynamic situation may be a process as in (1), it may be an action as in (2) or it may be both a process and an action as in (3).

We are now in a position to discuss the manner in which roles relate to grammatical functions, repeat semantic features of the verb, and involve the notion of causativity. To start off, consider again the sentences of (1) and (3) which we shall reproduce here for easy reference:

(1) a. *The door opened.*
    b. *The kerosene lamp lit up.*
    c. *The lamb died.*

(3) a. *Shrike opened the door.*
    b. *Miss Lonelyhearts and Betty lit the kerosene lamp.*
    c. *Miss Lonelyhearts killed the lamb.*

According to syntactic surface structure the noun *door* in (1a) is the grammatical subject and in (3a) the direct object of the sentence. Hence, *door* has two radically distinct grammatical roles. Yet we know at the level of meaning, the role of *door* with respect to *opened* is the same in (1a) and (3a). In both cases the door is what is opened. The patient relation to the verb is the relation between an object that gets changed and the process that changes it. The noun *lamp* in (1b) and (3b) bears the same patient relation with respect to the verb *lit* and so does the noun *lamb* with respect to the verbs *died* and *killed*. The notion of grammatical relations fails to capture the common semantic functions that the nouns *door*, *lamp*, and *lamb* each plays in the sentences of (1) and (3). The role of patient and the role of agent are independent of syntactic surface structure, unlike the grammatical relations of subject/object.

The most striking fact in the functioning of roles/cases, as noted by Greimas (1966:132), is their 'redundant' character. Each semantic role is manifested at least twice within the sentence. The first time it is present separately in each of the roles; the second time it is present with both of its terms in the predicator which relates the two roles. Thus, in the statement *Miss Lonelyhearts killed the lamb* a semantic category S is manifested, with its two opposed semes, s and $\bar{s}$, in the following manner

$$Role_1(s) + Pred(s + \bar{s}) + Role_2(\bar{s})$$

where $role_1$ is that of agent; the predicator, an action-process verb; and $role_2$, the patient. The actuality and goal of the action, represented by s, is a doing, and of the process, represented by $\bar{s}$, an undergoing, both of which take place at the same time. Process and action are conceptually distinct but when they coincide, the verb-predicate identifies the actualizing of the virtualization of one thing having its effective seat in another. For example, the potentiality of an agent, that of the 'teacher' is actualized not in vacuo or isolation, but in the 'taught'; it is the actualizing *of* this *in* that.

Many bivalent action-process verbs may be said to refer to actions, the effects of which 'pass over' or 'transit' from an agent to a patient, from that which is active to that which is acted on, and generally from that which changes something as the agent to that which is changed by it as the patient. Considered from this point of view, a bivalent verb is called an 'operative' verb. There is another valency schema in terms of which the situation described in each of the sentences of (3) can be analyzed. Looked at from this point of view, the action-process verb is commonly called a 'factitive' or 'causative' verb. It denotes an event whereby a cause produces a result or makes its effect happen. A very reasonable question with reference to the information conveyed in the sentences of (1) might well be *Who did it?*—that is, who was the agent or actor responsible for the process? The answer to the question is contained in sentences of (3) which identify the agent as the *cause* of the process, the instigator of the change. The processes illustrated in (1) seem basic and the actions in (3) result from an added layer of derivation which linguists term a *causative* derivation. This suggests that an action-process verb may be derived from a process verb by means of a causative transformation. Another way of saying this is that the derivation converts a verb that is a process into one that is derivatively both a process and an action. When the causative schema presupposes agency, it distinguishes between *doing* things and *producing, bringing about,* or *effecting* a change. What we thus bring about are the *effects* or *results* of our action. That which we do is the cause of those effects. The cause is also the initiating and activating state of action and the effects, the results of our action. Following Lyons' analysis and using his notation (Lyons, 1977), the two valency-schemata in terms of which we can analyze the dynamic situation in each sentence of (3) are:

(i) AFFECT (AGENT, PATIENT)   (operative),

(ii) PRODUCE (CAUSE, EFFECT)   (factitive or causative).

Furthermore, by reason of the connection between agency and causality, we have a third schema which combines elements of both (i) and (ii). This is

(iii) PRODUCE (AGENT, EFFECT)   (operative-factitive).

The verbs *opened* and *lit* each enters into process sentences and process-action sentences without any change in the verb itself. But we also find pairs of morphologically unrelated verbs which stand in the same semantic relationship to one another. One such pair is illustrated in sentence (1c) and (3c), *The lamb died* and *Miss Lonelyhearts killed the lamb*. The synonymy relation between *Miss Lonelyhearts killed the lamb* and a productive causative construction like *Miss Lonelyhearts caused the lamb to die* provided one of the most fundamental motivations for the generative semantics treatment of causative constructions. The last two sentences indeed share a number of semantic properties. They both entail sentences such as *The lamb died* and *The lamb is dead*. The seman-

FUNDAMENTALS OF STORY LOGIC

tic similarity can be accounted for in a unified way only if some common predicate, 'cause,' is posited for both at an abstract level. The meaning of 'cause' would include though it would not exhaust the meaning of such English verbs as 'cause,' 'make,' and 'get.' The French auxiliary verb 'faire' (make-do), like the abstract predicator 'cause' brings about the presence of an additional role:

    (4) a. Tuer, c'est faire mourir.
          To kill is to make-die.

        b. Renverser, c'est faire tomber.
          To knock down is to make-fall.

It would seem possible, therefore, to translate the factitive schema into a French variant like this

    (ii') PRODUIRE (FAIRE, FAIRE)   (factitive)

and play on the ambiguity of 'faire' as an active verb. This is exactly what Greimas does in his article on action modalities (Cf. Greimas, 1976). The factitive relation is set up between two arguments that are hierarchically distinct: the Sender, argument of the first 'faire' and the Receiver, argument of the second 'faire.' The arguments are to be linked and yet distinguished from the agent and patient, arguments of the operative schema which function at the same hierarchical level.

The general connection between causativity and increased valency has been strongly emphasized by Tesnière. If the number of roles increases by one, the meaning of the new verb is generally *causative* with respect to the old one. For example, the bivalent verb 'kill' is causative in relation to the monovalent verb 'die' and the trivalent verb 'give' is causative in relation to the bivalent verb 'have.'

The valency patterns we have been discussing relate to language at the level of conceptual-semantic deep structure. But they are presented to a reader through a discursive structure that expresses the underlying semantic organization indirectly. We are interested at this point in seeing the means whereby West arranged his linguistic surface in order to describe the action-process situations and the choices made to signal the valency patterns. The choices made powerfully affect the perspectival meaning and direct our attention to the infrequent usage of action-process verbs that are often split into two verbs. Let us look first at the process statement *The door opened* and consider the immediate context in which two instances of door opening occur in the novella. The first example occurs after Miss Lonelyhearts has unsuccessfully tried to seduce Mary and they both return to Mary's place where Shrike is waiting: *Then he [Miss Lonelyhearts] heard footsteps and limped behind the projection of the elevator shaft. The door opened and Shrike looked into the corridor* (24). The perspectival significance of the door in the eyes of Miss Lonelyhearts stands out. Miss Lonelyhearts hears footsteps; he does not know whose. He hides and from his hiding place he waits to see whether it is Shrike that is coming. It could be Mary. The option is made not to mention the agent who opens the door and so reinforce the impression that it is Miss Lonelyhearts who sees and, furthermore, that Miss Lonelyhearts does not know or is unsure. As soon as Miss Lonelyhearts sees Shrike, the process statement *The door opened* becomes a process-action statement by derivation from the conjoined sentence. Shrike, as the agent of *looks* is retroactively seen as the causative agent who opened the door. The second brief passage we shall consider occurs when Miss Lonelyhearts falls sick and is unable to leave his room. He has just waken up from a dream when Betty comes to see him: *There was a timid knock on the door. It was open and Betty tiptoed into the room with her arms full of bundles* (31). Miss Lonelyhearts' vision is again emphasized but in this case the selection of the static verb presents the door opening as a static situation. What we do not do, however, is interpret the situation as static since it is nested in a sequence of two temporal moments, two actions, which lend an unusually *processual* aspect to the situation. We might well ask for the implications of the static description. One plausible interpretation is that the focus is on Miss Lonelyhearts' somnolent state of mind which perceives Betty's actions as sudden and discrete states.

Action-process sentences are lexicalized on the discursive surface when a swift catalogue listing of events is reported. As the following passage illustrates, the numeration device tends to trivialize the events: *When they returned to the house, it was quite dark.* They lit the kerosene lamp *that they brought with them, then dragged the mattress into the kitchen and made their bed on the floor next to the stove* (37). Conversely, when the action-process situation is functionally important for the story, the action-process sentence plays the role of an abstract plan schematically outlining possible future events and manifests itself discursively as a closing, recapitulation sentence that punctuates the final stage in the serial chain of events. The sentence *Miss Lonelyhearts killed the lamb* could serve as a synopsis of the following mini-narrative; but it would compete with

better paraphrases that capture both the priest-like role Miss Lonelyhearts wants
to acquire and the violence erupting from failed actions—two semantic features
which are contextually more prominent in the novella.

*Jud suggested buying a lamb to roast over a fire in the woods. Miss Lonely-
hearts agreed but on the condition that they sacrifice it to God before barbecu-
ing it. Steve was sent to the cutlery stand for a butcher knife, while the other
two remained to bargain for a lamb. [...] When they had worked themselves into
a frenzy, he brought the knife down hard. The blow was inaccurate and made
a flesh wound. He raised the knife again and this time the lamb's violent
struggles made him miss altogether. The knife broke on the altar. Steve and
Jud pulled the animal's head back for him to saw at its throat but only a small
piece of blade remained in the handle and he was unable to cut through the
matted wool.*

*Their hands were covered with blood and the lamb slipped free. It crawled
off into the underbrush. [...]*

*After some time had passed, Miss Lonelyhearts begged them to go back
and put the lamb out of its misery. They refused to go. He went back alone
and found it under a bush. He crushed its head with a stone and left the
carcass to the flies that swarmed around the bloody altar flowers* (9-10).

Processes end, whether gradually as in

The snow melted
Miss Lonelyhearts' anger grew cold and sodden like the snow (16)

or abruptly as in

The knife broke on the altar (10)
The dead pan broke (and pain actually crept into his voice) (21)

leaving the objects that undergo them in some terminal state. The state is the
bridge between patient as undergoer of a process and patient as that which is
in a particular state. Process is a transformation from one state into another.
The *result* identifies the state of the object-patient after it undergoes a process.
It is after the result to which it tends, not that from which it recedes, that the
process of change is named. Thus we call a change into liquid 'melting' though
the initial state of the change is solid no less truly than its resulting state is
liquid. And we call it 'freezing' if its result is solidity, in spite of the fact that
liquid is its initial state.

We can say not only that an object 'becomes so-and-so' but also that it does so 'from *being* so-and-so': e.g. snow melts from being partially frozen; Miss Lonelyhearts' anger becomes "cold and sodden" from that of having "swung in large drunken circles"; the knife breaks from being whole; Shrike's face becomes expressive from being the "dead pan" blank. This 'something to start with' is the *initial state* of the patient which has disappeared and been superseded by the process of change.

Let us note, in addition, that things cannot act upon each other and turn into one another at random. For how, to take an example, could inner chaos and anguish as such 'become' cold? Miss Lonelyhearts does not become self-balanced or in control when he ceases to be hot, for what 'ceasing to be hot' means is not only becoming something not hot, but something on the line antithetical to heat that leads to cold. So, too, if inner chaos and anguish lapse from themselves, they cannot lapse into any chance result but only into a more or less complete 'lack' or 'absence of inner chaos,' equivalent to the 'presence' of inner order and peace, calmness and control. It would seem then, that whenever anything changes, the process is along a determined line between the terms of some contrast; or, if we start from the intermediate state, the process is toward one of the extremes. Opposed or contrasted states determine the termini of a process of change, the initial one being 'absent,' the final one being shown as happening.

3. Verbs of motion and the associated network of roles

Let us go back to the passage quoted earlier, describing Miss Lonelyhearts' sacrificial killing of the lamb and let us consider for a moment how the happening is presented. Miss Lonelyhearts and his two college pals, Jud and Steve, have laid the lamb on a meadow rock. They chant and work themselves up to performing the sacrifice. What happens then?

Phase 1 – *Miss Lonelyhearts brought the knife down hard [on the lamb].*
Phase 2 – *He raised the knife again* but hit the rock instead.
Phase 3 – *He sawed at its throat.*
Phase 4 – *He crushed its head with a stone.*

From the point of view just discussed, Miss Lonelyhearts' killing of the lamb can be seen in terms of Miss Lonelyhearts' action being the cause of whatever effect is produced on the lamb. The textual fragment, however, provides an alternative point of view. Phases 1 and 2 of the sacrificial killing are presented in terms of Miss Lonelyhearts' movement toward the lamb; more precisely, the movement of a knife which moves from Miss Lonelyhearts onto the lamb. The dovetailing of two types of verbs, representative of the two points of view, within a homogeneous sequence of events, relaxes what might appear to be at first sight a sharp distinction between a situation in which an agent affects a patient and a situation in which an entity moves to or from a place. The text thus introduces us to another important subclass of *dynamic* verbs as opposed to static verbs.

To *bring down* and to *raise*, like the more typical members of this class 'come' and 'go,' 'depart' and 'return,' are dynamic verbs, having to do with change of position. They are further specified as verbs of motion or movement. The suggestion I shall make about such verbs is that they require a noun which bears to it the relation of *object-of-motion* or *object-of-orientation*. For stative, locative verbs, such as 'sit' and 'be' (in, at, ...) we shall use the latter designation. In the above examples provided by phases 1 and 2, the object-of-motion is specified lexically as *knife*. As an object-of-motion the knife identifies the entity that is moving. Moreover, as the examples indicate, it will be necessary to distinguish between the object-of-motion from the grammatical object in the explicit sense of *patient* when the patient role is assigned the place of grammatical object.

A set of three other roles, which I shall refer to as motion roles, is dependent upon verbs of motion. *Terminal* identifies the location of the *object-of-motion* at the end of the movement or motion, the terminal boundary of the event—its 'whither':

(1) a. *Miss Lonelyhearts brought the knife down hard on the lamb.*
    b. *The lamb crawled off into the underbrush.*
    c. *Miss Lonelyhearts dropped the letter to the floor without reading it.*

In each of these sentences, the terminal indicates that as the event ended, the object-of-motion was in the position defined by *lamb*, *underbrush*, and *floor*.

Source identifies the location of the object-of-motion at the beginning of the movement, the initial boundary of the event—its 'whence':

(2) a. *Miss Lonelyhearts crawled out of bed like an exhausted swimmer.*
    b. *Miss Lonelyhearts snatched the paper out of the machine.*
    c. *Miss Lonelyhearts took a drink from the whiskey bottle.*

Each of these sentences indicates that as the event began, the object-of-motion was in the position defined by *bed*, *machine*, and *bottle*.

In order to handle the valency of verbs of motion we need to add to the three valency-schemata already discussed the following orientational and topological schemata:

(iv) MOVE (OBJECT-OF-MOTION, SOURCE)

(v) MOVE (OBJECT-OF-MOTION, TERMINAL).

Since all movement conceptually yields both a source and a terminal, (iv) and (v) can be combined to yield:

(vi) MOVE (OBJECT-OF-MOTION, SOURCE, TERMINAL).

A surface structure like the following reflects this combination:

(3) *Betty had left the couch for a red chair*

but more often the combination is lexicalized through two verbs:

(4) a. *Goldsmith* took *a pink envelope out of his pocket and* threw *it on the desk "From an admirer."*

b. *Shrike* pulled *a large batch of letters put of his pockets and* waved *them in front of Miss Lonelyhearts.*

c. *Miss Lonelyhearts* left *the city room and* went *into the hall to use the pay station.*

Locus is the term I have chosen, following its usage in the physics of fluid dynamics, for the relationship that others have labeled locative, location, place, or range. In an expression of movement locus indicates the path or area traversed, as in:

(5) a. Down the hill *they fled until they reached the meadow.*

b. *Mrs. Doyle slammed things around* in the kitchen.

c. *Doyle, the cripple, was slowly working his way* up the stairs.

With position, locus designates location, as in

(6) a. *Delehanty's was in the cellar of a brownstone house.*

b. *The room held a bed, a table, and two chairs.*

c. *An ivory Christ hung opposite the foot of the bed.*

The track followed from the source to the terminal is the actual path or the sequence of continuous states over which the movement or positional change extends. Note that the locus identifies the path but not the movement nor its 'whence' and 'whither.' Verbs of motion identify the kind of movement taking place or the kind of transition. The choice of the word 'transition' here is appropriately direct since 'trans-ition' denotes literally a 'going across' from where the object was before to where it is afterwards.

One additional remark. We can specify the limiting points of movement, its source and terminal, its place or locus, and, furthermore, its direction by means of prepositions. All these conceptual roles which enter as factors of movement are themselves *without movement*. It is clear that the movement takes place not in the form—which is its source and terminal—nor in the track followed but in the object itself which is actually in motion.

Verbs of motion cover a cluster of varied happenings. Sentences like the following appear to communicate bivalent *motion-processes*:

> (7) a. *Miss Lonelyhearts, Steve, and Jud fell exhausted in the tall grass.*
>
> b. *Miss Lonelyhearts and Doyle rolled part of the way down the stairs.*

That processes are involved is born out by the fact that these sentences are possible answers to the questions *What happened to Miss Lonelyhearts, Steve, and Jud? to Miss Lonelyhearts and Doyle?* That motions are involved is evidenced by the existence of an object-of-motion: *Miss Lonelyhearts, Steve,* and *Jud*, in the first sentence, and *Miss Lonelyhearts* and *Doyle* in the second. *Grass* is the terminal and *stairs* is the locus. Here we have a patient that 'overlaps' with the object-of-motion. This 'overlap' or 'merging' of roles is traditionally termed by linguists as *syncretism*.

Other sentences suggest that there are bivalent *motion-actions*:

> (8) a. *Miss Lonelyhearts visited Betty.*
>
> b. *The lamb crawled off into the underbrush.*
>
> c. *Miss Lonelyhearts vaulted the porch rail (and ran to kiss her).*

These are surely actions; for example, they pass the do-test *What did Miss Lonelyhearts do?* and *What did the lamb do?*. The semantic role of agent overlaps with that of object-of-motion. *Betty* and *underbrush* make up the terminal and the *rail* is the locus.

Many more sentences contain what appear to be trivalent *motion-action-processes*:

> (9) a. *Miss Lonelyhearts snatched the paper out of the machine.*
>
> b. *Miss Lonelyhearts threw Mrs. Doyle's letter into the waste-paper*

basket.

c. *Shrike buried his triangular face like the blade of a hatchet in her* [*Miss Farkis'*] *neck.*

d. *Miss Lonelyhearts brought the knife down hard on the lamb.*

We shall summarize the information identifying the set of all semantic roles discussed thus far and exemplified in the foregoing sentences with the sole purpose of ascertaining the overlapping of roles linked to process-action verbs with the roles linked to verbs of motion. The italicized roles are the roles matching the patient.

	Agent	Patient	Object-of-motion	Source	Terminal
a.	Miss L	paper	*paper*	machine	Miss L
b.	Miss L	letter	*letter*	Miss L	basket
c.	Shrike	neck	face	Shrike	*neck*
		(Miss Farkis)	(Shrike)		(*Miss Farkis*)
d.	Miss L	lamb	knife	Miss L	*lamb*

The traditional 'notional' theory of transitive action-process verbs associates the agent with the source of the movement, on the one hand, and the patient who undergoes or suffers an action with the terminal of movement, on the other hand. The standard linguistic term for terminal is 'goal' and it strongly reinforces a connection between patient and terminal within a 'goal'-oriented activity; the agent not only operates upon, but directs his action at, the patient. The problem with the word 'goal', however, is that it activates an association with the subject-agent and terms we use to connect a subject-agent's action with his or her will—that is, desires, aims, objectives—and this trailing cloud of meanings seems to have nothing to do with the linguistic definition of 'goal.'

The notional definition of action-process verbs, tested within the motion-action-process ones, is to some extent appropriate. In sentences (c) and (d) both the patient and the terminal of movement semantically overlap. Note, however, that the grammatical *object* is neither the patient nor the terminal, as the notional definition of the grammatical object would have it. In (c) Shrike via his face is both agent and object-of-motion and in (d) the knife, as the instrumental object-of-motion wielded by Miss Lonelyhearts, is encompassed again within the agentive causal chain.

As sentences (a) and (b) indicate, the notional theory is at times altogether inapplicable. The patient does not merge with terminal but with the object-of-motion which fills the place of grammatical object. In this case patient and object-of-motion both identify what is affected.

There are no actantial categories comparable to the roles of the orientational, topological schemata (4)-(6). Movement and the directional transfer it actualizes are, as we shall show later, analogous in some regard, to trivalent communication acts which involve notions of transfer, circulation, and exchange of messages and objects. So that in actantial grammar the 'topology' is absorbed into the 'syntax of communication.' The pertinent movements and objects-of-motion are the movements of the Sender and Receiver actants relative to a valued Object that is *in circulation*.

III

A Systemic Definition of Action:
The Practical Syllogism

On an intuitive, pre-analytic basis, we have no difficulty in picking out instances of genuine action and distinguishing them from things that merely happen to us and befall us. Is there any identifying feature of action which we would unhesitatingly accept as revealing action but which is missing in non-actions? In other words, what do we mean when we say we *do* something? The attempt to analyze action as simply that which is expressed by a verb and its relations does not reconcile fully with the 'ordinary' language concepts implicit in our everyday notion of action. We know whether events are actions only after we know much more than the verb provides. And this we decide after 'unpacking' the verb into a description of *antecedent states* and considering the additional propositions as a necessary litmus of agency or action. These antecedent states are the wants, goals, and plans of the agent which are interconnected in a peculiar pattern of reasoning used by the agent both before and during the performance of action, when the agent is said to 'be doing' something. The reasoning has been named in traditional Aristotelian commentary a *practical syllogism* or *inference*.

1. The practical syllogism

Let us look at what a schema of this kind works out:
Major premise: N wants to do O / bring about O.
Minor premise: N considers that he cannot do O unless he does P.
Conclusion: Therefore, N sets himself to do P / does P.
The starting point or major premise of the syllogism mentions some wanted

thing and characterizes it as an end of action. The minor premise relates some action to this end, roughly as a means to an end. The conclusion, finally, consists in using this means to secure the end: it expresses an *action* or a plan of action. Thus, in practical as in theoretical reasoning, we pass from premises to conclusion. In both the affirmation of the premises leads of necessity to the conclusion. Clearly in some sense the practical logic is different from theoretical logic. With it, we consistently work out not only what we ought to do but also what we want to do and we draw the conclusion in action, i.e. by enacting it.

We now have the materials for a very simple model of action explanation which not only appeal to ends or goals of action but also conform to our everyday account of action and the related notions by which we describe, explain, and 'textualize' our own behavior and that of others and by which we understand the written representation of narrated action. Taken together, the three steps of the practical inference not only exhibit a certain *pattern of reasoning* but they also form a *linguistically closed system* in which each step or action-dependent expression relates semantically and conceptually to the other two. Each sentence contains a so-called *modal verb* (a predicator) that operates upon a verb of action (its argument). As simple as the model appears, we are facing here an area of language traditionally considered quite complex in its network of semantic relations. We will investigate the nature of each step and we will examine only the modal verbs that are operating within and are enclosed by this pattern of reasoning which is said to lead to action.

The practical inference is an important problem-area for philosophers and particularly Aristotelian scholars. The concern with the type of reasoning exhibited and the systemic meaning manifested in the inference is totally extrinsic to concerns in linguistics. A rather different view of action modality is taken by linguists as opposed to both Aristotelian scholars and logicians. Research dealing with the practical inference focuses on the modal verbs appearing in each step and the ways the inference schema gives cohesiveness to an actional pattern. Linguists approach the problem of modality—well-known to include much more than what is traditionally called 'modal auxiliaries'—in terms of proposals for a general definition of modality and mood and a symmetrical and semantic classification of it into major types. One such general meaning of modals sheds light on the practical inference and supplies a suggestive metaphor. This meaning of modals supposes a succession of ideational chronology, a chronology of *aiming* which ranks modals along a passage marked by three degrees or moments: the possible, the probable, and the certain. In contrast to the *objective* or pragmatic meaning of modals, the second meaning has been termed *subjective*, hypothetical, inferential, predictive or epistemic. Viewed in this manner, the use of a modal like 'want,' 'believe,' 'consider' commits the reasoner of the practical inference to see the steps as making up *the trajectory of an aim*. This is the position championed by the linguist G. Guillaume for whom the problem of mood and modality is "essentially a problem of aim," that is, "a function of the contact or non-contact of the aim with actuality" (1965:30,3-7). For Guillaume, the particular theory of mood amounts to knowing which ideas when the aim traverses them, lead to *actuality* and which do not.

If we could give this schema a more specific linguistic interpretation, omitting the obvious and non-explanatory one—that, if chained linearly, it is a simplistic *text*, stated in artificial articulateness—it would have to be in the sense attributed to it by Greimas' textual linguistics and this sense is still vague and generalized relative to the schema as we have it set down. It is also amusingly playful with the linguistic metalanguage. The practical inference schema would then be the 'schema' which selects the lexemes that can be inscribed on the 'syntactical axis' tying the Subject and Object actants and is, therefore, termed a 'syntactical schema.' It is also referred to as the "discursive organization which manipulates the constitutive elements of the canonical narrative énoncé" and, in any case, is "a syntactical pathway that establishes itself during discursive manifestation." One of the functions the schema fulfills is to "transform the logomachic manifestation into a discursive manifestation of meaning" (Greimas, 1973:15,17,19). All these phrases are presently introduced as a background 'disattend track' which will be carried into the 'main track' in the next chapter when we take up the Subject-Object relation in actantial grammar.

One immediate correction that needs to be made is that practical reasoning is not restricted to exactly two premises and a conclusion. The number of premises is flexible but, however many there are, they must pass through three stages, the stage of initial premises, the stage of intermediate premises, and lastly the conclusion stage. We can also have complicated many-premise syllogisms sometimes represented as sequences of syllogisms. Reducing the practical syllogism to its minimum of three steps is like trying to choose a summary term for what each stage concerns itself with. Philosophers disagree on what modal verb is central or most important in the initial and intermediate stages.

The first or initial stage of practical reasoning concerns itself with a wanted thing or end of action. But in what form will mention of the want and goal appear? G. von Wright (1970) puts 'intends' in the syllogism and says that it is essentially the same as 'is aiming,' or 'pursues as an end,' or 'wants.' The notion of a *wanted thing* which I shall try to explain, is nonetheless not the same thing as that of an *end or goal of action*. The question may be raised, how things wanted and ends of action are mutually related. The question is complicated and I shall only touch upon it here. There is an obvious sense in which the object of a want establishes proleptically the goal or objective of an action. In other words, only objects attainable through action can be ends of action. If I am thirsty, I want to drink; the object of my want is the situation 'I'm drinking,' and the objective of my action is then the actualization or enactment of the situation in which I drink. For simple cases, it is customary to describe wants and desires in terms of their objects meaning by objects the things which figure as in imagination their goals. Barring the frustration of external circumstances, the end-result of desire is regarded as similar to the object consciously desired. But in a stronger sense, the object of desire and the end of action are no more alike than a sign on the highway is like the city to which it points and which it recommends to the traveler. The thing wanted must be at some distance from the action; in between, metaphorically speaking, is the 'locus' where the narrative trip happens and moves.

There is a double-directed and paradoxical meaning in *want* which covers the semantic components of both an origin and an end. Want is an origin insofar as the object of desire prods, propels, activates the subject in projecting an end of action to be reached. It is an end insofar as it connotes a kind of 'wherefore' or 'terminal.' The vacillation between these two meanings creates the tension of a 'not yet' yearning for an 'already.' There is another way in which the paradox manifests itself within the practical inference. Part of what is meant by 'want' in the initial premise is the disposition to bring about what is desired. To say the subject wants-desires something is to say that the subject is disposed to get it, in the following sense. Desiring it, when it issues in the appropriate action neither requires nor admits of explanation while the action not ensuing demands that we adduce some countervailing factor. In this sense, the want or desire is defined by 'reference-back' from the action, by its end or final state. It functions as a privileged anchoring point which pins down the sliding, ambulatory meaning of the actional signifying chain and system.

A. Kenny's attempt to formulate five variants of the initial premise which may be given plausibility by different passages of Aristotle clearly brings out the polysemantic nature of the want and goal. Each of these variants is analyzed and the pros and cons for retaining it as the starting point of reasoning are given:

(1) I want to heal
(2) Health is good.
(3) I shall heal
(4) This patient is to be healed.
(5) Health is of such-and-such a nature

Against the backdrop of these five variants, it will be useful to keep an action-process sentence, derivable from it, such as *The doctor heals the patient*. Note that in none of these variants is there more than one role mentioned, either the "I" as the doctor, that is, the wanting or desiring subject; or the patient; but in all cases the predicator is retained either verbally 'to heal' or nominally 'health.' The seven pages of analysis which Kenny devotes to the five proposed formulations indicate that all of them are pertinent and that all of them say something essential to the starting premise of a piece of practical reasoning (Cf. Kenny, 1979:126-32). The problem consists essentially in trying to sum up the variants in one phrase or of selecting one of them which will give a formal account of practical reasoning. Kenny suggests, in agreement with many other philosophers, that the essential characteristic of the initial premise is its prescriptive or deontic nature, expressible by means of deontic modal auxiliaries such as 'ought,' 'must,' 'should,' 'has to,' or 'is to.' A premise like (4), "This patient is to be healed," is a prescriptive premise and hence is formally suitable to serve as basis of practical reasoning. But, he adds, it needs completing with a definition, account, or theory of the end and a secondary statement of the want which shows its desirability or goodness for the valuing or appraising subject.

Let us now turn to the intermediate group of premises. This stage bears upon choice or deliberation about the means which are seen as necessary for the attainment of the end and which are in the subject's power to do or bring about. After something is declared worth wanting, the wanting subject must then ask himself or herself: "Is this a situation I can here and now bring about?" If the answer is No, the subject must look for some other means to that situation; if it is Yes, we have a statement of what is possible within the chooser's power and the choosing subject can then move on into action. Implicitly or explicitly the second or intermediate premise(s) is a premise of the possible, that which is in the subject's power to do. This possibility is suitably reflected in the modal auxiliaries like 'can,' the 'can' of ability and knowledge, of mental, physical, and personal powers and of human possibility, in general, and in the modal verb 'know how to.' M. Ehrman defines 'can' as follows: "The basic meaning of *can* is that there is no obstruction to the action of the lexical verb of which *can* is an auxiliary; that is to say, that action is free to take place" (1966:12). Alternative words which are used instead of 'considers' in the practical inference are 'thinks,' 'believes,' or sometimes 'knows.' For our purposes, we can summarize the human 'possible' as (a) that course of action which is conceived in advance of the actual doing or performance and can be done by the subject, and (b) that course of action which could be conceived as an alternative to whatever was actually done. Possibility exists because human beings can—have the power—to make anticipatory and retrospective commentaries and to imagine what is going to happen or what might have been. Thus possibility in this context is related to such concepts as 'plan,' 'project,' 'foresight,' and the like.

In the case of choice and deliberation, the intermediate premises, otherwise often expressed formally as conditionals—the modal expression of supposition and hypothesis—occur in answer to the question *How can N do it?* or *By what means?* Let us take up Kenny's example of the Aristotelian physician. Kenny cites the following reasoning suggested in the *Metaphysics*:

(1) This patient is to be healed.

(2) Health being the kind of thing it is, humours must be balanced.

(3) If he is heated, his humours will be balanced.

(4) If he is rubbed, he will be heated.

(5) Rubbing is in my power.

The first premise is the starting point; the next three premises can all be looked at as belonging to the intermediate stage and the last step as leading up to action. According to Kenny, the second, third, and fourth premises are premises of 'the possible' answering an enquiry about ways and means:

(1') This patient is to be healed.
      How can I heal him?

(2') I can heal him by balancing his humours.
      How can I balance his humours?

(3') I can balance his humours by heating him.
      How can I heat him?

(4') I can heat him by rubbing him.
   Rubbing is in my power.

(See Kenny, 1979:136-7.) What is done by the agent as the upshot of practical reasoning is action answering to the description given by the conclusion. It is debatable whether the action itself is initiated or whether the decision to act is verbalized in a description of a plan of action. There is also the position represented by G. Tarde, a contemporary and rival of E. Durkheim, that the conclusion of the practical inference is a necessity, "un devoir" ("a must") or "un il faut" ("an I-have-to"). In Tarde's own words:

> Le devoir est un vouloir qui a perdu conscience de sa majeure, du Désir qui le meut. [...] De là son autorité pratiquement absolue qui n'a pas besoin de s'exprimer pour agir et qui donne un air d'impératif catégorique à son dispositif sans motifs apparents. D'ailleurs, le *il faut* de la conclusion est toujours senti comme un *il faut* et non comme un plaisir.

> (The must is a wanting which has lost awareness of the major premise, of the Desire which moves it. [...] Whence its practically absolute authority which does not need to be expressed in order to act and which gives an air of a categorical imperative to its purview without apparent motives. Moreover, the *I-have-to* of the conclusion is always felt as an *I-have-to* and not as a pleasure.) (Tarde, 1897:215-6)

Whatever structural meaning there is to the modal *must* seems dependent on the relation between the second premise and the conclusion. Use of the means are a practical necessity, a *must-do* for the sake of that which is wanted, a requiredness in accomplishing the objective. In other passages, however, Tarde also speaks of the conclusion as a *mediated desire* in the sense that, wanting O and judging P to be the necessary means, we therefore *desire the desire of P*. Needless to say, this type of argument, though obviously true, leads us per force to carry each modal of the practical inference—whether it is the want or the must or the modals of the intermediate stage—into the conclusion, as *mediated*. We would never step beyond the reasoning to the action itself. Consequently, and for simplicity's sake, I have selected the view stressing the *onset of an action* and hence retained von Wright's formulation of the conclusion as 'setting oneself to do something' (von Wright, 1971). Alternative wordings might be 'decides to do,' 'embarks on doing,' 'proceeds to do'; or, most simply and most strongly 'does,' in which case we can truly say we *syllogize an action*.

2. Teleological explanation of action

The practical inference plays a key role as a model of explanation and understanding of action in the human sciences. An interesting and valuable methodological consequence ensues from "inverting" the schema, an ingenious idea which belongs to von Wright and that needs to be exploited (1971:96-7). The consequence consists in the *identity* of the practical inference schema with a type of teleological explanation. The schema of the practical inference *is* that of a teleological explanation "turned upside down." The starting point of a teleological explanation is that someone does something or that someone has set forth to do something. One of the simplest questions we may raise is "Why?". We shall turn shortly to a list of questions that appear instead of the why question and operate more accurately in ordinary-language use. For the moment, brief as it is, let us provisionally settle on "Why?". The answer usually is: "in order to do O / in order to bring about O." Given the conclusion, which is an action, we want to know the major premise. It is then assumed that the action which we are trying to explain is considered by the agent as causally relevant to the doing of O and that the doing of O is what the agent is aiming at or wants with this action.

The upside-down practical inference is, as we said, a teleological explanation of one type. 'Teleology' generally involves an apparent reference to the future as explanatory of the past. But this general, semantic denominator does not warrant the assimilation of all statements considered teleological to a single interpretation. We would not wish, for example, to attribute desires or beliefs to biological organs, animals, or to social institutions or practices. There are limits which it seems reasonable to impose on the scope of each variety of teleology. When we explain *human* or *anthropomorphic action* teleologically we start, so to speak, from the conclusion and work our way back to the premises. The wants and beliefs and plans, which enter into practical reasoning and which find expression in the statements which constitute the premises provide the *reason* or *motive* for action. To ask for this reason is to ask for the action's *point* or *rationale*. We may think the action crazy, stupid, wild, and so on, but knowing the reason, we can understand how the action could have been *appropriate* or *justified from the agent's point of view*, from the desire and goal (given in premise 1) and the choice and possibilities (given in premise 2) with which the agent started. The explanation renders an agent's action *intelligible* to us. A narrated action may be said to be *followable* or *readable* in R. Barthes' sense, when we can see for what reason the agent does it. The logical point of importance here is that accounting for the action is citing something from which the *propriety* of the action is supposed to follow.

As employed in explanatory contexts 'reason' often implies 'moving to action.' For in explanation we are looking for an *agent's* reason, that is, for those facts which *have* actually moved the agent to act as he or she did, whether they be called reasons or something else. From the platform of the practical inference, however, from the view of the reasoning subject deciding on what to do, *the subject cannot be said to be looking for things which he or she knows will move him/her.* When the practical inference subject asks other people to give him advice, to survey and weigh the reasons for him, he is not asking them to look for incentives, to provide him with motives, to mention facts which will move him. He is asking for facts of a certain sort, namely, facts which are properly called reasons, that is, facts such that if anyone were to follow them, they would be entering on the *best* course of action.

In the intermediate stage of practical reasoning, the subject tries before acting to determine which is the best course of action, the course supported by the "best reasons," that is open to him or her with a view to entering on it. In a teleological explanation, after someone has acted, we try to determine whether s/he has taken the best course open to her/him, with a view to determining whether s/he is to be condemned or praised. In this aspect of teleological explanation, we *justify*, we try to show, after the event, that the agent has taken the best course of action or that, at any rate, s/he is not to be condemned for not taking it.

We wish to contrast the use of 'reason' when it refers to the first step and second step of the practical reasoning, when these steps make up the information sought in a teleological explanation. The reason in step 1 will be called a 'motive-reason' or 'incentive-reason.' The genuine reason of step 2 will be called 'justifying reason' or 'appraisal reason.'

Although we are talking of the agent with indifference toward its real-life or discourse existence, a brief comment on one crucial difference that separates them is called for. The narrative character-agent appears as if s/he has 'real,' off-the-paper choices open to her/him and supported by the "best reasons" but these alternative choices are, in fact, structurally overdetermined and constrained by *the story's "best reasons."* On the one hand, we have an alternative choice that imputes a sort of free will and biography to the character; on the other hand, and in conflict with this alternative, we have the constraint of the discourse that dictates for its own well-being the choice of that alternative which provides it with a 'come-back' and insures its progress in 'rebounds.' This is a widely known and accepted higher law of narrative that can be summed up in Barthes' incisive words:

> At each crossroads of the action, the narrative ... chooses between several possibilities, and this choice involves at any given moment the very future of the story. ... It goes without saying that, where the action is faced with an alternative—having this or that consequence—the narrative chooses that from which it profits, i.e. that which *assures its survival as narrative*. Never does the narrative record anything—implied or real—which would snuff out the story, bring it to an abrupt ending. Narrative *art* consists precisely of endowing these structural determinants (the only concern of which is the 'well-being' of the narrative, not that of this or the other character) with the security, i.e. the alibi, of variables which are usually of a psychological, moral, or intensely emotional nature, etc. Where the narrative in fact opts for its own survival, it is the character who appears to choose his fate   (Barthes, 1971:7-8).

When the character chooses, that is, appears to choose, the wrong alternative, the narrative must explain it in the following sense. It must *cover* and *ground* this alternative in terms of those 'alibis' Barthes speaks of which provide a dual function in the story: that of creating the 'effect of the real' person, by resorting, as Barthes says, to the psychological, moral, and emotional nature of the person; and secondly, that of serving as *pointers* which allow the reader to reconstruct or convert those culturally cited personal traits, almost transparently and effortlessly, into motive-reasons or justifying reasons for the agent-character.

3. Textual and narrative arguments

Taking as our point of departure the practical inference and its inversion, the teleological explanation of action, we shall argue that the premises function as textual and narrative arguments in a complex propositional structure. In the major premise "N wants to do O / bring about O," N is agreed upon to be the subject—its status, other than grammatical, is noncommittal—and O will be designated as the *object-of-desire* or object-want. The verb 'want' may be followed by a direct object or by an infinitive: one may want a drink, a car, power and intellectual stimulation; one can also want to walk, to run, to see a sunset, and to own a Monet. The object-of-desire is not only something tangible, a physical entity, but also an experience of doing or undergoing certain things; N may be said to want O, to want to do O, to be O, to have O, or to have O happen. When read *with* the conclusion and so to speak backwards from it, the major premise will be said to make up the *goal-object* or *objective* argument in relation to the subject N.

Of great importance to the grasping of action dynamics is the nature of the first premise and the difference in *force* or *tension* that it carries when viewed in the context of the practical inference schema as against the view framed by the context of the observer, story-teller, or commentator giving a teleological explanation. It is impossible to waive the fact that only when the subject-agent is acting or after he has acted, but particularly during action, that the notion-argument of *objective* comes on 'full force,' i.e. with enormous semantic charge. It is also in this marked, incomplete actualization of action, when effort is involved, that action itself takes on the characterization of having a certain *direction* and directiveness, often spoken of as 'purpose,' 'aim,' or 'intent.' We speak of actions as being directed only when they are aimed at some object-of-desire, only when they are charged by an objective. For the notion of direction, metaphorically speaking, is given its specific force—which is its actional meaning —in terms of a teleological explanation of objectives. This force is close to zero in the first premise when viewed from the aspect of the reasoning subject, before the act. And it approaches another kind of deflated zero after the act but this time the objective is invested with a direction retrospectively.

Other questions than the "Why?" can be used to test for the presence of the objective. Taking his cue from an old English translation of Aristotle, Kenny suggests calling these questions "wherefore" questions to distinguish them clearly from the "why" questions seeking a causal explanation: "the end is the wherefore: for every purposive choice is a choice *of* something *for the sake of* something else" (Aristotle quoted by Kenny, 1979:114,85). Let us consider some "wherefore" questions which are verbal indices to the objective of an action:

What did N want to do?
What did N want?
What was N trying to do?
What was N meaning to do?

In giving an answer, we specify the objective aimed by the subject N. Otherwise put, we specify what N wanted or meant to do or bring about. We specify the objective most commonly by the use of 'want' plus the infinitive of the verb. What did Miss Lonelyhearts want to do?

> *He wanted* to work *on his leader*

but not (for example)

> He wanted worked on his leader. (ungrammatical)
> He to work on his leader. (ungrammatical)

An 'objective' sentence will answer the question *What did N want to do?* to which a simple process-patient sentence is not an appropriate answer. What did Miss Lonelyhearts want to do?

> *He wanted to kill the lamb*

but not (let's say)

> *The lamb was killed by Miss Lonelyhearts.*

The objective is not at all the same as the patient role, lexicalized as *lamb*, defined linguistically as 'goal,' or semantically as an object that undergoes a change. Who is doing and who/what is undergoing an action in *Miss Lonelyhearts wanted to kill the lamb*?

The verb in its infinitive form is a *project verb* which has before it the totality of its becoming and where none of the phases of action have been spent or wasted. 'To write' or 'to kill' is the image of the verb in tension only, the image of an action which is not done but can be done and can result from a desire or will. Even if we were to formulate the happen-test in the future tense in order to highlight the futurity in the future process, we still do not obtain an answer adequate to the 'objective' question:
What will happen to the lamb?

> *Miss Lonelyhearts will kill the lamb.*

The aim of 'to kill' operates through that of *to want*. Although 'to want' has a semantic feature of prediction or foreseeing in the sense that something wanted is something predictable, the prediction so largely overflows with desire and volition—"an excess of signification," in Guillaume's phrase—that the aim or objective stops long before it reaches the line of actuality. The want and desire are attitudes taken with respect to the possible and determined intrinsically in face of the possible, before acceding to the probable. The reverse obtains in the case of the future 'will kill' which is a view corresponding to the probable and the real, beyond hypothesis since it has already reached actuality.

For the case when action is identical with the objective and not a means to the attainment of this objective, we have a "collapsed" inference, i.e. *no* inference since the second premise is missing:

(Major premise:)Miss Lonelyhearts wanted to write.

(Minor premise:). . . . .

(Conclusion:)Therefore, Miss Lonelyhearts wrote.

The action of writing is not explained by saying that it was wanted, that it was an 'objective.' The answer to the question "What did Miss Lonelyhearts want to do?" "He wanted *to write*" specifies the objective of the first premise. The answer to the question "What did Miss Lonelyhearts do?" "He *wrote*" identifies the action in the conclusion. Both answers *identify* the action as type but they do not explain it. An act "done for its own sake" or "done as an objective in itself" is simply *understood*. If we want to *explain* the action, not just identify it, we must be able to unfold it by pointing to a more remote objective which is not in the action itself. This objective is the common or middle term in a syllogism "or form of reasoning in which from two given or assumed propositions called the premisses and having a common or middle term a third is deduced called the conclusion from which the middle term is absent" (Concise Oxford Dictionary, quoted by M. Sandmann, 1979:8-9). In the syllogism 'N wants to do O; N considers he cannot do O unless he does P; N sets forth to do P' the middle term which is repeated in the two premises and is absent in the conclusion is the term O. When the middle term is absent, action is identified and understood.

One often gets the impression when reading narrative texts of having full practical syllogisms when in fact we are facing barely veiled "collapsed" ones. Although the action is understood, it does not 'take,' like a photograph that has been overexposed. It fails to take because the collapsed inference is inconclusive; that is, we *cannot affirm* the action as conclusion. This partially explains the need of starting all over again, back to premise 1. We swivel back in order to peg the action, in order to account more thoroughly, i.e. *explain*, the objective. Let me give one such example from *Miss Lonelyhearts*. I shall first give a formal summary of it according to the practical inference schema and then quote the text (West, 10-11).

1. Initial premises: Miss Lonelyhearts wants to have / bring about
                                    perfect order. Everything had to form a pattern.

2. Intermediate premises: . . . .

3. Conclusion: Therefore, Miss Lonelyhearts sets himself to
                                    make a pattern of everything.

4. Outcome: He fails and panics.

2'. Intermediate premises: He considers that he cannot have order unless
                                    he visits Betty.

3'. Conclusion: Therefore, Miss Lonelyhearts sets himself to
                                    visit Betty.

Let us now take a look at how the narrative textualizes the above. I shall
bracket the modal propositions and interpolate them in the text if needed and
I shall also repeat segments of the text in order to mold it to the formality of the
practical inference.

1. Initial premises

    *Miss Lonelyhearts found himself developing an almost insane sensitiveness to
    order. Everything had to form a pattern: the shoes under the bed, the ties in
    the holder, the pencils on the table.*

2. Intermediate premises

    . . . .

3. Conclusion

    [Therefore, Miss Lonelyhearts sets himself to make a pattern of every-
    thing.] ... *the shoes under the bed, the ties in the holder, the pencils on the
    table. When he looked out of a window, he composed the skyline by balanc-
    ing one building against another. If a bird flew across this arrangement, he
    closed his eyes angrily until it was gone.*

4. Outcome

    For a little while, he seemed to hold his own but one day he found himself with his back to the wall. On that day all the inanimate things over which he had tried to obtain control took the field against him. When he touched something, it spilled or rolled to the floor. The collar buttons disappeared under the bed, the point of the pencil broke, the handle of the razor fell off, the window shade refused to stay down. [...] He fled to the street but there chaos was multiple. Broken groups of people hurried past, forming neither stars nor squares. [...] He stood quietly against a wall trying not to see or hear.

2'.   Intermediate premises

Then he remembered Betty. She had often made him feel that when she straightened his tie, she straightened much more. And he had once thought that if her world were larger, were the world, she might order it as finally as the objects on her dressing table.

3'.   Conclusion

He gave Betty's address to a cab driver and told him to hurry.

Note how a collapsed inference generates a full one. Moreover, the conclusion in 3' is no longer identical with the objective in 1. Miss Lonelyhearts' action of taking a cab to visit Betty is explained by the initial and intermediate premises of 1 and 2'. The initial set of premises is nonetheless still perplexing. The nub of the perplexity caused by Miss Lonelyhearts' obsession with order consists of the fact that neither the immediate chapter-episode in which it is embedded nor the subsequent ones in the novella articulate the relationship of the needed order to the events represented in the story. But let us focus our attention on the segment as it is, outside of its positional meaning, syntagmatic and paradigmatic, in the story, and let us compare the differences in formulation and expression from the formal practical schema.

The thing that strikes me the most in reading *Miss Lonelyhearts found himself developing an almost insane sensitiveness to order* is the progressive aspect of desire which is being formed or *developed* and the dysphoric, compulsive connotation of the desire referred to as *an insane sensitiveness to*. Both of these characteristics urge us to inquire into the actual emergence of the object-of-desire. Quite unlike its 'want' counterpart which represents the modal in this stage, the textual formulation makes it plain that the 'want' or 'desire' and objects-of-desire arise only when "there is something the matter," when there is "trouble" in the existing situation. When analyzed "this something the matter" is found to spring from a lack, a shortage, a want in the existing situation as it stands, an absence which produces *conflict* in the elements that do exist. If Miss Lonelyhearts is obsessed with order, it is, we reason, because there is some 'disorder' in his situation and this disorder is designated by the semantic configuration of "chaos," "lack of self-control," "meaninglessness," "lack of sureness," and is, in addition of a "mental" and "psychological" nature, as connoted in the intermediate premises. If things were going well for Miss Lonelyhearts, objects-of-desire would not arise and there would be no occasion to project an objective or consider means to enacting them. For 'going smoothly' signifies that there is no need for effort and struggle. So that our interest in knowing why Miss Lonelyhearts is obsessed with order is the need to understand the conditions under which the object-of-desire took shape. These conditions are those of need, privation, deficit, and conflict which are explored by Miss Lonelyhearts with a view to finding ways of resolution.

Desires thus appear to be *mediated* in their interaction with environing or contextual situations in which they arise. This is to say that a desire is not of an original, primary nature. But when viewed from the system of practical logic, the desire constitutes an origin relative to the acts which follow it; it is the 'starting point' in reasoning out ways of resolving the situation of lack, deficit, and conflict.

The objective stated by the initial set of premises serves as a *key enigma* for the novella as a whole. There is an emphatic mark on the object-of-desire which will be the object of the enigma. The formulation of the enigma "What does the disorder consist of?" questions the situation in respect to the conditions that constituted lack of order and need for order for Miss Lonelyhearts. The thematization and formulation of the enigma function as constituent units of what Barthes called in his *S/Z* the 'hermeneutic code' of the narrative which articulates an enigma and leads up to its solution. The disclosure of the mania-for-order enigma will take the entire novella. Moreover, it will not take place directly, literally like the disclosure of La Zambinella's identity in the classical short story by Balzac which Barthes analyzes. There are promises of answers and partial hints but no final "Now I will tell you . . . " The decipherment will have to be *inferred* from the formal properties of a narrative model which make up the formal and distributional framework within which the content units of the enigmatic chain can be poured and analyzed. Miss Lonelyhearts' *insane sensi-*

tiveness to order can only be explained *formally* by analyzing its syntagmatic and paradigmatic position or placement within the general economy of the narrative. Having said this, I would like to stress that this view is at this point only postulated and needs to be fully argued and analytically carried out to be acceptable of itself. The general methodology of establishing a formal model and meaning of narrative units is at the heart of Greimas' textual semiotics whose contributions in this respect are often analytically elegant tours de force.

The segmentation of the textual passage along the schematic steps of the practical reasoning manifests the surface, lexematic variability of the modal verb in each premise and the action of the conclusion, and sheds light on their deep structure mode of functioning, a compressive decoding which tends to naming, of messages in expansion. The intense desire corresponds but does not commensurate with an *insane sensitiveness to*. Only the deontic modal 'had to' in *Everything had to form a pattern* matches with the formal initial basis of practical reasoning. The 'can' and 'know how' of the intermediate premises in 2' materialize discursively as a 'remembering' by the subject of past occurrences that are now anticipated as a possible means to the bringing about of the desired order. Since the means are not explicitly signalled in an "if ... then" conditional nor the "cannot ... unless" conditional, the conclusion does not repeat the hypothetical "if" or "unless" clause as the action to be initiated. Nevertheless, Miss Lonelyhearts' decision to visit Betty—*He gave Betty's address to a cab driver and told him to hurry*—is clearly explained as a pattern of practical reasoning, anchored by initial and intermediate premises.

In the balance of this sub-section, I wish to concentrate on the difference between two senses of *end*, namely end as objective or end-in-view versus end as 'final' outcome, termination, or completion. The first sense of end, considered within the practical syllogism, arises before action is initiated and during action as mediated; it is not something lying beyond action at which the latter is directed, nor is it, strictly speaking an end of action at all.

When Miss Lonelyhearts sets forth 'to make a pattern of everything,' he is embarking on the *executive* stage of action where he can pull it off or muff it. During the executive stage, the remote objective functions as an end held in view, currently serving to direct activity; or, in ordinary language, as a plan, estimated to lead to certain ends. The objective or end-in-view is framed with reference to a negative factor—the lack, want, privation, and conflict which mark some 'trouble' or problem in the situation of the subject—but the negative factor operates as a condition of forming the appropriate *idea* of a desired end, which when acted upon determines a positive content and import. It is positive in the degree in which it marks the doing-away of the existing lack and conflict that evoked the end-in-view. The lack, shortage, or privation appears to be an essential factor in actional 'movement,' the movement here being taken metaphorically. The lack, shortage is relative, that is, utterly dependent on the character-in-situation. Miss Lonelyhearts is without order, short of it, and wanting it *in situation*. It is a condition of his acquiring the 'order' that he should 'not yet have it.'

The envisaged objective to be reached constitutes the *idea* or image of a desired end prior to and following onset of action and not ends to future action. The subject is guided and directed to his/her objective by a plan, a consecutive series of instrumentally related images. The pathway of images is clearly or vaguely seen *ahead of time, ahead of action* in the mind's eye: it is fore-seen and fore-acted. Until the action or serial chain of actions has reached actuality, the objective or end-in-view has no existence outside the mind. When it does reach actuality, the imagined objective is superseded and replaced by a certain *outcome*, an end as consequence or accomplished result.

This imaginary pathway can, of course, be re-presented in speech or writing. That narratives can be told is conditioned to a large extent by the capacity of human beings to provide an account of their actions either as pre-activity, anticipatory images (of which the practical inference is one kind), while they are going on (during the executive stage of action), or as post hoc retrospective readings of completed actions (in terms of the outcome or as a teleological explanation). As images either before or after the outcome, these commentaries emerge as statements by the actor or observer which give meaning to his/her actions. Most important, these commentaries constitute the *actual meaning* of these actions and thus provide the very basic of units for articulating narratives.

When the objective is identical with the action, as instanced in step 1 and 3 of the segment from *Miss Lonelyhearts*, the scope of actions it spans is very narrow. But even here the immediate objective is distinct from the end as attained outcome. Since the wanted order and patterning is not acquired, the objective does not reach actuality; instead it figures as a turning point or redirecting pivot in considering other plans of action. It makes sense to ask, then, about the outcome of any action whether or not the agent succeeded or failed and, derivatively, we may ask whether the action itself succeeded or not.

Because the execution of an action brings errors and difficulties into light, it is important to be alert to the possible alterations of the plan and to attend closely to the nature of the objective which brought it about.

Having an immediate or remote end-in-view is a characteristic of *present* activity. It is the means by which action or a sequence of actions becomes guided and acquires meaning. Once the objective has reached actuality, the ensuing outcome will stand as a significant point at which action will need redirection. The termination of the present action, the outcome, is the beginning of another end-in-view. C. Stanislavski viewed the objectives that make up an actor's role as the basic building blocks of the play which he likened to notes in music shaping the larger and overall pattern of events:

> Objectives are like the notes in music, they form the measures, which in turn produce the melody, or rather the emotions—a state of sorrow, joy, and so forth. The melody goes on to form an opera or a symphony, that is to say, the life of a human spirit in a *role* (1961:51).

In any play or narrative we can identify what, following Stanislavski, I shall provisionally call the *superobjective*, a hierarchy or network of minor and major objectives which organizes actions and other events into a signifying and coherent whole. The actualization of the superobjective is made possible by the fact that a complete series of objectives has been reached.

The superobjective guides the action of the protagonist and it is the interest of the reader or audience in watching him/her 'move' toward the objective that determines where the narrative or play shall begin or end. In the syntagmatic unfolding of a narrative, from beginning to end, there would be nothing to follow if the superobjective of the protagonist was construed as being the same as the final outcome; or, if no obstacles altered the protagonist's major and minor objectives towards the attainment of the desire, usually intense, to bring about the object-of-desire. That it is the "movement toward the object-of-desire" or conformably "the trajectory of an aim" that we follow in a story has been vigorously underscored by E. Mabley with respect to a dramatic play:

> Near the beginning of every well-constructed play the author directs our attention strongly toward one of his characters. He does this principally by showing this person, the protagonist, in the grip of some strong desire, some intense need, bent on a course of action from which he is not to be deflected. He wants something—power, revenge, a lady's hand, bread, peace of mind, glory, escape from a pursuer. Whatever it may be, some kind of intense desire is always present. [...]

> It is the protagonist's pursuit of his objective that we follow during the course
> of the play. The importance of this fact can hardly be overestimated, for when we
> are shown whether he has achieved or failed his objective, the play is over. It is the
> protagonist's pursuit of his goal that is the real subject matter of the play (1972:8-
> 9).

When we are shown whether the protagonist has achieved or failed his/her superobjective, the play is over; that is, the superobjective is replaced by a final (super)outcome. The semantic content of the objective of the attained outcome or end as consequence is existential. The difference between the two senses of end is striking proof that in the narrative process, the termination or conclusion is not just apprehended and enunciated but is stated as a way of procedure: the story-telling itself.

4. The sentence object reconsidered

At the juncture in which the practical syllogism suggested itself as a simple conceptual tool that helped split actions from processes, an intertwining problem was simultaneously being attended to. This problem consisted of a host of subtle, baffling, and arduous issues centering and gravitating around the highly amorphous concept of *object*. We have taken great care in clearing away and foregrounding some potential ambiguities and obscurities that might have stayed unsuspected and masked if the various 'objects' run across were not palpably delineated and assigned a separate conceptual status and singular name. These distinctions will be highly serviceable in the following section.

In our discussion of the transitive action-process verbs we pointed out that the 'direct object' could be given a semantic interpretation in terms of the patient case/role. Later, we argued briefly that the goal-object or objective could not be confused with the object as patient. Our very last distinction between objective and outcome of an action provides a lead which we would like to seize upon in order to reconsider the semantic interpretation of 'direct object' or simply 'object.' Following the lead makes us raise the question "Is there a grammatical/semantic relation that is analogous to the objective or outcome of an action?" The answer is yes, though I hesitate to assert it fully; a qualified yes will do.

In the semantic analysis of sentences, it is difficult to give a *single* interpretation to the relation 'direct object of,' a theoretical and practical fact which gives much weight and insight into O. Jespersen's discerning statement: "the relation between subject and object cannot be determined once and for all by pure logic or by definition, but must in each case be determined according to the special nature of the verb employed" (1963:160). Using points made or suggested by Lyons we shall now inquire into the meaning of 'object of result.' A concrete example by way of two simple sentences again will serve as illustration:

(1) N is reading a book.

(2) N is writing a book.

In (1) the book that is referred to exists prior to, and independently of its being read; but the book referred to in (2) is not yet in existence—it is brought into existence by the completion of the activity described by the sentence. By virtue of the difference, the *book* in (1) is traditionally regarded as an 'ordinary' object of the verb *is reading* whereas the *book* in (2) is described as an 'object of result.' From the semantic point of view, any verb that has as its object an 'object of result' might be appropriately described, in Lyons' term, as an 'existential causative.' Some of the most common verbs that fall into this class are 'make,' 'produce,' 'create,' 'construct,' 'cause.' Sentence (1) answers the question "What is N doing?". Sentence (2) answers the question "What is N making?". The make-question, unlike the do-question, presupposes that the activity involved is 'resultative' or factitive and has as its last term, the 'existence' of some object. The *outcome* of the action is the realized 'object of result,' a certain product called *book*.

At this point, it might be useful to mention, by way of digression, that not all objective-directed actions lead to an outcome consisting of *products*. Actions can be accomplishments, such as running a four-minute mile, or activities, such as talking. The chief point that I want to make is that objectives and outcomes are *more like* the object of result than the object as patient.

The 'existential causatives' are also transitive action-process verbs. They are factitive or operative-factitive but not purely operative. The object is clearly not a patient: it does not make sense to say that *What N did to the book was to write it*. The proposition expressed in (2) is related, by causative derivation, to the propositions expressed by

(2) a. The book is coming into existence

b. The book exists

in the same way that the proposition expressed by *Miss Lonelyhearts killed the lamb* is related to the propositions *The lamb died* and *The lamb is dead*. Proposition (2a) identifies the particular process involved as a change, of which the initial state is non-existence and the result is existence. *The result of the process coincides with the outcome of the action*. But the one emphasizes the nature of what emerges from the process and the other the agent as initiating the process and producing the result-outcome, changing it from what it was to what it is to be.

IV

The Subject-Object Relation in Actantial Grammar

The general discussion of the semantics of event and role relationships in the sentence and the examination of the textual unfolding of action as a pattern of practical reasoning and as a teleological explanation provide a suitable springboard from which to launch an analytical overview of the Subject and Object actants in Greimas' actantial grammar. We must keep in mind that the discussion of Section II polishes considerably the linguistic and conceptual devices which provided the starting point for Greimas' actantial grammar; and, secondly, that the considerations of section III which shall determine the strategy I shall follow, are altogether absent or rather, so heavily coated and veiled by a linguistic terminology that they appear virtually and consciously disclaimed.

Starting from a dual epistemological approach to construct a theory for the description and methodology of text semantics, Greimas proceeds in his *Sémantique structurale* to the fundamental, viz. elementary "semantic syntax" of a micro-universe. Induction aims for the construction of bigger semantic units upwards from the smallest, the semes, and the reverse method of linguistic deduction views the text in its totality in order to analyze it into smaller components, uncover the disposition of new concepts, and check against the results of induction. The two big classes which make up the "semantic syntax" are the *actants* and the *predicates*; they combine with each other to form the semantic and thematic kernel or nucleus of a textual micro-universe, The *predicates* are divided along the static vs. dynamic binary opposition: *Function* (symbol:F) designates the dynamic predicate and *Qualification* (symbol:Q) the static predicate (1966:123,154-6). This division yields two possible classes of semantic kernels, usually referred to as the simplest narrative énoncés:

(a) *dynamic* or *functional* énoncés in the canonic form:

Function (Actant) or F(A) or $F(A_1, A_2, \ldots, A_6)$

(b) *static* or *qualification* énoncés in the canonic form:

Qualification (Actant) or Q(A) or $Q(A_1, A_2, \ldots, A_6)$

Following the research in the French case grammar of the 50's—which was known there as an area of structural syntax—and most notably that of the linguist Tesnière, from whom he borrows the term 'actant,' Greimas of the 1966 actantial grammar postulates the number, roles, and configuration of the actants. The two major actantial categories, Subject vs. Object and Sender vs. Receiver are fixed along vertical and horizontal axes in a Cartesian-like functional network of syntactic and semantic relations where the Object actant is over-determined (see figure 4.1).

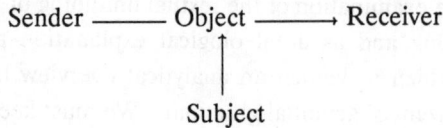

Sender ———— Object ————→ Receiver

Subject

Figure 4.1

The positional value of the Object is doubly defined by the convergence of the actantial axes: both as an "object of desire" and as an "object of communication." In addition to these four actants, we also have the Helper and Opponent which play auxiliary and adversary roles in the action of the subject-agent.

The actantial grammar is, as Greimas reminds us, "in the first place, an extrapolation of the syntactical structure" (1966:185) which casts subject, verb, and object as roles in a kind of dramatic representation where the proposition-énoncé becomes a theatrical play. A semantic micro-universe can only become or be defined as a meaningful whole insofar as this underlying structure can rise into view as "a simple spectacle, as an actantial structure" (1966:173). And Greimas adds: "This spectacle is, however, unique in that it is permanent: the content of the actions changes all the time, the actors vary but the énoncé-spectacle always remains the same because its permanence is guaranteed by the unique distribution of a small number of roles" (1966:173).

It is difficult to see how the model was hypothesized *essentially from the syntax of the sentence.* Considering the fact that Greimas often illustrates the Subject-Object relation by means of a sentence like "Peter hits Paul" (1966:132, 1971:798) which uses a transitive action-process verb, the *subject* in the semantic role of *agent,* the *object* in the role of *patient,* one is at pains to see how these semantic cases could overlap with the actants in the folktale or those in the dramatic play. Yet, Greimas takes the analysis of Propp's "dramatic personae" and the speculative yet incisive reflections of Souriau's "dramatic functions" as empirical evidence confirming his hypothesis. The equivalence he posits of the Subject and Object actants is set out in figure 4.2:

Syntax	Subject	Object
Propp	Hero	Sought-for person
Souriau	The oriented thematic force	Representative of the desired good, of the orienting value

Figure 4.2

The provisional explanation of the Subject and Object actants in 1966 and the one which is operative til today is based on the *general meaning* given to these categories by Propp and Souriau. The semantic cases of the sentential subject and object, the agent and patient, are abandoned, it seems from the very beginning, especially the patient. The narrative Subject or protagonist will later be recognized as being both agent and patient, but neither of these sentential roles will be very pertinent to its characterization. The refusal to acknowledge this non-equivalence of the sentence subject and object with Propp's and Souriau's actants has had a truly amazing effect on the introductory and critical commentaries, published ten to fifteen years later, on Greimas' narrative semiotics. These works studiously abstain from commenting on the Subject-Object relation, in a kind of methodological and verbal paralysis, by quoting the relevant passages of Greimas extensively and appealing either to the provisional/hypothetical formulation—here, too, imitating Greimas—or treating it as self-evident.

Although the roles of agent and patient are abandoned, the notational machinery is, however, retained and used as cover terms for categories of a *text* structure of a different nature. This use of syntactic apparatus has the unintended effect of confusing and obscuring the problems at issue. By using the analogy with syntactic theory, one suggests the sweeping, far-reaching answer "it is like syntactic structure" with the quite detailed notion of structure that implies. As it turns out, the way the theory is manipulated, the vehicle of the metaphor has switched position with the ground. The theory of narrative structure is not like syntactic structure but the reverse obtains: syntactic structure is redefined as being like the structure of simple narrative.

Propp's study provides the quasi-lawful, empirical generalizations and the maximally conclusive evidence from which the hypothesis of sentential actants (Greimas' term for 'arguments') *borrows* its force *metaphorically* and its *ground of explanation*. One could try to argue more convincingly, I think, that Propp's study lends some supporting evidence to Souriau's thesis—not based on any analysis of plays—that it renders it more tenable but does not establish it (i.e. confirm it). In sum, the argument I am putting forth is that the analogy with syntactic-semantic theory is solely restricted to vocabulary divorced from the attendant conceptual machinery of the theory of sentence syntax; on close examination, the parallel appears to be no more substantial than this. It should be clear that my alias-and-misnomer argument does not provide any counterevidence against the actantial model but questions the supposedly linguistic derivation. Since the model was developed to account for *texts* or semantic micro-universes and constitutes a formalization of Propp's and Souriau's textual-narrative categories, throwing the model back onto the sentence in order to suggest the universality of the model does not invalidate the postulation or hypothesis with respect to texts.

The comparison of the proposition—whether statement or énoncé—to a spectacle or drama was inspired, of Greimas' own avowal, by a remark of Tesnière. Greimas says that he has been "struck by a remark of Tesnière, which he probably meant to be only didactic, comparing the elementary énoncé to a spectacle" (1966:173). Without the help of a reference which Greimas omits, I have inferred, by a process of elimination, that the relevant passage is most likely the following one, which was quoted once before, earlier in chapter I:

> Le noeud verbal . . . exprime tout un petit drame. Comme un drame en effet, il comporte obligatoirement un procès, et le plus souvent des acteurs et des circonstances. Transposés du plan de la réalité dramatique sur celui de la syntaxe structurale, le procès, les acteurs et les circonstants deviennent respectivement le verbe, les actants et les circonstants.
>
> (The verbal node . . . expresses a complete short play. Like a dramatic play, in fact, it includes obligatorily a process and most often actors and circumstances. Trans-

posed from the plane of dramatic reality to that of structural syntax, the process, actors, and circumstances become respectively the verb, the actants, and the circumstancial indicators.) (Tesnière, 1965:102)

What do we make out of the fact that one third of Greimas' material for actantial grammar was Souriau's work on dramatic situations? One cannot escape the writer's feeling of the hindsight imperative; that is, the imperative obeyed when a later part of the text requires, as its necessary condition, some earlier one. It does *appear* that the metaphor of drama or spectacle was "striking" because it fitted in so nicely with Souriau's dramatic situation. My grumble, however, is not on this score at all, but the much more weighty fact that this remark of Tesnière and the syntactic-semantic structure of the sentence are claimed to provide the theoretical, nay, *linguistic* grounds for narrative actants.

This last point looms large as we return to the connection between predicator and argument. Now, however, we work from the perspective gained after a global consideration of the nucleus of the sentence and of the text and after drawing attention to the most striking feature in the relation of action-process verbs to their accompanying nouns. Let us raise the issue of the nature of the dependency holding between the *actant* and the sequence of *functions* or actions that constitute it in the narrative or dramatic situation.

But first, a note of importance. The dependency cannot be demonstrated by means of a simple or even complex sentence. The most forceful reason for disregarding the sentence is to consider the ensuing consequences of accepting it. This tack would lead us back to the roles/cases and their tie to the verb. And the actant and functions, as I have emphasized earlier, are textual categories. Since any discussion of the textual actant and functions will be vitiated without a specific example and since adopting the sentence for illustration will neutralize the genuine nature of the dependency, what remains for us to do is to suggest only some general differences.

I shall take my lead from Souriau's view of actants as forces and roles in the dramatic situation and his parallel argument that the actantial situation and action, in its broad theatrical sense of 'the thru-line of action,' are "correlative." It will not be hard to intuit the following dramatic principle: the action has to lead to the situation and the situation has to lead to action. This general statement gains a dramatic impact of its own in Souriau's phrasing:

What is theatrical action? It is not enough, in order to get action in the theater to stir up the characters, to make them come and go, physically; nor to accumulate events, reversals of fortune, duels, killings, violations, misunderstandings, or recognitions: even disasters. ... Such events are theatrically admissible only insofar as they take hold of the genuine theatrical action, that is, of those inner forces which converge in the scenic moment and which thrust forward the becoming of the play. For the action to happen, it is necessary that to the question "What happened next?" the answer results through *force* (as Pirandello liked to say) of the very situation and of the dynamisms within each scenic moment   (Souriau, 1950:43-4).

How does the 'correlative' interdependence of force and action, actant and functions compare with the 'redundant' feature of the role-predicate relation? In the context of action-process verbs we observed that the roles of agent and patient were manifested twice, within the verb and in the accompanying nouns. Greimas names this phenomenon 'redundancy' in his *Sémantique* and 'isotopy' in his "Eléments de grammaire narrative." In the latter article Greimas defines the function-actant relation as if it was identical to the verb-role one. The actant is said to be isotopic of the function *in the same way* that the agent is isotopic of the verb (1970:168). The example given as illustration is the relation 'fisherman - to fish.' A sentence derivable from it might read redundantly "The fisherman is fishing" and, more abstractly, "The agent is acting or doing (something)."

The redundancy of the agent role in the agent-act relation or the isotopy of the agent to the verb, and vice versa, is not immediately apparent in the actant-function relation. The actant is like the namable sum of a sequence of functions-actions of a character or set of characters; or, the converging point toward which the sequence tends. But, at the same time, it is instituted by each of the functions in the sequence. An exhaustive catalogue of actions makes up the actant and in this connection we can speak of the "actantial convergence" or "reduction" as a type of operation performed upon the text, upon the sequential dynamism of actions. Inversely, one can speak of the "functional divergence" or "expansion" when we start with the actant. Functions and actant are thus interchangeable only at a high level of abstraction and the substitution made is between vastly unequal dimensions, unequal in textual length.

The textual interchangeability between actant and functions is not redundant like the sentential isotopy of the agent-act. On the contrary, it is capable of being understood in more than one univocal sense. Greimas has pinned down this ambiguity very clearly in his *Sémantique*:

Si, en effet, au niveau des messages pris individuellement, les fonctions et les qualifications semblent bien être attribuées aux actants, le contraire se produit au niveau de la manifestation discursive: on voit que les fonctions, tout aussi bien que les qualifications, y sont créatrices d'actants, que les actants y sont appelés à une vie métalinguistique du fait même qu'ils sont représentatifs, on dirait même compréhensifs, de classes de prédicats. Il en résulte que les modèles fonctionnels et qualificatifs, tels que nous les avons postulés, sont, à leur tour, dominés par les modèles d'organisation d'un niveau hiérarchique supérieur que sont les modèles actantiels.

(If, in fact, at the level of messages taken individually, the functions and qualifications actually seem to be attributed to actants, the contrary happens at the level of discursive manifestation. We see that the functions, as well as the qualifications are, at the level of discursive manifestation, creative of actants, that the actants are here summoned to a metalinguistic life from the very fact that they are representative—we would even say comprehensive—of classes of predicates. It thus follows that the functional and qualificative models, such as we have postulated them, are, in turn, dominated by the models of organization of a higher hierarchical level, which are the actantial models.) (Greimas, 1966:129)

For the time being, we have to be satisfied with the incomplete and unsettled appproximation of the actant-function relation and the actant-actant relation that a second glance has yielded.

What I want to do now is to demonstrate that the sentential object is semantically distinct from and irreconcilable with the actantial object. I am going to show that the object actant is a dense and complex overlapping of concepts related to goal-oriented action, change, value, desire, a specific syntagmatic position within the narrative, in addition to being a simple physical object; and, if this is indeed the case, then it can hardly be said to have been extrapolated from the semantic-syntactic interpretation of the sentential object. The implications and consequences from this canvassing are many but I shall single out two of them. First of all, all objections and disputations which have been made against the actantial grammar on the grounds that it is based on Tesnière's theory of valency or on case/role theory, evaporate. Secondly, we shall have good reason to go beyond and remain "undazzled" by the linguistic notation and, by extension, what one reviewer called "powerful and impressive formalisms" which, ironically enough, appear to their inventor as "a jargon that may be forbidding but pretty easy to master" ("un jargon peut-être rébarbatif, mais assez facile à assimiler") (Greimas, 1977:227-8).

On both counts, the upshot of the demonstration will be in fortunate agreement with Greimas' more fundamental and broader onception of the methodology afforded by semiotics.

I propose to carry out the demonstration by considering the nature of the relationship between subject and object that has been formulated in the four different stages of actantial grammar and comparing the relations obtained to the nature of the premises and conclusion in the practical inference. The aspect of the subject-object relation to be investigated is one that has received a primary focus in the 1966, 1970, 1973, and 1976 actantial grammar:

1. desire and teleology in 1966;
2. desire as the modal predicate "to want," being the desire of realization of action, the project of the subject, and the narrative program in 1970;
3. (a) the object as value which mediates the relation between subject and object; (b) a relation of conjunction or disjunction of the subject and the object-value; (c) the polemical (agonistic, game) model of the narrative reflected in dual and opposed subjects, and an object of conflict in 1973;
4. the subject and object as defining states, actions, and the pragmatics of action (the virtualizing and actualizing modalities) in 1976.

1. Desire and teleology

The two key passages in *Sémantique structurale* which attempt to provisionally define the nature of the subject-object relation are worth quoting in their entirety. Both passages struggle with the conversion of the linguistic notion of transitivity into some relation that proves to be either partially or totally outside the domain of syntax: desire and teleology. Unless, that is, one interpreted any kind of conceptual reasoning or anthropomorphic reasoning, as Greimas would say, as 'semantic syntax.' Let us take up these passages:

> The relation between subject and object ... appears with a semantic investment of 'desire.' It seems possible to conceive that transitivity or the *teleological relation* ... located on the mythical dimension of manifestation, appears, due to this semic combination as a sememe realizing the meaning-effect 'desire' (1966:176-7).

> The fact that we have wanted to compare the syntactical categories with the inventories of Propp and Souriau forces us to consider the nature of the relationship between subject and object—which seemed to us, in its greater generality, to be a relation of a teleological order, i.e. a modality of 'being able to do,' which, at the level of the manifestation of the functions, would have found a practical or mythical 'doing'—as a more specialized relation, carrying a heavier semic investment of

'desire' transforming itself, at the level of manifested functions into 'quest' (1966:180-1).

Neither of these definitions is very precise but, taken in conjunction with Propp's and Souriau's definitions—in the posited table of equivalences—they are enough to give us an idea, intuitive though it may be, of the conceptual categories involved. The axis of 'desire' or wanting ties the subject and object and this desire is manifested as a 'quest.' The relation is also the manifestation of a goal-oriented aim conceived as being broadly teleological. Identifying the object which, in practical analysis, often is hidden or obscure, consists then, in looking for what is the aim of the subject's quest, what the subject wants.

All of these concepts are to be found operating not in transitive action-process verbs but in the systemic definition of action as a practical syllogism and as the teleological inversion. The two relations between the subject and the object are contained in the set of relations constituting a piece of practical reasoning but do not fully overlap it. We have the object-of-desire of the major premise, "N wants to do O / to bring about O," and the objective or end-in-view which is formulated as a 'wherefore' question in a teleological explanation, seeking the answer "in order to do O / to bring about O."

It is remarkable that this partial overlapping of the subject and object actants can be easily observed without having recourse to either Propp's *Morphology* or Souriau's *Situations*. The strongest generalization of the folktale or the dramatic play reduces it to an *action* as a pattern of reasoning and retains the features that are part of the starting-point for the subject of practical reasoning and an explanatory reason or motive in a teleological context.

2. The modal want: desire of realization of action

In 1970 "desire" receives a linguistic recasting as the modal predicate *to want* which governs the subordinate and descriptive clause. In the sentence "John wants Peter to leave" the modal énoncé consists of "John wants ___ " and presents itself as "the desire of realization of a program"; "Peter is leaving" is the program, the object actant, and the object of desire. The relationship between the modal énoncé and the descriptive énoncé is interpreted as a *syntactical doing* that consists in "the transformation of a virtual program into an actualized program" (Greimas, 1970:169).

I shall restrict my comments to making two major points. The first is the verbal status of the modal predicate *to want* which is explicitly stated and denoted in the analysis of sentences as a function. Let us bear in mind Greimas' definition of the function as a dynamic-evental predicate in opposition to the definition of qualification as a stative verb. The question I want to raise, which is in theoretical consistency with Greimas' definitions, is this one. Is the verb *to want* a function or a qualification? Can the answer be simply stated without backing it up with evidence? I think I am justified in pausing for a moment here to mark off one of the controversial problem-issues and much discussed complexities in philosophy that passes off as a linguistic or semiotic *certainty* in Greimas, an axiomatic certainty that is smuggled discreetly through the back door.

Since we are aware of the linguistic background, let us avail ourselves of the rules-of-thumb criteria and retrace the linguistic analysis. Although John looks as if he were an agent from the point of view of surface structure, there seems to be some doubt as to whether he is an agent. John is not the instigator of an action, not someone who does something. Rather, he is someone who was mentally disposed in some way, one with respect to whose mental experience something was wanted. Following Fillmore and Chafe, I shall say that the verb is experiential. The verb *to want* appears, linguistically, to be a state, as suggested by the fact that it does not answer the question *What does John do?* or *What is happening to John?* It is also true that *want* does not occur in the progressive specification: we do not normally say "John *was wanting* Peter to leave."

Although Greimas explicitly designates *to want* as a function, he also suggests an implicit and contradictory view which bypasses the entire dynamic vs. static opposition but which brings it closer to a non-function, if not exactly a state:

> The *modality* of wanting allows the construction of modal énoncés with *two actants*: the *subject* and the *object*. The axis of desire which joins them allows us to interpret them semantically as a virtual *performing subject* and an *object instituted in value* (Greimas, 1970:170-1).

The words that are italicized are Greimas' emphasis. What we wish to focus on instead is the *virtual* which occurs in "a virtual performing subject" and also in the above definition of the syntactical doing as "the transformation of a virtual program into an actualized program." Let us take up the same sentence of

Greimas, "John wants Peter to leave," as an illustration for making explicit what is implicit in the quote just given. According to this quote, John can be said to be the virtual performing subject. We shall set into work, put into play, the simplest, yet most productive, of the principles of reason, the Principle of Identity which philosophers like to put into the empty form of redundancy A = A. To say that John is the virtual performing subject is to say that John is a virtual agent and hence *not an agent*—yet. By the principle of redundancy or isotopy of semantic roles—the textual variant of Identity—which repeats a semantic feature in both verb and noun, we can infer that what holds for *John* holds for the verb *wants* in "John wants ___ ." We can deduce that *wants* is not an action, not a function but a virtual action, a virtual function, a virtual performance. This commits Greimas to saying that *'to want' is a virtual action or performance* and if it is virtual, it cannot actually be a function. The conclusion is clear: *to want* is both a function and not a function.

By Greimas' definitions and the principle of contradiction, the conclusion is also unacceptable. Something went wrong somewhere with the definition of the function in opposition to a state. The general definition of the function as a dynamic-evental predicate has not changed since its initial formulation. In 1976 Greimas, talking of the Proppian function *lack*, the eighth in a series of thirty-one functions, objected to its status as a function because "far from designating a doing [an action], the 'lack' designates more properly a state and cannot be considered as a function" (Greimas, 1976a:7). The same argument can be leveled against *want*. But we have shown that Greimas retains it as a function *and* a state—if all we have is the opposition between functions and qualifications—and the pain of contradiction stimulates re-thinking. Though the contradiction sting is there, can it be removed if viewed in another way?

Let us restart from the assertion that

(1) Wants are virtual actions

and, in order to manifest one semantic-conceptual feature of the want, let us contrast it with a broader statement like

(2) States are virtual actions.

Assertion (1) seems much more acceptable than assertion (2). What the *want* or *desire* has that a state does not have as such is a force, power, or efficacy to originate or bring the action into being by virtue of its power or force to do so. We would not be able to understand the conception of wants-desires as virtual, potential actions if we did not *already* have precisely the idea that wants *cause* actions. The disposition to bring about an action which is part of the 'subject-ive,' 'private,' 'mental' *force* of desire or want is part of a commonview concep-tion of desire which has come down to us from the ancient metaphysical idea of an efficient cause. This is the sense of 'cause' conceived in relation to human action, of which the best known defense is R. Collingwood's. Desire as cause is seen as something that exerts power and makes the act happen:

> That which is caused is the free and deliberate act of a conscious and responsible agent, and 'causing' him to do it means affording him a motive for doing it. For 'causing' we may substitute 'making,' 'inducing,' 'persuading,' 'forcing,' 'compelling,' according to differences in the kind of motive in question (Collingwood, 1940:290).

Desires or wants cause, make, induce, force, compel the action to be initiated. Notice that the definition of 'causing' is framed in a teleological explanation, starting from the act and not before it, and lists the various kinds of 'causes' as constituting a motive-reason or incentive-reason for the agent.

Desires may cause action but the likelihood is certain only when action has been initiated. The probability distribution is evenly divided relative to the threshold of the passage from non-action to action. In other words, it is equally possible to say that desires may not cause the action at all.

This brings us to the second major point. Given one premise of the initial set of premises of a practical inference, "John wants Peter to leave," no interme-diate premises, and no conclusion, can Peter's departure be seen as anything more than John's object-want, the object of his desire? On the other hand, suppose that the initial and intermediate premises were filled out, and the conclusion lead to: "Peter is leaving." What, in this case, is the relationship, the *connection* between the premises and the conclusion? Is it, as Greimas says, a *syntactical doing*? This is a difficult and perplexing question to which we shall return at the end of this section. For the moment, it will suffice to note that the object of desire is John's and the "transformation of a virtual program into an actualized program" is a doing which incurs upon Peter to do. The status of Peter's leaving is not the same in the initial premises as it is in the conclusion. The nature of this status which will preoccupy us later includes more than just "a transformation" and what Greimas referred to elsewhere as a different "syntagmatic position." In "Les objets de valeur" Greimas made the point this way: "The two situations of lack while being comparable are not identical because the syntagmatic positions are not" (1973:29). So I draw attention to the fact that the two situations of Peter's leaving are not identical.

3. The aim of goal-oriented action

3a   The object as mediating value

In 1973 the object and subject are discussed in relation to "value." The basic presuppositions and implicit, guiding themes which inform the article "Les objets de valeur" are focalized around the subject's aiming at the acquisition of *cathected* relationships to goal-objects. The non-active, stative subject is viewed likewise in terms of being without these objects or having them. The subject *orients* to the object in a unique, evaluational mode: it *invests* the particular object with value through attributing to it affective-cultural significance for direct satisfaction or blockage of desires-wants.

Greimas puts great emphasis on the linguistic values invested in the description of the object to the exclusion of the appraisal and prizing value that stems from desire, the object of desire or the goal-object. The meaning of the object is said to be like the meaning of the lexeme which has "an undefinable character." The scope of the earlier postulations with respect to the conditions that manifest meaning—the elementary structure of signification in 1966, later charted as the semiotic square—is now extended to cover the meaning of the object. These conditions are:

a) every object is knowable only by its determinations and not in itself;
b) the determinations of the object can only be apprehended as differences that outline the object and it is this differential character which confers on them their status of linguistic value;
c) the object, while remaining unknowable as such, is nonetheless presupposed as a kind of support by the existence of values   (Greimas, 1973:15).

The differential, linguistic value of the object, practically speaking, is ancillary to the less abstract value that involves desire and the goal-object. Thus, when Greimas says that "the syntactical object is just the project of the subject" and that "the object can only be recognized by one (or more) semantic values which manifest it" (16), whatever linguistic, differential sense is invested methodologically into the word *value* lapses into the clearer, triumphant sense of value associated with an object of desire and goal-object.

The dual meaning of value investment in the goal-object stands in need of a brief comment, tangential to Greimas' text. The word 'value' and 'valuing' are verbally employed to designate both *prizing* in the sense of holding precious, dear, and *evaluating* or *appraising* in the sense of putting a value upon, *assigning* a value to. This is an activity of rating, an act that involves comparison, as is explicit, for example, in appraisals in money terms of goods and services. To evaluate some goods is to attribute to them a value of distribution or exchange and to presuppose that the goods have a common measure which makes them *equivalent*, equal in value. The double meaning of value is significant because there is implicit in it one of the basic issues regarding the value that involves desire and objects of desire. For valuation in the sense of 'appraisal' occurs only when it is necessary to bring about something which is lacking, something which is wanted. It takes place in relation to the conditions under which desires take shape and foreseen consequences are projected as *valued* goal-objects to be reached. In case a goal-object exists and is valued, or exists in relation to a desire, the activity engaged in is mediated by the anticipation of the outcome which as a foreseen end, as an end-in-view, enters into the makeup of the object of desire.

Analytically, the locus of value is neither in the object nor the subject nor in the immediately observable subject-object situation; its locus is rather a conception, a construct inferred from events, based upon what is done and said by actors. Concretely, of course, any given value is in some sense "built into" the state of the subject-actor *in relationship* to some object. In which case, Greimas says

> The object aimed at appears as a pretext, as a place of investment of values, an elsewhere which mediates the relationship of the subject to himself/herself. ... The value which is invested in the object aimed at semantizes in some way the entire énoncé and becomes at once the value of the subject who meets it when aiming at the object (1973:15,16).

The example given makes this evident. When somebody buys a car in our modern society today, it is not the car as object that is wanted but a means of rapid displacement and often a bit of social prestige or a feeling of more intimate power.

There always remains a *distance* between the set of values organizing the representation of the object and the elusive object (of desire) itself. The object appears as a shifting space of determinations that are grasped through values:

> The grasping of meaning meets on its way only values determining the object, and

not the object itself; hence the lexeme which sets itself as a fool-the-eye (trompe l'oeil) deception in the place indicated by the object is only readable in some of its values (1973:16).

In following a story or in the interpretation of any action, written or spoken, from the viewpoint of the practical inference or from the viewpoint of a teleological explanation, *the locus of readability* of the object of desire is in the neighborhood of values which *show* that what is wanted is wanted under a *desirability-characterization*. I am borrowing the last expression from D. Gauthier who has defended the necessity of retaining this criterion in the initial set of premises that make up a formal piece of reasoning (1963:29ff.). The readable values of the object are those which make clear, which specify an answer to the question *What/Why does N want that for?* In what way does N consider the wanted object desirable, *worth* wanting?

These questions lead us back to the initial premises of the practical syllogism. Of Kenny's five possibilities for stating the major premise, the second variant "Health is good" and the fifth variant "Health is of such-and-such a nature" circumscribe the neighborhood of values that are at play in the object of desire, that is, "health." Expounding on the fifth variant will specify the object-values sought under a desirability-characterization. It will show in which way health is worth wanting.

In a teleological explanation we said that the initial premises provide the motive-reason or incentive-reason for the agent to act, those reasons which have 'moved' the agent to act as s/he did. If we have a premise of desirability-characterization, the object of desire and the goal-object can be said to have an *incentive value*. The motive-reason or the incentive-reason is the reason of value. To take up Greimas' example of a car, answers to "why is the car good (a value) for a particular actor?" are value-reasons: because of convenience, power, prestige, evasion. These reasons enter into the functional component, practical and mythical, of the semantic analysis of car.

That we desire this and do not desire that are "brute facts" which cannot be accepted point-blank unless accounted for by value-reasons. Other people often have desires different than our own. Such being the case, it is never obvious why something is valued or good for someone in a particular situation. Even an inherent object-value or universal good such as "health" elicits questions as to why it is valued or seen as worth wanting for a particular subject-agent. Phrasing the point this way forcefully brings us back to the "lack of health" situation and the "trouble" which evoked the object of desire.

3b   Conjunction and disjunction

The subject and object relation is also viewed in this stage of the grammar in a perspective of *state* as opposed to an *action*. The function itself is redefined but the new distinctions which are drawn do not melt theoretically with the older ones. Before going any further, let us take up again the canonical formulation of the énoncé from 1966 as the model of comparison in clarifying the ambiguous behavior of "function":

(a) *dynamic-functional* énoncé
     Function (Subject, Object) or F(S,O)

(b) *static* énoncé or *qualification*
     Qualification (Subject, Object) or Q(S,O)

It is postulated now that the *function* can be broken down into two "functions-predicates" or functions-verbs: *to do* and *to be*. Rephrasing this, the function can be either an action (and not the more inclusive event or dynamic verb) and a state. Furthermore, the action is posited as a transformation and the state as a junction (1973, 1976). It will be easier to see this division if we put it schematically as two strings of identities:

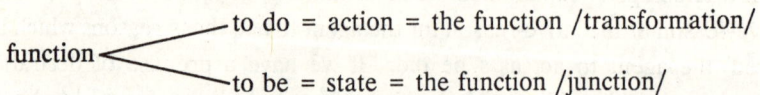

$$\text{function} \begin{cases} \text{to do = action = the function /transformation/} \\ \text{to be = state = the function /junction/} \end{cases}$$

The function is said to be a "function-predicate" but the operative sense is *not* that of the predicate or verb. For how can the function as a *dynamic* or evental predicate be a *state*? On the other hand, the function cannot be identified as a "logical function" and still retain the linguistic meaning of action and other events. But this is a shaky and uneasy objection to make for the following reason. The criteria by which Greimas suggests to construe the function as a "logical function" or relation are not at all specified when they should be. The similarities and differences between a "logical function" and an action or state must be investigated and clearly set down. The task cannot be evaded if one is seeking and implicitly claiming logical (semiotic?) rigor and a responsible honesty with the subject matter considered. Hence the very vague notion I get from Greimas' reference to "logical function" mirrors what I feel is a vague and hesitant conception in Greimas' works.

On the whole, the status of 'function' as a theoretical construct is ambiguous and confusingly ill-defined. Incompatible and incommensurate senses of 'function' are made to merge with glaring and embarrassing inconsistency or with fuzziness. We found this ambiguity operating in the verb *to want* earlier. This pervasive conceptual/theoretical inconsistency within one and the same article and between different publications spanning a decade leads us to conclude, to quote Greimas himself, when talking of the notion of 'corpus' that

> la sobriété et la rigueur logique de la définition ne font que masquer le caractère intuitif des décisions que le descripteur sera amené à prendre à cette étape de l'analyse.
>
> (the logical soberness and rigor of the definition essentially do nothing but mask the intuitive character of decisions which the describor will be led to take at this stage of the analysis.)   (Greimas, 1966:143)

If I am giving the word back to Greimas, it is not by accident. I think that the tone and attitude conveyed here are behind Greimas' efforts to situate the 'function' theoretically in one metalanguage or another and that what passes off as a certain though misleading dogma is actually a search—suggestive and provisional.

Disregarding for now the problematical status of function and leaving it out of view, let us consider closely what is the new typology of elementary énoncés at this stage of the actantial grammar—the typology which results from a redefinition of the function in combination with two actants, the subject and object. Let us look first into the énoncés of state based on the equation of function as junction. Taken as a semantic category, junction is articulated into two contrary semes: disjunction and conjunction. This opposition leads to formulating two types of *énoncés of state*:

$$\text{disjunctive state} \quad F_{disj} \, (S \cup O)$$
$$\text{conjunctive state} \quad F_{conj} \, (S \cap O)$$

where $\cup$ is the function /disjunction/ and $\cap$ is the function /conjunction/.

In an *énoncé of doing* the subject operates the "passage" which is located *between* the states of disjunction and conjunction (1973:20). The informal way of representing the doing or action is

$$S \cup O \implies S \cap O$$

which is to be read as the passage of two successive states of a subject which is disjoined from the object-value and then conjoined with it. The *doing* is postulated as a *transformational* doing performed by the subject and aiming to transform a state. The canonical formulation of the énoncé of doing is represented as follows:

$$F_{transf} \: [S_1 \Longrightarrow O_1(S \cap O)]$$

where

$\qquad \Longrightarrow \quad$ indicates the transformation or doing

$\qquad S_1 \quad$ indicates the subject operating the transformation

$\qquad O_1 \quad$ is by error denoted as "an énoncé of state" (1973:20, 1976:92) when it refers in fact to the object actant.

The énoncé distinguishes the subject of doing, S_1, from the subject of state, S, and, in my terminology, O_1 as the objective from O as the outcome. It represents any kind of act, whether real or narrated, a "paper act" as Greimas says (1976a:14). When it refers strictly to the "paper act," the énoncé in question is spoken of as a *narrative program* which accounts for "the syntactical organization of the act" (1976a:14).

The account of the semiotic status of the object-values leads Greimas to consider story-telling or "narrativization" as the syntagmatic positioning of object-values in conjunction and disjunction from the subject (1973:19). To see exactly how Greimas' terminology operates, let us take up our practical inference schema and set it up along with the corresponding formulas of Greimas in two columns.

S wants to do O / bring about O.	$S \cup O$
S considers that he cannot do O unless he does P.	
S sets himself to do P.	$F_{transf} \: [S_1 \Longrightarrow O_1(S \cap O)]$

Let us assume, furthermore, that S has achieved his objective; the outcome will be phrased and symbolized as follows

S has done O / brought about O.	$S \cap O$

The conclusion of the practical inference which is an action is for Greimas a *doing* and specifically a *transformation*; to set it apart from other kinds of transformation, it is sometimes referred to as a *transformational doing*. In his *Maupassant* Greimas has yet another name for the doing-as-transformation: *actualization*. A twofold distinction of doings is made which mirrors the subdivision of junction into conjunction and disjunction. When the subject's doing aims at a conjunction with the object, as exhibited in the above example, the doing is called a realization; when aiming at a disjunction, the doing is a virtualization:

$$F_{transf} [S_1 \Longrightarrow O_1 (S \cup O)]$$

Notice that it is no longer possible to "invert" the practical inference schema and get a teleological explanation of the action. Asking the question "Why is S doing P?" does not give us the equivalent of the answer "because S wants to do O / in order to bring about O." What we have instead is the disjunctive state S $\cup$ O which may best be paraphrased as "S is without the object." Even seeing something like a "lack" into the disjunction would be tantamount to making an interpretation at cross-purposes with the aim of logical formalization. But we do this, anyway, in spite of the symbols. It seems impossible not to interpret the disjunction as a lack of sorts and not to see in it the desire or the want which aims at the liquidation of the lack, or alternatively, the acquisition of the object desired.

A very interesting phenomenon is taking place in Greimas' linguistics of the text and semiotics of action and narrated action. Progressively more and more metaphysical concepts are introduced and translated or mapped into linguistic terms (like 'transformation') or semi-logical ones (like 'disjunction') but, curiously, the Greimasian metalanguage can be read only through and *with* the old metaphysical one. The features of the action which are made prominent in 1973 are those of *actualization* and the *aim* of action. Anything that happens between the conjunctive and disjunctive states is an actualization. There are two poles between which the actional aim, viewed metaphorically as *a kind of change or movement with respect to O*, takes place. Reverting to the older distinction established between 'being at the goal' in the realized state and being in potentiality (virtuality) 'such as is capable of attainingthe goal' we can construe *the aim of action* not as a transformation but as the progress of the realizing of a potentiality. We cannot place the action either among virtual-potential states or among the realized states; for this is the before or after of action. And the fact turns out that action is an aiming or actualization but an uncompleted one;

because a virtual-potential state, as long as it is such, is by nature uncompleted and therefore its actual functioning—which action is—must stop short of its completion. On the attainment of the end or outcome, the action toward O no longer exists and is merged in the realized state.

3c   Methodological by-play: deconstruction and the subject-object relation

In view of the trailing current of deconstruction criticism, it will be worthwhile to furnish a piece of stage-setting which will make the relation of actantial grammar to deconstruction not only clearer but utterly formidable. We will do this with the help of L. Marin's engaging interpretation of a parable of Pascal which uses actantial grammar as a means to deconstruct the notion of meaning as an "ontological presence" and to explicate "absence of center" (Marin, 1976). A good portion of the analysis revolves around an interpretation of the actantial object and the stative énoncés of conjunction and disjunction. We shall consider mainly the beginning of the parable that reads as follows:

> *A man was cast by a tempest upon an unknown island, the inhabitants of which were in trouble to find their king, who was lost; and having a strong resemblance both in form and face to this king, he was taken for him, and acknowledged in this capacity by all the people. At first he knew not what course to take; but finally he resolved to give himself up to his good fortune* (in Marin, 1976:218).

In this sequence of events, it is obvious that the lost king is the "object," that is, the objective for the islanders; and that the islanders as subject are in a state of disjunction from their king. In addition to the semantic-conceptual arguments and some metaphysical concepts which we have shown to be packed and methodologically invested into the O of the first premise of a practical inference, Marin adds a few more from deconstruction.

In the initial situation, the king as an object is a "lack" because he is lacking to the islanders. Marin reads disjunction as being automatically a lack. On that ground, the point we made on the natural, even necessary, tendency to read much more into the 'logical' notation of $S \cup O$ receives a beautiful affirmation from Marin. The object is also valued because he is "the center of the island universe and its leading, organizing principle" (199). The locus of readability of the want-object, the king, is—for Marin much as it is for us—in the neighborhood of values which show that what is wanted is wanted under a desirability-characterization. The readable values, the incentive values of the object for the islanders are interpreted via the political role the king fulfills in a society. Because the king is "the privileged element that links the parts together in an organized whole," his disappearance eliminates the "center" of a "closed system [which] is no longer a system since it is deprived of its center" (201); "the king is the absolute value, the structural center of the system, its axiological norm. But he is not there, he is absent" (213).

Thus far we have the following paradigm of equivalent or nearly equivalent substitutions: disjunction; object lacking; object being sought; object as center of a society; object as center of a system; object as center. Once the actantial object is infolded and driven into the deconstruction notion of a pure "center," it gets invested anew with all the plural meanings of the qualifiers which are juxtaposed with it, making of it a symbolic configuration: ruling center, structural center, political center, social center, ontological center, axiological center, signifying center, semiotic center, textual center. One example will suffice to illustrate the symbolization process:

> When the center of a system is defined as missing, as being lost, when there is no longer an ontological and axiological central locus for the regulation of its operations, then such a system as an organized whole is changed into chaos; [...] More specifically, we have a system which is paradoxically organized and regulated by a *missing center*, by an *absent principle* (203, my emphasis).

The substitution of the real (true) goal-object, the lost king, for the castaway, the false goal-object, is the outcome of the islanders' action-search and they accept the castaway in full ignorance of his identity. The outcome is perceived by Marin as "an extraordinary attempt to deconstruct the very notion of 'meaning' as an 'ontological presence' providing the signifying system with its transcendent guarantee of truth" (206). The *lost king* in this context "is the origin and the telos which precede the system and construct it." And Marin adds: "in order to construct these signifying systems, we first need such a 'meaning.' But at the same time we must recognize that this ultimate truth, this originating logos is a simulated truth, presence, and telos" (206). It seems to me that the set of philosophical terms in the quotes just given do not offer any solid reference point or instructive technique to textual analysis: the significant features of 'ultimate truth' or 'transcendent truth' which Marin does not discuss are easier to feel and to express in terms of the practical inference than they are to manipulate abstractly or dialectically. To put it briefly: it is not clear what these terms mean as such. I also take the 'originating logos' and the 'telos' as making sense when referring to the initial premise of a practical inference, paradoxical in its conceptualization insofar—let us repeat it once more—that it is both a beginning and end to the practical inference subject as virtual agent and to the observer of it; to the 'paper' subject and to the reader of narratives. The first premise is the origin and the telos which construct the practical inference and become explanatory in a teleological account of action. As the results of our analysis of the *Miss Lonelyhearts* segment showed, the first premise can be taken to mean an origin or originating logos in the sense that it is *axiomatic* for practical reasoning. No reasoning can proceed without some axiomatic givens. The desire or object of desire constitutes an origin relative to the acts which follow it; it makes up the axiomatic starting point in reasoning out ways of resolving the situation of lack and trouble.

Finally, as a conclusion to this detour, I think it is correct to say that the initial disjunction of the S and O, interpreted either as a lack, privation, the absence of the object, or "a missing center" is a feature not peculiar to the Pascal parable and the Proppian folktales. It is basic to the interpretation of what it means *to want* to do something (to be, to have, to happen).

3d   The polemical (agonistic) model of narrative

From the interval of 1969 to 1973 the polemical model of the narrative has become more and more pronounced. This model postulates a unit of structure intermediate between the simple narrative statement of the form Event (Role$_1$, Role$_2$, ...) and the plot as a whole insofar as it refers to the sequence of happenings in the story. The polemical model, like the actantial model, is a paradigmatic grouping of the Proppian functions. Unlike the actantial model which is based on the characters to whom spheres of action are attributed, the polemical model is a sequential and syntagmatic unit made up of functions. Enough, I hope, has been said to mark the theoretically problematical definition of the function and to warrant the abandonment of our efforts to understand what it means outside of its foundation in Propp's text. We shall agree that "function" here and elsewhere will mean specifically one of Propp's thirty-one functions and anything that Greimas' poetry of linguistics-cum-logic imagination chooses it to mean.

Greimas has analyzed the grouping of Propp's functions and has uncovered a syntagmatic chaining of five functions that form a recurrent unit in the narrative (see figure 4.3). This sequence of functions is termed a Test or performantial syntagm or, yet again, a narrative schema (Greimas, 1966:196-8). The discovery of this recurrent unit that Propp himself did not recognize is a significant and decisive accomplishment in recent narratology which has not been sufficiently acknowledged and utilized. To my knowledge, only one study by Larivaille (1974) rethinks this large unit thoroughly, from the ground up, and postulates an altered one as an important by-product issuing from a trying application of Propp's schema to a set of folktales.

CONTRACT, A	injunction acceptance
STRUGGLE, F	confrontation success
c	consequence

Figure 4.3

The Test presents the parallel or correspondence between the actants and the functions which they imply in the following abstract manner:

TEST = A(Sender,Receiver) + F(Subject,Anti-Subject) + c(Object,Subject)

    = Contract + Struggle + consequence

(Cf. Greimas, 1965:166). The quest of the subject is threatened or prevented by the other subject. On the program of the first, the second is an opponent or anti-subject, as the first is on the program of the second. The analysis of the Proppian fairy tale schema manifests three Tests which Greimas calls the Qualifying Test, the Main Test, and the Glorifying Test. All three Tests are a variation of the generalized schema given above that is postulated to be an invariant unit.

As of 1970, the Test will refer to the last three functions only and the actants involved in the énoncé. The succession of three narrative énoncés representing the Test is designated as follows:

$$NE_1 = F : confrontation \; (S_1 \Longleftrightarrow S_2)$$
$$NE_2 = F : domination \; (S_1 \Longrightarrow S_2)$$
$$NE_3 = F : attribution \; (S_1 \Longleftarrow O)$$

The last énoncé is also represented as a transfer $(S_2 \Longrightarrow O \Longrightarrow S_1)$. By S_1 we designate the hero-subject, by S_2 the traitor anti-subject, and by O the object-value.

The Test represents a central point of "transformation" in the narrative, a locus of decision and dénouement. The two protagonists, the subject and anti-subject, are in opposition to each other and confront each other. Of the two doings that are thus opposed, one must succeed and the other must fail. The outcome of the Test will be the situation where a victorious subject acquires an object-value that was withheld by the traitor anti-subject. In this manner the Test manifests the existence of two "narrative programs," two objectives, of which the énoncés are partially or totally overlapping and correlated. The crossing of the two chained and superimposed "programs" splits the narrative into a dual narrative; their opposition to each other makes the narrative not only dual but polemical—polemically, agonistically dual.

The Test is claimed to be the most characteristic "episodic" unit of narrative "syntax" (1966:194). It can be considered as a *minimal narrative* for several, specific reasons that Greimas convincingly demonstrates: (1) it is the irreducible nucleus or kernel which accounts for the definition of the narrative as *diachrony*; (2) it operates the transformation of axiological contents which fix the limits of the 'reversal of the situation' by marking the end of the narrative *before* and the beginning of the *after*[1] (Greimas, 1966, 1971)

---

[1]The comparison of the "minimal story" as postulated by Greimas with those of Prince (1973), Larivaille (1974), and Hendricks (1977) is most interesting and illuminating.

Prince, *A Grammar of Stories*. — Prince's view is closest to the definition of a process: "A minimal story consists of three conjoined events. The first and third are stative, the second is active. Furthermore, the third event is the inverse of the first. Finally, the three events are conjoined by three conjunctive features in such a way that (a) the first event precedes the second in time and the second precedes the third, and (b) the second event causes the third" (31). One example is "John was happy, then John lost a lot of money, then, as a result, John was unhappy."

Larivaille, "Analyse (morpho)logique du récit." — Larivaille uncovers an "elementary narrative sequence" made up of six functions: initial state, provocation of the hero, reaction to the hero, sanction, final state, and spatial connectives. This recurrent sequence is analogous to Greimas' Test in its older and more expanded definition. Furthermore, according to Larivaille, the Proppian schema manifests five such sequences—not only three as Greimas has shown but this is due to Larivaille's omission of the contract—which are termed Proposal, Qualification, Affirmation,

Interpolate the polemically dual Test into a simple narrative world with *bounded* axiological values, such as the folktale, circulating in a closed circuit from one subject to another "in the manner of a ball which, during a football game, continuously changes hands" and the evental picture unrolling before us holds to view two subjects simultaneously present, each deploying a program of action that aims at the same object (Greimas, 1976a:12). The syntagmatic pathway of the object-value is set up in such a way that its acquisition by one subject is at the expense of the other, its loss by one subject is at the benefit of the other. The conjunction of S_1 with the object simultaneously and necessarily corresponds with the disjunction of S_2 from the object.

The *stakes* that are at play in the Test consist of the object-value that is coveted by both sides and the consequence boils down to transfers of an object from one subject to another. The aftermath of the confrontation can be rewritten in a simple canonic formula:

$$S_1 \cap O \cup S_2.$$

Cutting through this symbolic formulation and the other énoncés that make up the Test and supporting it by a smoother because more continuous grasp is the everyday concept-notion of what Tarde aptly called a *teleological duel* and a

---

Confirmation, and Glorification.

Hendricks, "'A Rose for Emily': A Syntagmatic Analysis." — Hendricks does not claim the status of 'minimal story' to his "cluster of functions," which he proposes to call "an episode." Rather, he speaks of it as a large, recurrent unit of the narrative. The episode is a patterned sequence of three functions, the fourth one in parenthesis being optional and where braces indicate alternatives:

(a) $\bar{a}$ c $\begin{bmatrix} r \\ \bar{r} \end{bmatrix}$

The symbols designate the following "functions" (Hendricks, 1977: 262,268):

a, associative relationship (supportive).
$\bar{a}$, dissociative relationship (nonsupportive).
c, confronts.
r, repulsed; dominated.
$\bar{r}$, yielded to; was dominated by.

Shortly after in the article Hendricks groups these elements together into one major type of narrative structure which he terms *dramatic*: conflict (= virtual confrontation) a/$\bar{a}$; confrontation, c; domination r/$\bar{r}$ (272). In Greimassian notation Hendricks' episode can be roughly translated as

± Opponent + confrontation ± domination

where ± is to be read as '+ or –' and to mean 'either present or absent.' Note that the episode contains two of the three Test énoncés: confrontation and domination.

struggle of desires. The duel is between two or more practical syllogisms and the gist of the duel is for one subject to sacrifice the object for another. The value that is invested in the object is in this sense understood economically as a *value-struggle* and as *"price,* the cost of desires in conflict" (Tarde, 1898:375). Furthermore, the status of the object in the consequence of the Test is defined and circumscribed as the competition-object, the competition-value: "Value is always the result of the competition of several desires, of the sacrifice of some, and of the triumph of one of them" (Tarde, 1898:375).

The triangular or tri-actant formulation of desire and action also brings to mind Kojève's celebrated distinction as to what makes a human or 'anthropogenic' desire specifically human as opposed to what he calls an animal desire. For a desire to be human it has to be oriented towards another *desire* and *another* desire. In order to be anthropogenic, the human being has to act with the aim not of acquiring an *object* but rather of acquiring another's desire of the object:

> Le Désir anthropogène diffère du Désir animal [...] par le fait qu'il porte non pas sur un objet réel, "positif," donné, mais sur un autre Désir. [...] Le Désir qui porte sur un objet naturel n'est humain que dans la mesure où il est "médiatisé" par le Désir d'un autre portant sur le même objet: il est humain de désirer ce que désirent les autres, parce qu'ils le désirent. [...] Désirer le désir d'un autre, c'est en dernière analyse désirer que la valeur que je suis ou que je "représente" soit la valeur désirée par cet autre: je veux qu'il "reconnaisse" ma valeur comme sa valeur, je veux qu'il me "reconnaisse" comme une valeur autonome.
>
> (Anthropogenic Desire differs from animal Desire [...] by the fact that it deals not with a given, real, "positive," object but with another Desire. [...] The Desire which deals with a natural object is human only insofar as it is "mediated" by the Desire of another dealing with the same object: it is human to desire what others desire because they desire it. [...] To desire the Desire of another is, ultimately, to desire that the value that I am or that I "represent" be the value that is desired by this other: I want him to "recognize" my value as his value; I want him to "recognize" me as an autonomous value.)   (Kojève, 1947:13-14)

4. The explanatory logic of action

In "Les actants, les acteurs et les figures" new "categories" are introduced, in addition to the structural-syntactic junctions of the subject and object, which are said to "overdetermine the actants in their syntagmatic progression" (1973a:164).

The categories are named after the Chomskyan opposition of linguistic *perfor-mance* and *competence* but they will refer specifically to the verbalization of action and to the antecedent states and modalities of action. A detailed and rigorous analysis will look into these categories three years later under the rubric of "modalizations and overmodalizations of action." In 1973 competence is initially defined as the overlapping, the "syncretism," of the modalities of *to want* and/or *to be able* and/or *to know what/how – to do* (1973a:164). The doing or performance "presupposes" beforehand a competence to do. This view of the connection of the act to the modalities holds according to what Greimas calls *the logic of presuppositions*, when the act is done.

If you view the act, however, from the point of view of the desiring subject, thinking ahead of what s/he ought to do, "the subject must first acquire a certain competence to become a performer" (1973a:165). This is the view worked out in the practical inference and Greimas calls it *the motivating logic*. Parentheti-cally, he specifies the principle of *causation* associated with this logic: "post hoc, ergo propter hoc" which means "after this, therefore because of this." We can call this a basic principle of causation but it is usually dubbed a fallacy, the fallacy that results from the assumption that because there is a temporal rela-tionship between two events or states, there is a cause-and-effect relationship between them. Yet no one would have had occasion to label the "post hoc, ergo propter hoc" a fallacy if it did not already suggest a spark of truth. Take out the word "ergo" and you are left with the unsophisticated notion that whenever A is the case, B sometimes, usually, or always happens soon afterwards. In other words, A is the cause of the B that happens soon after it.

Much controversy surrounds the root of the asymmetry between A and B. It is debated whether the asymmetry is due simply to a temporal difference or whether it consists of something other than time. It will take us too far afield to broach this problem and it will be extraneous to our purposes. I would like to stress, however, that the (cause, effect) schema that was seen operating in the relationship of the agent and patient roles manifests an asymmetry that is *not* temporal in nature. And secondly, let us note that a conceptual mapping is set up between *competence* and *causation* of action in such a way that they become implicitly synonymous. Furthermore, the causation is grasped and framed through a teleological explanation of action. In much the same way as Colling-wood defines "causing to do" as "affording a motive for doing it," Greimas' motivating logic starts from the act and not before it and seeks motive-reasons or incentive-reasons which explain why the agent acted as he or she did. The tie or connectedness from competence to performance winds up being the same as the tie from performance to competence; in other words, the motivating logic is the logic of presuppositions, both of them starting with the action.

In "Pour une théorie des modalités" the competence, qualified as "potential" and "pragmatic," is articulated into three *levels* of existence, "each level being characterized by a particular *semiotic* mode of existence" (1976:100, my underlining). The three levels are specified and set up in a table of three columns which we shall permute into rows in order to give emphasis to the perfect correspondence with the three steps of the practical inference schema (see figure 4.4). The modals that are selected in each row commit Greimas to a certain position in the formal representation of the reasoning which leads up to action—and not the 'act' only, as Greimas has it. The first row contains the desire and the prescriptive modalities and the second, the power and know how. The third row, however, surprises, when translated into English and when taken out of the context explaining the act. Greimas chooses to define the act or performance in its "naive and least compromising" sense as *ce qui fait être, that which makes one be* (1976:90). He retains the two predicates "faire" in its dual English sense of "to make or cause" and "to do" and "être" as "to be" and hyphenates the two into the composite *faire-être, to do-to be*, to represent the act itself.

PRACTICAL INFERENCE	PRAGMATIC ACT		
S wants to do O/ bring about O	have-to-do want-to-do	*virtualizing modalities*	**Competence**
S considers that he cannot do O unless he does P	can-do know-how-to-do	*actualizing modalities*	
Therefore, S sets himself to do P / does P	to do-to be	*realizing modalities*	**Performance**

Figure 4.4

The virtualizing modalities are referred to also as *efficient modalities*—which recall Aristotle's efficient cause—and the actualizing modalities are said to qualify or ground the narrative subject.

At this point we reach the end of our demonstration that aimed to show that the textual-actantial Object is incongruous and incommensurable with the sentential object and, concurrently, we arrive at the most beautiful and conclusive confirmation that the Subject and Object actants are not derived essentially from the syntax of the sentence, namely the semantic roles of agent and patient. The Subject and Object actants are conceptual categories stemming from the practical syllogism, its teleological inversion, and its opposition to (or union with) one or more practical syllogisms.

The demonstration itself and the final confirmation to which it led us should fill the hearts of all narratologists, and particularly those engaged in narrative semiotics, with the glow of familiarity. Hence, it may be worthwhile to review the observation Greimas makes about the "pragmatic act" at this last stage of the actantial grammar from the point of view of some recent and past philosophical contributions to the topic.

Greimas observes that the sketch of modalities that make up the pragmatic act or practical syllogism is determined and oriented backwards from the *act*, implying the inevitability of the action explained in the light of antecedent states or modalities. The relation between levels or steps, says Greimas, is one of "presupposition oriented from the performance (which presupposes competence)" (1976:100). Greimas would like to consider this "syntagmatic organization of action modalities" as *canonical* in the narrative grammar. This organization, he says, appears "justified *in abstracto*, as the simulacrum of the passage to the act" (100). He hesitates to do so because he notes the "fait curieux": "it does not correspond to what happens at the level of manifestation. [...] The subject may, for instance, be provided with a *can-do* without, however, having the *want-to-do* which should have preceded it. We are dealing with a difficulty which catalysis, the explicitation of presuppositions, cannot solve alone" (100).

5. On defining the problems involved in the practical inference or the pragmatic act

I would like to take up this last observation of Greimas and discuss the difficulties we are facing with the 'practical inference' or 'pragmatic act.' One of the ways to bring out the problems and set them in bold relief is to contrast practical reasoning with theoretical reasoning. Let us take up a very simple example to illustrate the latter:

Major premise: All men are mortal

Minor premise: Miss Lonelyhearts is a man

Conclusion: Therefore, Miss Lonelyhearts is mortal

In making this inference, we would say that the conclusion holds (is true) *because* the premises are assumed to be true. To the question raised "Why is Miss Lonelyhearts mortal?" we would answer "because all men are mortal and Miss Lonelyhearts is a man." The "because" here signifies a *logical* relationship, not a causal or teleological one. The *tie* or (textual) *connectedness* between premises and conclusion is conclusive or certain in the sense that it is logically *necessary*; that is, the conclusion *has to hold*. Accepting the conclusion of theoretical reasoning is a necessity that consists of this: that if the premises are true and the argument is valid, the conclusion has to be true.

One of the major problems we are facing with practical reasoning is showing in what sense practical reasoning necessitates its conclusion. Is the practical inference *logically conclusive*? And if not, wherein lies its *binding* force? Although the practical inference has the same structural features as the theoretical inference, it admits of a special problem not shared by the theoretical inference. There is no set of rules for practical reasoning which correspond to rules of logical and mathematical deduction. What, shall we say, are the rules by which we pass from premises to conclusion in practical reasoning? What are the criteria for validity in the practical inference? It is by no means easy to say.

Without formulating the key questions which arise with practical reasoning, Greimas has nevertheless provided one answer by considering the act which has already been done and by matching "presuppositions" to it. The *necessary tie* or relationship between the action and the modalities is one which is established from the *fait accompli*. From this angle, his implicit answer agrees with that of von Wright: "It is only when action is already there and a practical argument is constructed to explain or justify it that we have a logically conclusive argument. The necessity of the practical inference schema is, one could say, a necessity conceived *ex post actu* (von Wright, 1971:117). Reversing this pattern, as Greimas does, to see "what happens at the level of manifestation" when the subject is considering to act, vetoes the logical conclusiveness or compulsion. Von Wright has argued this point persuasively and sums it up as follows:

Despite the truth of the Logical Connection Argument, the premises of a practical inference do *not* with logical necessity entail behavior. They do not entail the "existence" of a conclusion to match them. The syllogism when leading up to action is "practical" and not a piece of logical demonstration   (von Wright, 1971:117).

What this means is that the act does not follow with logical necessity from the virtualizing and actualizing modalities, from the desire to bring about O and the possibilities considered to achieve it. More briefly, there is no logical compulsion tying 'competence' to 'performance.'

From the viewpoint of the practical inference subject, the connection between premises and conclusion is non-deletably and irremovably loose rather than logically necessary. The most important way in which the connection is loose is that the reasoning itself is *defeasible*[2]. That is to say, a pattern of reasoning which would justify a certain course of action might cease to justify it if further wants and beliefs were added to the premises. The reasoning is defeasible because if we add further premises we cannot be sure that the conclusion will remain satisfactory. Let us reconstruct one defeasible inference from this passage of *Miss Lonelyhearts*:

> *He stopped reading. Christ was the answer, but, if he did not want to get sick, he had to stay away from the Christ business. Besides, Christ was Shrike's particular joke. "Soul of Miss L, glorify me. Body of Miss L, save me. Blood of ... " He turned to his typewriter* (3).

The practical inference involved here goes as follows: "Miss Lonelyhearts wants to answer the correspondents' letters. He considers that he cannot answer them unless he writes a Christian message. Therefore, he sets forth to write a Christian message." Although writing a Christian message may be a reasonable conclusion from the premises first set out and, particularly, in view of the kind of letters he receives, it ceases to be reasonable to Miss Lonelyhearts if and when he adds the premises that *the Christ business* gets him sick and that it is

---

[2]I am borrowing the term from Kenny who takes it up, in turn, from Geach. Feinberg (in White, 1968:96) comments on its legal and real estate meaning: "Defeasibility is a term which Hart borrowed from the law of property where it is used to refer to an estate or legal interest in land which is 'subject to termination or "defeat" in a number of different contingencies but remains intact if no such contingencies mature.' [Hart] then extended its meaning to cover all legal claims that are regarded as *provisionally established* at a certain stage of the litigation process but still vulnerable to defeat, annulment, or revocation at some later stage of the proceedings."

also the object of his editor's hostile joking.

Theoretical deductive reasoning is not defeasible like practical reasoning. Adding a premise does not and cannot invalidate a previously valid inference. If a conclusion follows from a given set of premises, it can be drawn validly from any larger set containing those premises, no matter how many are added to the set. The kind of conclusion that a practical inference leads to is, in this respect, essentially different from a theoretical conclusion that ends with 'statement proved' or 'theorem or result deduced.' The binding force, the 'practical' bond of continuities, the 'logical' mesh of connections between the premises and the action to which it leads always remains loose. No matter how conclusive the reasoning may appear, there is always the possibility that it may have to be corrected or supplemented in the light of further wants and beliefs.

In what sense, then, can we speak of practical reasoning as being conclusive? What shall we say is the nature or connectedness that carries with it a binding force? The discussion of this problem is receiving decisive impetus from analytic philosophy concerned with the concept of action and with forms of practical discourse. The works of Kenny are an important contribution to this area and it is instructive to follow his examination of practical reason. The logic of satisfactoriness and the logic of satisfaction which he developed to solve the problem of conclusiveness provide an interesting alternative to the *ex post actu* view. The appeal of this position lies in its attempt to deal with the inference in its actual unfolding, dealt with *prospectively* with a view to things which have to be done rather than *retrospectively* with a view to things already done.

Kenny in *Will, Freedom, and Action* starts with the fact that mental states like 'want,' 'will,' 'believe,' 'consider,' and 'plan' are identified by their expression and proposes that the way to understand them and their mode of functioning in the practical inference is to study the nature of their expression. Following Hare and Stenius, Kenny breaks up any linguistic expression, any sentence, into a *phrastic* which contains the descriptive content of the sentence and a *tropic* which is a mark of mood or a modal operator (1975:39,74). In our terminology the 'phrastic' is roughly the same as the 'proposition' and the 'tropic' as the 'modal (verb).' A broad division is drawn between two different kinds of sentences or two different "speech-acts": *assertion* and *fiat* which contain the same proposition but a different mood. Assertoric sentences include many which are not normally thought of as assertions; suppositions and guesses are ranked along with assertions. Kenny adopts the artificial term 'fiat' to refer to all non-assertoric sentences. Lumped together under 'fiat' are sentences as varied as those expressing wishes, wants, requests and commands, plans and projects. The binary opposition of assertion vs. fiat seems to overspread the division of verbs according to mood: on the one side, verbs that are in the indicative mood and, on the other, verbs that are in the subjunctive, imperative, or conditional mood.

Fiats and assertoric sentences are sentences with different moods but the same descriptive content. So does the corresponding expression of the desire in the initial step of practical reasoning and the expression of the means and possibility in the intermediate step. Practical reasoning, as it appears to Kenny, can be regarded as a process of passing from one fiat to another, just as theoretical reasoning consists in passing from one assertoric sentence to another according to rules. The point of the rules for theoretical reasoning is to ensure that one never passes from true assertions to false assertions; the rules are truth-preserving rules. To determine what the point of the rules is for practical reasoning is to specify in what sense practical reasoning necessitates its conclusion.

We must first ask what is the practical analogue of truth: "What is the value which rules of practical reasoning have as their purpose to preserve in the way in which truth is the value preserved by rules of theoretical reasoning?" (Kenny, 1975:71). Fiats contain possible states of affairs whose actualization satisfies the desires expressed by them. Among fiats of the practical inference schema, we have noted, are goal-objects, objectives, and plans and projects that relate to the goal-object as a means to an end. Much of practical reasoning consists in the search for a *satisfactory* plan to execute, i.e. which will best serve our objective and gratify our desire. We might be inclined to say: what is satisfactory is not the plan, but the states of affairs projected by the plan. But it would be absurd to say that a plan was not satisfactory on the grounds that it was only a plan and not yet executed. As Kenny points out, "if a plan were never satisfactory unless executed, planning would be impossible. For we would have to do everything in our power before we could decide which of the things in our power was the best thing to do; and by then it would be too late" (1975:80).

A satisfactory plan as anticipated and imagined by the practical inference subject, summarized by the value-concept of *satisfactoriness*, is the practical analogue of truth. Unlike truth and falsehood, execution and non-execution, which are absolute notions, satisfactoriness is relative. A plan is not just satisfactory or not satisfactory *simpliciter*: it may be satisfactory to some persons and not to others, satisfactory for a given set of wants and not for others. By virtue of the relativity intrinsic to satisfactoriness, the crucial characteristic of defeasibility of practical reasoning takes place.

Reflections on these considerations led Kenny in 1966 to suggest that the logic operative in practical reasoning was the logic of satisfactoriness. The construction of this logic consists in formulating the rules which will ensure that in reasoning about what to do we never pass from a plan/fiat which will satisfy our desires to a plan/fiat which will not satisfy them. This is because the purpose of practical reasoning is to get done what we want. The logic of satisfactoriness is only a part, though a central part, of practical reasoning. Because in getting done what we want, we have to make use of the practical logic of satisfaction—which is an exact parallel of the familiar and predicate logic—as well as the practical logic of satisfactoriness. The development of the logic of satisfactoriness and the wider and "richer" logic of which it forms a part continues. At this stage of research Kenny provides an answer to the 'forward' conclusiveness of the practical inference:

> In practical inference it is only the logic of satisfactoriness which is *conclusive*, in the sense of insuring that the conclusion has the value the reasoning aims at, namely the satisfaction of the reasoner's wants. The logic of satisfaction—reasoning to necessary conditions for satisfaction—is never conclusive in the sense of ensuring the arrival of what is wanted. Having carried out a piece of practical reasoning to necessary conditions, and put the conclusion into action, the reasoner cannot then rest secure in the confidence that what he has done will bring about the state of affairs he wants; there may be more that he has to do to achieve his goals. In particular, to take Hare's example, one never comes to the end of satisfying a negative prohibition (1975:89).

The conclusion of a practical inference is satisfactory and binding relative to a given set of wants. As mentioned earlier, defeasibility comes about because satisfactoriness is a relative notion. The only way to avoid defeasibility in practical reasoning would be to insist that the initial premises setting out the object-of-desire and the goal-object should not only be correct but also complete; that *all* the wants, *all* the desires, to be settled by one action should be fully specified. If we could do this, then we would eliminate the danger of a further premise being added, of another desire surging forth, which would negate the satisfactoriness of the conclusion described in the last step of the practical inference. If we could do this, however, it would be next to impossible to act. The notion of an initial premise which is fully complete and yet complete enough to entail a practical conclusion is chimerical. Only in restricted contexts can we even begin to approach completeness in the specification of practical premises.

V

Sequel to the Semantics of Event
and Role Relationships

1. The simple narrative statement: communication

In our theoretical target of chapter II we have said that the two major
components of the narrative consist of the component referring to *event* which
is defined by the canonical units

$$NE_1 = F_{doing} \, (S \longrightarrow O)$$

and the component referring to *contract* which is defined by the canonical units

$$NE_2 = F_{communication} \, (Sr \longrightarrow O \longrightarrow R)$$

These two components can be represented graphically as the two key axes of the
actantial model (figure 5.1).

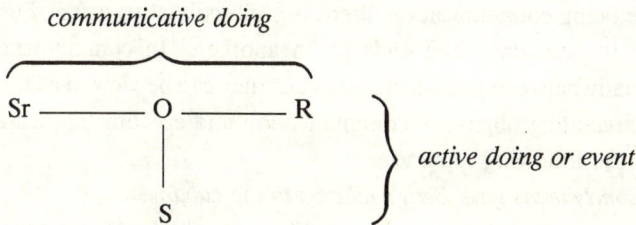

Figure 5.1

In the preceding chapters we have examined the component of event and
have introduced the basic concepts for analyzing the semantic structure of
sentences and for the simplest actional text which the practical inference articu-

lates. In the next chapters we will be dealing with the other macroscopic component of the narrative, that of the contract and
communication. Similarly to the subject-object relation, we shall start, once again, at the level of linguistic statement in which elementary verb-predicates are associated with a configuration of cases or roles.

Some of the essential features of communicative verbs were briefly introduced in the discussion of the causative or factitive schema of transitive verbs and in the orientational schemata of verbs of motion. At this point we will explore more closely the nature of the sentential roles and textual actants which form the network of communicative doing or communication.

Acts of communication, whether verbal or transactional, are analogous to verbs of motion. The logical schema in terms of which we analyzed a trivalent motion-action-process verb and its dependent roles is

MOVE (SOURCE, OBJECT-OF-MOTION, TERMINAL).

In some semantic theories such as the one propounded by D. Nilsen and A. Pace Nilsen the motion schema is the prototype of all movement and transfer and the most inclusive class of trivalent verbs. By virtue of its generality it is broken down into four categories: transportation, transfer, exchange, and communication. Thus, communication is a component of the class of motion verbs. The inverse holds true in actantial grammar where communication is the prototype and the class divisible into speech, transfer, transportation, exchange and other events, as we shall see. In either case, the prototype being motion or the prototype being communication, there is a directional transfer of an object which begins in one place and ends up in another. In communication the transfer is usually between people or actors but they can be viewed as the source or terminal circulating objects of communication and exchanging messages.

Consider the following sentences:

1. *Miss Lonelyhearts gave Betty's address to the cabdriver.*
2. *Shrike went among his guests and distributed the letters (as a magician does cards).*
3. *Miss Lonelyhearts bought a quart of scotch for the Shrikes.*
4. *Miss Lonelyhearts explained his job situation to Betty.*
5. *Miss Lonelyhearts submitted drafts of his column to God.*

In these sentences we have a "communicative" situation in which the cabdriver can be said, in a broad sense, to be the *receiver* or recipient of the *object-of-*

communication, Betty's address, transmitted by Miss Lonelyhearts; likewise, Shrike's guests are the receiver of letters from Shrike; the Shrikes, of scotch from Miss Lonelyhearts; Betty, of an explanation from Miss Lonelyhearts; God, of column drafts from Miss Lonelyhearts.

In principle, trivalent communication verbs are *to say* and *to give* and these include their counterparts, *to know* and *to have* or *receive*. Verbs like *buy, sell, send, explain* are also three-place communication verbs combining a subject, a direct object, an indirect object or prepositional phrase involving motion to the receiver. The semantic-logical cases contracted by a three-place predicate of a communicative network are a particular case of a structure of attribution much more general, well known in linguistics as the *schema of communication* or, even more generally still, as the *structure of exchange*. We shall call the schema the *benefactive schema of communication* because the relation is usually benefactive, as attested by the more widespread names for the sender and receiver: benefactor and beneficiary. This schema may be represented as a linguistic statement with three roles:

COMMUNICATE (SENDER, OBJECT, RECEIVER), and

Event $F_{communication}$ (Sr —— O ——→ R)

Although, to take one counterexample, *Miss Lonelyhearts received a punch in the mouth*, the relation in the exchange can be malefactive, it is normally and by convention defined to be 'for the benefit of' or 'in the interest of' the receiver. Thus, to stress its most predominant usage, we may choose an alternative definition of the benefactive schema of communication:

GIVE (SENDER, OBJECT, RECEIVER).

One general point to be made is that, as two-place constructions can be derived from one-place constructions by means of the notion of 'causativity' so three-place constructions can be derived from two-place constructions by means of a further application of the same notion. As *Shrike opened the door* is to be related syntactically to *The door opened*, so (a) is to be related to (b).

(1) a. *Miss Lonelyhearts gave Betty's address to the cabdriver.*
    b. *The cabdriver has Betty's address.*
(2) a. *Shrike went among his guests and distributed the letters (as a magician does cards).*
    b. *The guests have the letters.*

(3) a. *Miss Lonelyhearts bought a quart of scotch for the Shrikes.*

    b. *The Shrikes have a quart of scotch.*

(4) a. *Miss Lonelyhearts explained his job situation to Betty.*

    b. *Betty understood the situation.*

(5) a. *Miss Lonelyhearts submitted drafts of his column to God.*

    b. *God received the column drafts.*

Loosely, one might say in most cases something, the direct object, tends to be done for, given to, or received by the indirect object which fills the semantic role of receiver. Miss Lonelyhearts and Shrike are not only agents but also the senders. The sentences in (4) are a paraphrase from the text laying bare the nucleus of the communicative situation. The following is a verbatim quotation of the same frame:

(4) a'. *Perhaps I can make you understand. Let's start from the beginning. A man is hired to give advice to the readers of a newspaper. The job is a circulation stunt and the whole staff considers it a joke. He welcomes the job, for it might lead to a gossip column, and anyway he's tired of being a leg man.* [...]

    b'. *Although he had spoken soberly, he saw that Betty still thought him a fool.* (West, 32)

Communication takes place in a conversational or dialogue context so that the giving can be and often is acted out through speech rather than summarized by the narrator. And, as far as Betty, the receiver, goes she obviously understands but, in another way, she does not understand. That is, she does not accept the situation and the impositions it creates for Miss Lonelyhearts and herself. An explanation usually pairs off with understanding but here more than a cognitive understanding is sought after. Miss Lonelyhearts wants Betty to accept and to cooperate and if she does not understand in this way then, for all practical purposes, she does not understand at all. Something else is happening between Miss Lonelyhearts and Betty than a mere transfer of information and an explanation for her benefit. The event is still a communication but more than just the benefactive type.

Note that in the benefactive type of communication the recipient does not reflect a semantic agent in (b) any more than in (a). The cabdriver does not do anything; neither do Shrike's guests, the Shrikes, Betty, and God. The meaning of each verb in (b) expresses a relation of two objects coinciding. To be exact, it localizes the object of communication in some place, the place filled by the receiver.

As the textual example of Miss Lonelyhearts' job began to show, not all communication reflects the pattern of benefactive communication. The other type of communication consists of a *factitive* and persuasive doing or what can better be described, not without reason, as *manipulation*. In order to illustrate the factitive meaning of communication, it will be more illuminating to discuss the linguistic derivation of 'complex' three-place verbs with reference to French. The factitive construction in French, *faire-faire* (make-do), uses the auxiliary modal *faire* to generate a three-place construction from a bivalent transitive verb. For purposes of comparison, let us translate the first two sentences of benefactive communication from the previous page.

(1) a. *Mademoiselle Coeur-Brisé donna l'adresse de Betty au chauffeur de taxi.*

   b. *Le chauffeur de taxi a l'adresse de Betty.*

The factitive construction is exemplified by

(6) a. *Betty fait manger la soupe à Mademoiselle Coeur-Brisé.*

   b. *Mademoiselle Coeur-Brisé mange la soupe.*

The translation of (6) is

   a. *Betty makes Miss Lonelyhearts eat the soup.*

   b. *Miss Lonelyhearts eats the soup.*

The grammatical structure of (6a) in French may be indicated by means of the quasi-English gloss 'Betty makes-eat the soup to Miss Lonelyhearts.' The parallelism in grammatical and syntactical structure between (1a) and (6a) is obvious. As *l'adresse de Betty* is the direct object of the simple three-place verb *donna* so *la soupe* may be regarded as the direct object of the factitive three-place verb *fait manger*. This is not obvious in the English translation but it is in the quasi-English gloss. *Au chauffeur de taxi* is the indirect object of *donna* and, similarly, à *Mademoiselle Coeur-Brisé* is the indirect object of *fait manger*. It is characteristic of the causative or factitive construction in French that the subject of the underlying bivalent verb, *Mademoiselle Coeur-Brisé*, is transformed into an indirect object with three-place causative verbs whereas the object of the underlying bivalent verb, *la soupe*, remains as the direct object in the three-place causative construction. By contrast, in English the subject becomes the direct object, *Betty makes Miss Lonelyhearts do* as compared to *Betty makes-do to Miss Lonelyhearts.* When you consider that in most cases the receiver stands for the indirect object or the dative, it is easy to see how the three-place factitive construction is linked to the benefactive schema of communication:

Betty	fait manger	la soupe	à Mademoiselle Coeur-Brisé
Sender	communicate	object	receiver

The role of receiver *au chauffeur de taxi* and *à Mademoiselle Coeur-Brisé* maintains in both cases the same position and the same role.

Semantically, however, complex factitive three-place verbs differ from the benefactive type. One of the distinctive features of manipulative communication is more clearly brought out in the English construction with *make-do*. Statements using *make* or any expression that involves explicit causation by use of complement verbs like *have, get,* and *cause* commonly introduce an implication of force, pressure of authority, or sometimes coercion. J. O. Urmson talks of the restricted use of such expressions in English:

> 'What made you do that?' is a question of the same type as 'What possessed you to do that?', implying that the agent was carried away. [...] 'Who made him do it?' suggests external compulsion; 'What made him do it?' suggests inner compulsion; while 'What caused him to do it?' does neither, though it does not, perhaps, exclude them (J. O. Urmson in A. White, 1968:155,163).

The French modal auxiliary *faire* does not generally partake of this feature although the sense of an efficient doer activating and propelling someone else's action is basic to both the faire and make constructions. We shall retain this particular pragmatic meaning. Other traits of the make-do construction are chosen for forensic purposes, contrary to their ordinary-language use and congruent with the conceptual and teleological nature of what von Wright labelled the "making-people-do-things mechanism" (von Wright, 1971:147). Of tangential interest at the moment, is the widely used *make-feel* construction in English to indicate how the sender's actions affected the receiver's feelings, often without any conscious manipulation though they do not exclude it. Examples come readily to mind: to make someone feel proud, ridiculous, awkward, embarrassed, like a fool, like a million.

The second key semantic difference between benefactive and factitive verbs is highlighted by the grammatical difference between them. We have pointed out the grammatical similarity in order to seize the communication aspect common to both but the grammatical difference introduces a distinction between kinds of communication. A sentence containing a factitive or causative verb is a complex sentence with an independent or superordinate clause governing a subordinate or dependent infinitive clause. The factitive relation is set up between a subject, *Betty*, and an object which is itself a lexical proposition, *Miss Lonelyhearts eats the soup*. This embedded proposition has its own subject or agent, *Miss Lonelyhearts*. It seems, therefore, that the factitive relation is a relation between two hierarchically distinct subjects, S_2 the modal subject and S_1 the subject of doing, or the Sender and Receiver, respectively. The device of subordinating one clause with the Receiver whose strings are pulled to another clause with the Sender trying to pull his or her strings in such a way that one is part of the other no doubt establishes the grammatical basis to the non-symmetrical relation between the modal subject and the subject of doing. There is no such hierarchical asymmetry between the Sender and Receiver of a benefactive verb.

Although the coercive or compulsive "make-do" is not often used in English, there are very many verbs that function the same way as "faire-faire" and which fall into the "making-people-do-things mechanism." These verbs have been aptly called *verbs of control* by D. Nilsen and A. Pace Nilsen. They behave exactly like the complex factitive verbs though some of them allow the deletion of one argument in surface structure. Like the factitive verbs, verbs of control have a dual subject and one agent who has the most control over the other cases, that is, the Sender over the Receiver and the Object. Consider a sentence like

> *Shrike hired Miss Lonelyhearts.*

The verb in this sentence seems to be a two-place predicate co-occurring with an agent, *Shrike*, and an object who is not, however, a patient. In some case grammars Miss Lonelyhearts' role would be that of experiencer. While it is true that Miss Lonelyhearts is the direct object of the verb *hired*, he is also in some sense an agent. When we use the sentence "Shrike hired Miss Lonelyhearts," we are saying explicitly that Shrike did something, i.e. *hire Miss Lonelyhearts*, but we are also stating implicitly that Miss Lonelyhearts will do something, i.e. fill a particular role. As *Miss Lonelyhearts gave Betty's address to the cabdriver* is to be related syntactically to *The cabdriver has Betty's address* so (a) is to be related to (b):

    a. Shrike hired Miss Lonelyhearts.
    b. Miss Lonelyhearts will do something.

The employee's role can be specified

    a. Shrike hired Miss Lonelyhearts to write an advice column for the newspaper.
    b. Miss Lonelyhearts will write (writes) an advice column for the newspaper.

Like factitive verbs, verbs of control also have an embedded action in the form of an embedded infinitive clause. In this clause, the object of the main sentence, Miss Lonelyhearts, now acts as the *agent*. This is either stated explicitly or implied, depending on the particular verb of control. Following Nilsen and Pace Nilsen, we will say that the main feature which distinguishes the different sub-classes of verbs of control from each other would be strength. A weak verb of control would be *allow*, a stronger verb of control would be *encourage*, and a still stronger verb of control would be *force*. To my knowledge, only Nilsen and Pace Nilsen have singled out these control verbs and studied their linguistic manifestation. The long list of control verbs which they give and the judicious subdivision made of them are both to the point and ample enough to suggest a far-flung expansion of *faire-faire* and *make-do*. Here, then, is what they introduce in their *Semantic Theory*: a fivefold division of verbs of control (Nilsen and Pace Nilsen, 1975:129).

    1. Verbs of allowance include the following:

    allow, appoint, authorize, call on, challenge, choose, commission, constrain, dare, engage, elect, employ, empower, enable, entitle, hire, let, name, nominate, permit, privilege, tell, write, licence, permit.

What I find particularly striking are verbs like *tell* or *ask*, as in "N told P to do something," which appear quite innocent in safeguarding P's freedom to action, especially if the verbs are taken by themselves, and yet they are incredibly manipulative or have great potential to be so. This, of course, indicates that all manipulation starts with knowledge, with the pair to tell/to say or the pair to know/to have which is, in principle, the verbal pair of the benefactive schema of communication.

    2. Verbs of aid are like verbs of allowance except the agent of the main sentence not only has control over the secondary action, but is actually an agent

in helping to carry out the secondary action. Such verbs include

aid, assist, coach, design, help, lead, prepare, remind, teach, train, demonstrate, show.

3. Now consider verbs of encouragement, such as

admonish, advise, arouse, appeal to, ask, beg, beseech, caution, communicate, condemn, counsel, direct, encourage, enjoin, entreat, exhort, fire up, goad, induce, inspire, instruct, invite, persuade, lead, prompt, provoke, request, say to, stimulate, stir, tempt, urge, warn.

4. Verbs of expectation are stronger than verbs of allowance, aid, or encouragement. They include the following:

count on, desire, expect, intend, (would) like, look for, mean for, oblige, prefer, seek for, trust, want.

They imply that the secondary agent has some sort of an obligation to the primary agent to accomplish the action of the embedded sentence.

5. Finally, the strongest control verbs of all are those of force, such as:

assign, cause, coerce, command, compel, consign, forbid, force, get, incite, make, order, require, prevail upon.

Given such a rich and suggestive list of control and factitive verbs, we thought that a careful combing of the text would yield many examples. The search proved to be anticlimactic and it had to be reconciled with the inescapable observation that every single page of the novella was steeped with persuasive and manipulative doing. There are at most half a dozen instances of factitive and control verbs, one of which includes a double factitive, "Betty made Miss Lonelyhearts get Shrike to extend his sick leave" (36). This unexpected discovery alerted us to the fact that control and manipulation are something you do and not something you verbalize. Factitive and control verbs are verbs that *name* or *describe* happenings which take place in a normative context of duties and rights and which are *interpreted* surely and effortlessly through body language, body politics, and verbally through requesting information and criticizing the other. The following passage from the first chapter of *Miss Lonelyhearts* illustrates the profusion of manipulation and control in the total absence of factitive and control verbs.

On seeing Miss Lonelyhearts for the first time, Shrike had smiled and said, "The Susan Chesters, the Beatrice Fairfaxes, and the Miss Lonelyhearts are the priests of twentieth-century America." The editor, Shrike, hires Miss Lonelyhearts as an advice columnist and the event of hiring is connoted through the qualifications of Miss Lonelyhearts and an amused acknowledgement of a role-identity pleasing to Miss Lonelyhearts and acceptable to the editor. It is Shrike's smile, however, his facial gesture, which clearly says 'Yes, I'm hiring you.'

A copy boy came up to tell him that Shrike wanted to know if the stuff was ready. A verb of expectation is implicit here but the force is attenuated verbally by a soft question 'wanted to know.' All polite and diplomatic communication aims at absorbing and at best erasing the blow of the force scaffolding one's influence or manipulation of the other. But the receiver can always gauge the degree of the blow fairly accurately and in so doing, he or she understands the message by restoring the other's erasure. *He bent over the typewriter and began pounding its keys.* Miss Lonelyhearts has assessed the force very well and communicates an equally strong discouragement to the copy boy through his body language and suppression of all spoken communication. In order to drive him away, Miss Lonelyhearts pretends he is busy.

But before he had written a dozen words, Shrike leaned over his shoulder. Shrike's counter-move is to apply force and this is executed through body language and by an uncomfortable and intimidating proximity to the receiver. When the body is captured, the mind and emotions closely follow but not without a natural resistance and a fiery struggle to stay free. *"The same old stuff," Shrike said. "Why don't you give them something new and hopeful?"* Force is also applied by negative criticism and domination which touch both the mind and the body of the other and yank them into the behavioral pattern dictated by the critic. *Tell them about art. Here, I'll dictate:*

"Art is a Way out.

Do not let life overwhelm you. When the old paths are choked with the débris of failure, look for newer and fresher paths. Art is just such a path. Art is distilled from suffering. As Mr. Polnikoff exclaimed through his fine Russian beard, when, at the age of eight-six, he gave up his business to learn Chinese, 'We are, as yet, only at the beginning ... '

"Art is One of Life's Richest Offerings.

"For those who have not the talent to create, there is appreciation. For those ... " Shrike's criticism is somewhat attenuated by his own active participation in the writing of the column. Shrike is helping and coaching Miss Lonelyhearts but he is imposing his viewpoint on Miss Lonelyhearts, as his last words show.

"Go on from there." A command issued in an imperative usually indicates the strongest control by the issuer of the command. Shrike assigns a topic to Miss Lonelyhearts and since Miss Lonelyhearts cannot refuse, Shrike prevails upon him to do it.

Some linguists have argued against a role like the factitive sender, causative agent, or instigator of another's action on the basis that the English language does not have a construction of neutral causation, like the 'faire faire' modality in French. Hence, the conclusion is drawn that English does not provide a strong motivation for distinguishing between the manipulating agent and the manipulated agent. For that conclusion to hold, however, we would have to dismiss the fact that English does have many communication verbs of control which make that distinction clearly. And this is not a superfluous class of verbs nor a superfluous set of roles. To treat the "causer" or factitive sender like a regular agent is to ignore the whole area of tension between human freedom and agency, on the one hand, and its curtailment through manipulation and politics, on the other. Surely, this mode of communication could not be considered superfluous in any culture and any language.

The passage from *Miss Lonelyhearts* seems to indicate that the verb-predicate is not the only linguistic unit which stands for an event or signifies an evental meaning. The avoidance of using manipulative and control verbs by breaking them down into a proliferation of other kinds of verbs and events paradoxically allows the genuine nature of manipulation and control to emerge with the power of inference and connotation. Manipulation and control float like connotative signifieds that function literally as an index: they point but they do not tell. They undertake to fill the void of what they silence by the plenitude of what they say. In this annulment of the power (the intimidation) of one language dissolving behind another, connotation behind denotation, manipulation and control succeed in forming a kind of causal *glissando* which allows the connotation of power to turn back on itself and indicate its own existence. Within this game of duplicity, subverting the opposition between denotation and connotation, by making one refer to the other to fulfill the needs of a certain illusion, manipulation and control wind up "telling us something simple, literal, primitive: something true," something which R. Barthes defines, in fact, as denotation; and he goes on to say, "[it is] the superior myth by which the text pretends to return to the nature of language, to language as nature. [...] This is why we must keep denotation, the old deity, watchful, cunning, theatrical, in charge to *represent* the collective *innocence* of language" (Barthes, 1970:16).

Keeping denotation as the hearth and norm of a primary, original meaning we can say that with factitive and control verbs the *object* that is communicated to the Receiver is a plan of action which can be issued in a variable tone of control force. Matching the conceptual symbolism used in the practical syllogism we may verbalize this mode of communication as

(1) The Sender makes / made the Receiver do O/ bring about O or, using an average degree of force,

(2) The Sender proposes / proposed to the Receiver to do O / bring about O. We define this type of communication to be *manipulative communication* or manipulation. It is differentiated from the benefactive type and represented schematically as follows:

MAKE-DO (SENDER, OBJECT, RECEIVER)

It provides a distinct explanatory pattern to the question *why* something was done which is often that the agent was made to do it. There is a variety of ways in which people are said to be made to do things, to be motivated by someone, persuaded, inspired, urged, and so on. In all cases, when we say the Sender wants the Receiver to do this thing O / bring about O / make O happen, we *ground* the second want on the first. The Receiver wants to do something because the Sender wanted him or her to do this thing first. The Sender exercises a cognitive doing which aims at provoking the pragmatic, evental, somatic doing of the Receiver. He or she is the instigator of the action and the promoter responsible for the action executed by the Receiver-Subject. Thus, the Sender is characterized not only by its factitive modal status but also by its syntagmatic position which precedes that of the Receiver. Let us note, in addition, that contrary to what happens in the benefactive type of communication schema where the Sender is the one who tends to do and give something to the Receiver, in the factitive type, it is the Receiver who tends to do something for the Sender. Insofar as actional cost is concerned, namely, the total amount of action or activity which one gives to the other, the two types of communication are in perfect opposition to each other. As Greimas himself observes, "Whereas the Subject gives in the transaction the totality of his doing and being, the Sender, generous Sovereign, if he offers everything, he loses nothing of his substance" (1976a:23).

Under what circumstances will the Sender's proposal to the Receiver, using incentives or threats, that the Receiver-Subject do O / bring about O, cause the Receiver to accept and become the Sender's agent? This is an issue which Propp did not consider in his analysis of the folktale. Actantial grammar bypasses this important component of 'trading in the future' which clinches the contract and later becomes an exchange of social and pragmatic rewards. No one ordinarily stages a rewarding performance for another until s/he receives some indication that the Sender will, in return, stage a performance rewarding to her/him. A negotiation or bargain must be struck before the goods will actually be allowed to change hands. Yet, as G. McCall and J. Simmons pointed out, in *Identities and Interactions*, the negotiation "does not assume the outward appearance of a crude 'naming of prices.' The tactics of rhetorical persuasion are more evident in the process than are those of the market place though the moves of each party are motivated by cost-reward considerations" (1966:141). The Sender and Receiver must also strike a bargain over getting not just a profitable exchange but "fair exchange." The principle underlying the exchange is spoken of as the rule of distributive justice which states that one's investments, rewards, and costs should all be roughly comparable. If one's costs are higher, for example, one's rewards ought also to be higher so that the profits (rewards less costs) will be roughly equal among all the parties to the exchange.

The *make-do* or proposal by the Sender to the Receiver and the free acceptance by the Receiver together establish a mutual *consensus* between the two parties or, in Greimas' terminology, a *contract*. We just spoke of it as a negotiation, bargain, and as a mutual staging of rewarding performances. Every contract presupposes the idea of an exchange of goods and services and every exchange, in turn, has at its basis, the principle of equivalence. The contract is an exchange whereas manipulative communication in itself is nothing but a one-sided gain for the manipulating agent-Sender. We shall see later that equivalence makes up one of the two fundamental types of the idea of Justice applied to given social interactions while the other is that of equality. For the moment, it is important to understand that the contract in its first stages consists of a mutual and free agreement between the Sender and Receiver and an exchange of commitments to each other. Only when the services of the Receiver are exchanged later for the goods at 'the right price' from the Sender does the agreement get fulfilled as a contract.

In the Proppian folktale the contract appears as a generalized and recurrent coupling of functions that are articulated as *injunction* vs. *acceptance*. The contractual relation into which the Subject-hero enters with the Sender is a normative or deontic one, intimately connected with the authoritarian social hierarchy reflected in the Proppian folktale. The Sender is usually an agent who issues commands, orders, prescriptions, injunctions, or prohibitions to the hero and thereby enjoys some recognized position of *authority* over him. Command, prohibition, and permission are related modal categories governing, influencing, or otherwise controlling the possible courses of action. But other modal systems can be conceived as fulfilling a similar constraint on the course of narrative action. Thus, for example, any verb of control is an operator modalizing action along a different register. When I ask my friend to shut the door I do not command her; not to speak of the case when I ask a stranger for street directions. In both instances, however, I influenced the receiver: I "made him/her do" something.

In summary, communication may be benefactive or manipulative. When the Sender's giving or the make-do is not accepted by the Sender, the communication is unilateral and when it is accepted, it is bilateral. Contract is a bilateral communication which is both manipulative and benefactive; that is, it is meant to be a mutual and fair exchange though the benefactive return is yet to be explained.

2.   Codicil to the theoretical target

A supplement to the target in chapter II is desirable to account for the special questions raised with the communication component of the narrative. The key reason for the codicil is that all attempts at reconstruction of the Sender and Receiver actants on the textual level did not crystallize into a neat, elegant pattern like the practical syllogism, giving concrete and definite form to complex and refractory concepts invested in goal-oriented action and change. That is, the practical syllogism provided a clear vision of the intermediate, linking terrain to the broadest and pervasive question stated at the very opening of our text as a two-way flow between linguistic-semantic case roles and textual categories covered under the Subject and Object actants.

There is no comparably clear and concise terrain linking the different textual strata and complemental arguments of the Sender, Receiver, and object of communication. The key question for the communication component of the narrative can initially be formulated as a variant of the overarching two-way flow inquiry.

1) First, from bottom to top, or if we wish, from the particular to the general, which is the direction of linguistic induction: the issue of integrating case roles into higher units called actants is a loophole due to the fact that Greimas identifies only the benefactive schema of communication on the sentence level. Let us explain. Building from the research on syntax and semantics from Tesnière and Martinet, Greimas first mentions in *Sémantique structurale* that the opposition

benefactor vs. beneficiary

is more appropriate semantically than the triad of roles

agent vs. patient vs. beneficiary.

His suggestion is to rename the benefactive roles as

sender vs. receiver.

The example he gives falls within the same paradigm of our own examples of the benefactive schema of communication. Thus, in the propositions

"Eve gives an apple to Adam," and

"Adam receives an apple from Eve"

the syntactical substitutions of the roles change nothing to their semantic distribution which stays the same. Eve is both the subject and the sender and Adam is the receiver.

In the chapter on the actantial model, the first two examples also illustrate the benefactive schema of communication whereas the third actually illustrates the factitive schema while passing off inconspicuously as the benefactive type:

Subject		Hero		Sender		God
Object	~	Holy Grail		Receiver	~	Humanity

The shift of attention from the communication roles in themselves to the syncretic manifestation of the actants in the one-page account of the Sender and Receiver allows the difference of this example to escape notice (Greimas, 1966:178). In one article of 1973, Greimas elaborated the three kinds of actantial or role overlappings broached in this section: a distinct one-to-one matching between actant (A_1, A_2, A_3 ...) and actor or role (a_1, a_2, a_3, ...), a one-to-many matching, and a many-to-one matching. (See Greimas 1973a:161.) Propp introduced these three possibilities in chapter 6 of his *Morphology*, entitled "Distribution of Functions among Dramatis Personae" and I have simply renamed the distribution as a type of matching between actant and role. In "Pour une théorie des modalités" and, to a lesser extent, in his preface to Courtés' book, both written in 1976 or a decade after the inception of the actantial model, we find a heavy focus on factitive modalities and, inferentially, the manipulative type of communication but it is not differentiated from, nor even related to, the benefactive schema of communication. In the linguistic restatement of communication verbs, I have introduced a distinction between two types of communication verbs where there is none made in actantial grammar. This distinction was motivated by going upwards from the smallest units, the actors or roles, to the actantial categories Greimas uncovers in the largest units of the folktale and narrative text.

2) Inversely, going from top to bottom, or from the general to the particular, which is the direction of linguistic deduction: confusion arises when we turn to the two global and achronic summaries of the narrative seized in a single sweep. In the communication component of the narrative which is the same as the communication axis of the actantial model, i.e.

$$NE_2 = F_{communication} (Sr \longrightarrow O \longrightarrow R)$$

communication and contract are interchangeable. Communication, transfer, exchange, and contract are totally fused, all being broadly the *same*.

In the following chapter on the functional analysis of the entire Proppian chain of functions, Greimas deduces another paradigmatic and achronic interpretation of the tale solely in terms of C, communication, and A, contract, which are opposed to each other as *contraries*. C and A are two functional structures or semic categories, each of which is a pairing of two functions, and hence a higher meaning-unit than the function alone:

$$C = \frac{c}{non\ c} \qquad\qquad A = \frac{a}{non\ a}$$

The top term, c or a, is a function belonging to the Sender and the bottom term, non c or non a, is a function belonging to the Receiver. With C, we may read the pair as the Sender gives O to the Receiver, accompanied by the bottom function which is reciprocal, the Receiver has O. With A, we have the Sender makes the Receiver do O and, bottom term, the Receiver accepts doing O. The extensive recurrence of these two units, spread on the scope of the entire Proppian chain, and the use of the most general and useable methodological procedures describing meaning lead Greimas to postulate what shall provisionally be called the *achronic homological model* of the narrative text. Denoting the negative term of C and A with a negation sign above it, the units of the model take the form of a four-term homology:

$$\bar{A} : A :: \bar{C} : C \qquad \text{or} \qquad \frac{\bar{A}}{A} \sim \frac{\bar{C}}{C}$$

The tale as a simple achronic structure is grasped as a correlation between two pairs of opposed functional categories: the contract and communication (Greimas, 1966:207-8).

In the actantial model and in the canonic component of the narrative A is the same as C whereas in the achronic homological model A is opposed to C. On the sentence level A is also treated as identical to C and only the benefactive schema of communication is isolated. The point is rather crucial and I will devote a good part of the analysis in distinguishing clearly between the two. Understanding how communication and contract units function within the tale and how they were theoretically generated will necessitate the reconstruction of two successive rounds of "approximation" to clarify possible preceding stages in the normalization of the Proppian chain which Greimas presented in one final complex sweep. Our aim is to show how Greimas' schema of semantic operations which comes close to the "Boolean algebra" Lévi-Strauss dreamed of when he reviewed Propp's *Morphology*, lays bare the mechanics underlying the interplay of functions, communication, contract, and all actants in the actantial model. (See Lévi-Strauss, 1960:28.) As matters stand now, the "Boolean algebra" does not fully convince if only because it is deceptively simple, yet also problematic, thorny, and confusing. In a "remarque" following the achronic homological model of the tale, Greimas himself admits to this difficulty in a cautious *caveat*:

> L'analyse de la structure de la communication C vs. $\bar{C}$ n'est pas aussi simple que sa présentation le laisse entendre. Elle nécessiterait de long développements, impossibles dans le cadre de ce chapitre. Nous y reviendrons à une autre occasion.
>
> (The analysis of the structure of communication C vs. $\bar{C}$ is not as simple as its presentation would suggest. It would necessitate long developments, impossible within the scope of this chapter. We shall return to it another time.)   (1966:205)

Notwithstanding the fact that the presentation on communication is not as transparent and, therefore, not misleading by its simplicity, as Greimas feared it might be, we would have wished to see those "long developments" on communication and its precise relation to the contract. Greimas has not returned to this topic again and although this is understandable, a development of the topic is highly desirable for its own sake and to reassess its later and implicit acceptance as a well-grounded Boolean algebra of narrative events. Since the two rudimentary and complementary procedures of *normalizing* the Proppian tale, or any material analyzed—reduction and structuration—presupposed the entire sequence of functions and were carried out in this internally closed whole, the analytic review of the communication and contract units will automatically take in the whole tale in the form given by the Proppian chain. Unlike the Subject and Object actants, the comparison with the Sender and Receiver is a heady, soaring leap between the sentence and the entire tale.

3. Normalization and derivation of contract [A] and communication [C]: first approximation

The most substantial analysis of the Sender and Receiver actants as well as the richest source of ideas for stimulating further research on the topic come not from the chapter on the actantial model itself but from the next one on the "functional analysis" of the Proppian chain of folktale functions which takes the entire tale in one grasp and seizes both the semantic interplay of functions and the logical principles of their ordering. The heuristic and methodological value which Greimas attaches to Propp's work is matched by his own seminal contributions which he brought to bear on it. Greimas emphasizes the need to advance beyond the limits reached in Propp's analysis and make headway for the more sophisticated and common narratives:

> La valeur du modèle proppien, on le voit bien, ne réside pas dans la profondeur des analyses qui le supportent ni dans la précision de ses formulations, mais dans sa vertu de provocation, dans son pouvoir de susciter des hypothèses: c'est le dépassement en tous sens de la spécificité du conte merveilleux qui caractérise la démarche de la sémiotique narrative dès ses débuts. L'élargissement et la consolidation du concept de *schéma narratif canonique* apparaissent ainsi comme une de ses tâches présentes.
>
> (The value of the Proppian model, we see it well, does not lie in the depth of the

analyses which buttress it nor in the precision of its formulations, but in its virtue of challenge, in its power to stir up hypotheses: it is the overstepping in every sense of the specificity of the fairy tale which characterizes the course and practice of narrative semiotics since its beginning. The outstretching and the consolidation of the concept of *canonical narrative schema* thus appear as one of its present tasks.)
(1976a:10)

Even more than the linear succession of 31 functions by which Propp defined the folktale, it is the sequence of the three recurrent Tests—qualifying, main, and glorifying—which defines the regularity of the tale or the canonical narrative schema. On the other hand, the actantial model is a paradigmatic regularity derived by a slight spatial regrouping and a simplification of the generalized schema or Test.

In order to make headway and consolidate all the research done on the actantial model, the narrative Test, and the canonical narrative schema, we have to backtrack and return to Propp's *Morphology* and the functional analysis which Greimas carried out on this folktale chain. The value of both works, Greimas' chapter as well as Propp's book, lie in their synergetic tenor of being thought-provoking, each throwing light on the other. Interweaving these two works is considerably advantageous in our synoptic goal of elucidating the communication component of the narrative and the two types of communication schema. And there is also a very practical reason for keeping the Proppian chain in view: the concrete aspect of Propp's functions is suggestive and serves as a balancing corrective to the general principles emerging from the functions when emptied of specific content. Larivaille, for example, thinks the Proppian chain as it stands is unbeatable for a concrete analysis of tales:

> Tout bien pesé, la *Morphologie du conte* nous apparaissait comme la seule voie pratiquement utilisable, et ce pour deux raisons essentielles: premièrement parce que, malgré les nombreuses tentatives faites pour l'améliorer ou le simplifier, le schéma proposé par Propp restait le plus aisément et efficacement applicable à une *approche concrète* des contes; en second lieu parce que, ayant été établi à partir d'un corpus relativement important et diversifié, ce schéma constituait un rempart contre les erreurs auxquelles aurait fatalement conduit l'étude d'un seul type de conte coupé de tous les autres.

> (All things considered, the *Morphology of the Folktale* seemed to us as the only useable path, practically speaking, due to two basic reasons: first because, despite the numerous attempts made to improve it or to simplify it, the schema proposed by Propp remained the most easily and effectively applicable to a *concrete approach*

of tales; secondly, because, having been established from a relatively important and
miscellaneous corpus, this schema provided a bulwark against errors to which the
study of a single type of tale, cut off from all others, would have led.)   (Larivaille,
1974:368-9, my emphasis)

I would add that Greimas' generalization is readable and enlightening only
through the specifics of Propp's folktale chain: a point made very obvious when
you see the formulaic sequence of the semantic analysis and reduction in
Sémantique structurale (p. 203).

The Sender and Receiver are deduced from the iteration of the Tests in the
Proppian chain of functions and hence the *Morphology* remains the concrete
source of their derivation and of their further elaboration. Where Greimas'
semantic reconstruction, elaboration, and 'consolidation' of the folktale chain
and spheres of action (actants) leave us perplexed, whether it be due to exces-
sive abstraction or insufficient exposition, there is always Propp's work to fall
back upon, "the usual source of our [Greimas'] inspiration" (Greimas, 1973:17).
So that, even if the value of the Proppian model for narrative semiotics depends
on its being developed, refined, and generalized beyond the confines of the
folktale, it stands as a constant, invaluable, and unassailable point of reference
and point of departure.

Before looking at this derivation, let us recapitulate in a table (figure 5.2)
the equivalence Greimas sets up between the linguistic actors and Propp's
spheres of action as well as Souriau's "dramatic functions":

Syntax	Sender	Receiver
Propp	Dispatcher Father of the sought-for person (princess)	Subject-hero
Souriau	Arbiter Awarder of Good	The virtual beneficiary of Good

Figure 5.2

While Arbiter and Awarder of Good point to the role of Benefactor in the communication schema, the Dispatcher and Father of the sought-for person do not initially give the hero anything. Instead, as Greimas says, they "charge the hero with a mission," namely, they *make* him *do* something. Likewise, in the example of the Holy Grail, the hero is not the receiver of a Good or an object of communication from God. God influences him or motivates him to seek and find the Holy Grail and give it to humanity who will benefit by it. In the simplest and most familiar of terms, the Dispatcher, Father of the sought-for person, and God of the Holy Grail are, to borrow an Aristotelian expression, the *prime movers* who activate the Subject-hero on his/her quest (to do O/ bring about O). They represent the locus of those values which activate and cause the Subject-hero to do what he or she wants.

In an update article, ten years later, Greimas distinguishes between "two figures of Senders," what we called the benefactive Sender and the manipulative Sender, which fill two different positions in the unfolding of the story and suggest a narrative pathway proper to this actant. The Sender's pathway "frames" the action of the Subject-hero by its contractual nature. Following the contract between the Sender and the Receiver-Subject, the latter undergoes a series of Tests to fulfill the commitments and finds himself, at the end of the tale, rewarded by the Sender who thus also brings his share of the contractual contribution:

> From the syntagmatic point of view, the narrative schema presents itself in its whole as a double pathway of the Sender, of which the two segments—initial and final—bracket and mount the pathway of the subject. [...] The contract established at the start between the Sender and the Receiver governs the narrative whole, the remainder of the tale appearing thus as its execution by the two contracting parties: the pathway of the subject which makes up the contribution of the Receiver, being followed by the sanction of the Sender, both pragmatic (the reward) and cognitive (the recognition). [...] Two figures of Senders—often joined together in one arch-actant—thus manifest themselves, the first as trustee of values he will seek to endorse in programs of action, the second as the judge of the conformity of actions with respect to an axiology of reference. (Greimas, 1976a:22,23.)

We are now in the position to carry out the first "approximation" of the normalization of the Proppian chain, to reconstruct the derivation of the Sender and Receiver, and to get a basic perspective on how A and C come up through the analysis of the entire narrative schema. By the same token, we will check the accuracy of Greimas' statements in 1966 and 1976. Let us see, first, whether the Sender is an arch-actant manifested in two different figures and, secondly, whether Greimas' functional analysis of the narrative schema permits the analytic reduction that is the actantial model. We shall focus on the Tests; but in order not to lose sight of the fact that the Tests are the topical part of the tale, we'll let a blank space represent the initial and final parts of the tale and label summarily the events which they stand for. (See figure 5.3 for the table of the partial narrative schema. The full table is included as an appendix.)

Some remarks on the notation:

1. The letter f followed by a numerical subscript n refers to the n-th function in Propp's *Morphology*. I have dropped Propp's alphabetical designation in order to see at a glance the position occupied by the function in the sequence and to minimize confusion introduced by the symbolism of Greimas.

2. The functional couple making up the structure of the contract appears in its negative form, $\bar{A}$, at the beginning of the tale and in its positive form, A, in the last function of the tale, "the wedding," which is the contractual fulfillment of the last Sender, Arbiter and Rewarder of the hero's acts. We shall go into greater detail into the initial and final sequences of the tale but we mention this now due to the presence of the contract or the breaking of it. Moreover, each Test is initiated by a distinct contract: contract A_1 for the Main Test, contract A_2 for the Qualifying Test and contract A_3 for the Glorifying Test. So there are altogether four contracts in the folktale which follow an initial breach of contract.

3. The theoretical motivation for labeling the consequence *non c* at this point instead of c is not obvious nor self-explanatory but will become clear shortly. It will suffice to say for now that the consequence is a communication unit and that the category of communication, C, is articulated into its opposing semes, c and non c; similarly for negative communication, $\bar{C}$, which is articulated into $\bar{c}$ and $\overline{non}\ \bar{c}$.

4. Let us recall the generalized Test that underlies all three Tests from chapter IV.3c: the contract A, the struggle F, and the consequence non c. We have broken up the table into three rows to exhibit this visually. The relation between the contract and the struggle is sequential, the latter usually following the former 'contiguously' but this is not a necessary condition. In the Main Test the contract A_1 is separated from the ensuing struggle by a great distance which

	Hero designated	QUALIFYING TEST	MAIN TEST	Hero saved	GLORIFYING TEST	Final sequence
	A_1 $\{$ f_9 = mediation, f_{10} = beginning counter-action $\}$	A_2 $\{$ f_{12} = first function of the donor, f_{13} = hero's reaction $\}$	A_1 $\{$ f_9 ... f_{10} $\}$		A_3 $\{$ f_{25} = difficult task, ... $\}$	C + A Restoration of order and Re-integration
					..... f_{26} = solution of task	
		Simulated and symbolic struggle where the Sender plays the role of Opponent	f_{16} = struggle, f_{17} = the hero is branded, f_{18} = victory		f_{27} = recognition	f_{31} = marriage
Initial sequence $\bar{A} + \bar{C}$		f_{14} = receipt of magical agent	f_{19} = liquidation of lack			
Break-up of the order and alienation		non c_2	non c_3		non c_1	A (non c_3)

Figure 5.3

nests the entire Qualifying Test. In other words, the Qualifying Test is embedded into the Main Test at the point the contract to the Main Test has been established.

5. One additional observation. The spread of the contract and the struggle in the Main Test is an analytical division which only Greimas saw fit to operate on the Proppian sequence of functions. Other researchers working in the post-Proppian field of narrative studies do not follow up Greimas' suggestion. Larivaille, for example, objects to this spread but his analysis drops out the contract entirely and fuses it with the struggle. The methodological presuppositions underpinning this merger make up a variant of the simplest "stimulus-response" theories of behavioral explanation and, in fact, Larivaille labels them such, "provocation (mise à l'épreuve) vs. reaction." While Greimas is interested in recovering social behavior, or true exchange, where the activity of each of at least two actors reinforces (or punishes) the activity of the other, Larivaille seeks to systematize the Proppian functions in individual goal-oriented behavior, that of the hero. In other words, Larivaille simplifies matters in such a way as to lose the social domain and contractual organization of society which Greimas relates to individual values.

The contract A which includes the generalized functions of injunction and acceptance corresponds to the actants of the factitive Sender and the Receiver. The analysis of the comparative table of the Tests indicates the following three Senders carrying out contractual functions (figure 5.4):

(Part of) Greimas' schema	Main Test	Qualifying Test	Glorifying Test
A $\begin{cases}$ injunction $\\$ acceptance $\end{cases}$	f_9 = mediation $f_{10} = \begin{cases}$ beginning $\\$ counteraction $\end{cases}$	$f_{12} = \begin{cases}$ first function $\\$ of the do- $\end{cases}$ nor f_{13} = hero's reaction	f_{25} = difficult task . . . . . (acceptance)
A $\begin{cases}$ sender $\\$ receiver $\end{cases}$	dispatcher hero	donor hero	father of the sought-for princess hero

Figure 5.4

The full table of the narrative schema disproves what Greimas said in 1976. The functional sequence does not begin with a contract and continue with the enactment of both parties. Only the individual Tests indicate this pattern. It is possible to see the final Sender, the Father of the sought-for person, as an implicit global Sender and reinstitute an implicit global contract which precedes the final reward, marriage, symbolized as $A(\text{non } c_3)$. The contract would be inferred *ex post facto* as a logical constituent of a positive exchange. In actuality, the narrative schema begins with a *broken contract* and is followed by four individual contracts, the last of which is asserted to be the negation of the initial broken contract, i.e. $-(\bar{A}) = A$. In the close-up table zeroing in on the contract component of the narrative we see that all three Senders are factitive or manipulative. Moreover, the donor enacts the actantial role of Sender also, a fact which is not reflected in the actantial model where the donor is matched to the Helper. The third pair of actants which complete the actantial scheme consists of the Helper and the Opponent who work for and against the fulfillment of the Subject's desire (to do O/ bring about O) or by facilitating and blocking the communication of the object, O. The Helper is said to correspond to Propp's "helper" and "donor" while the Opponent covers the actional spheres of the "villain" and the "false hero." Although there is nothing unusual in the many-to-one matching between the donor (actor, a_1) and the Helper and Sender (actants, $A_1 + A_2$), once we have equated a_1 with A_1, as Greimas has done in the actantial model, it is impossible to infer that a_1 is manifested by both A_1 and A_2 without the recourse to the table of the narrative schema. In the classification of dramatis personae proposed by Meletinsky and his team which does not fully correspond to the one proposed by Propp or to the actantial model of Greimas, "the class *donor* represents the union of two functions, test and giving. The acting characters of this class act as testers, resume the role of villains, and actually help the hero as donors" (Meletinsky, 1974:115). As Greimas points out, the fight or struggle between the hero and the donor in the Qualifying Test is "simulated, that is, symbolic, where the sender plays the role of opponent" (1966:206). Although the donor is named from his role of providing the hero with a magical agent which will insure the hero's success in the Main Test, his initial function is that of making the hero do something, testing him usually on the appropriateness of his social behavior.

Like the donor, the father of the princess acts as tester, opponent, and finally as the ultimate and greatest rewarder. Propp remarks the father is most often the one to assign a difficult task to the hero due to the hostile feeling towards the suitor. When the hero resolves the task, passing the test, the father rewards him with the supreme tale value, consisting in marriage to the princess.

In sum, all three Senders, the dispatcher, donor, and father of the princess, are factitive: they make the hero do something and thus fulfill the initial role of the Sender as "trustee of values to endorse in programs of action." However, only the dispatcher and donor "charge the hero with a mission" and not the father of the sought-for person. By the time the hero and the father of the sought-for person meet, the hero has accomplished his mission and liquidated the misfortune or lack. The father of the princess acts as the ultimate judge, arbiter, and rewarder who sanctions the identity of the hero (recognition) and rewards him (marriage to his daughter) after the hero passes his test. Our earlier quote of Greimas now stands corrected. Within the general economy of the story the father of the princess fulfills the final roles of Arbiter and Awarder of Good; so does the donor by giving a magical agent to the hero. The only way, in fact, we could reconstruct a double pathway for the Sender framing the pathway of the hero is by starting at the very end of the tale; by assuming the final Sender is the global one or arch-actant; and then, by matching presuppositions to that exchange.

Having seen how the contract, A, arises within the iterated Tests of the narrative schema, let us now briefly lead onto C, the communication part by focusing on the Tests once more. The syntagmatic sequence of the Test which follows the contract may be represented as a sequence of énoncés:

$$NE_1 = F : \text{confrontation } (S_1 \longleftrightarrow S_2)$$
$$NE_2 = F : \text{domination or victory } (S_1 \longrightarrow S_2)$$
$$NE_3 = F : \text{attribution } (S_2 \longrightarrow O \longrightarrow S_1)$$

The initial agreement between the Sender and Receiver is defined as the contract. Next are the first two narrative énoncés, NE_1 and NE_2, which make up the functional couple of the Struggle, F (where the F here does not refer to "function" as it does in the narrative énoncés just above). The final narrative énoncé of the Test is an attribution or an acquisition of the Object by the Subject, symbolizable as $S_1 \cap O \cup S_2$. The consequence of the Test is also a particular case of the *benefactive schema of communication*, symbolizable as non c. Because the Main Test is the key one of the tale, it usually stands as the paradigm for the canonical sequence of Test énoncés. In other words, S_2 will designate the villain anti-subject only as prototype and if this is emphasized, it will be logical to designate S_2 uniquely as the contradictory of S_1, that is, as $\bar{S}_1$ due to the polemical actantial structure which is strongly polarized by contradictory or contrary investments of the Subject and Anti-Subject.

In all three Tests S_1 refers to the hero-subject but S_2 designates a variable character or actor. In the Qualifying Test S_2 is the donor and the communication is one of exchange where the hero acquires the magical helper. In the Main Test S_2 is the villain and the interaction is akin to a confrontational duel which results in a transfer even if it is not an exchange as such. In the Glorifying Test S_2 is the father of the sought-for person and again the communication is a true exchange. At the moment S_1 has successfully completed the anticipated act—has done O / brought about O—he has attributed to himself the object-value and is in conjunction with it. At the same time S_2, having given up O, either willingly if he is a Sender or unwillingly if the Anti-Subject, is deprived of the object-value and is in disjunction from it.

The symbolism of the énoncés and the table of the narrative schema would suggest that communication actually consists in the Subject's successful attainment of an objective (or object-goal) and only involves one object of communication. With the exception of the Main Test, however, the outcome of the Subject's action is a reward by the Sender and is contingent on the Sender's reaction to what the Subject does. In the Qualifying Test, for example, the hero's actions involve a set of complementary reactions concerning his own actions and those of the donor with whom he interacts in a symbolic struggle. There is an exchange of actions and objects such that the consequence always comes from another actant, the Sender or the Opponent. It is in the reciprocity or complementarity of roles and expectations through the medium of a shared social and cultural code that sanctions enter and acquire their place in systems of action. What an actor is expected to do in a given situation constitutes the expectation of that role. What the relevant other or Sender is expected to do, contingent on the Subject's action, constitute the sanctions. Role expectations and sanctions are, therefore, in terms of the content of action, the reciprocal of each other. The sanctions are rewards when they facilitate the realization of goals which are part of the Subject's action. The object-goal of the hero is the object-consequence communicated by another actant. The consequence of the Qualifying Test, for example, consists of the hero's receipt of the magical agent from the donor. It is a sanction of the hero's behavior by the donor and in that regard the hero's success in getting the magical agent makes him the participant of a social process of exchange. In other words, the hero would not have received the magical agent had he not interacted with the donor. A successful action is thus a team effort and a team success: of the individual hero and of those with whom he interacts.

The particular consequence of each Test in the order in which it appears in the tale can be symbolized in two ways:

receipt of magical agent $= $ non $c_2 = S \cap O_2$
liquidation of lack $= $ non $c_3 = S \cap O_3$
recognition $= $ non $c_1 = S \cap O_1$

In the reduction and normalization of the Proppian chain, the category C was defined as communication or a process of exchange characterized by the transmission of some *object*. Communication has then been specified by the transmitted object, each variable-object being indicated by a different number: 1, 2, 3. The objects of communication are the object-values:

1. In the case of C_1, the object of communication is a *message* which makes up the key to knowing or recognizing the hero.

2. In the case of C_2, we are dealing with the transmission of *vigor* which deprives the individual of the energy necessary for action or, on the contrary, attributes it to him/her. The object-vigor is the mythical equivalent of the modality of "can" and "know what/how."

3. In the case of C_3, the communication consists in the transfer of the *object of desire* which would correspond to the modality of "want." (See Greimas, 1966:209.)

The consequence is an outcome not only of the struggle but also of the contract established before the struggle, which is also a constituent of the Test. The consequence is thus the sanction of this contract and the proof of its realization. In other words, the consequence presupposes the existence of A + F such that if F follows A, the consequence is necessary. We will show later that the consequence as the positive seme-function non c is diametrically opposed to its negative manifestation $\overline{\text{non } c}$ in the initial sequence of the folktale. So that the consequence is an *element common to both larger structures of the tale, A and C, and relates them to each other.*

The injunction of the Sender is clearly an injunction to the Receiver to do O and thus the consequence is not only a positive sanction or reward; it is also

an object of trade. In other words, the entire meaning of the Test can be loosely summed up in terms of the economics of human exchange:
1. The Subject-Receiver trades O' to Sender for O.
2. The Sender made the Subject-Receiver do O' with the implicit promise he will give O to the Receiver.

Hence, the consequence ending each Test is the hero's *earned* gain and well-deserved reward and his/her success is in part due to the cooperation of the Sender who followed through on his/her end of the bargain and fulfilled the implicit promises s/he made to the hero.

VI

Excursus on the Legal Philosophy of Contract and the Sociology of Exchange

To achieve understanding of a fact, a problem or a semantic network of events, we must understand not only *that* it is the case and *what* it consists of, but also *how* and *why* it is. From the first approximation of the semantic algebra of Proppian functions, it is impossible to grasp clearly

(1) the *descriptive* explanation of what A, contract, and C, communication, are like and how they function with respect to each other and other components of the chain;

(2) the *practical* explanation of how A and C were named and classified as categories within the chain;

(3) the *theoretical* explanation as to why the consequence of the Test was chosen to be the common pivot linking A and C together. It involves the conceptual machinery deployed in the explanatory account and the strength of the explanatory link between Propp's chain of functions and the algebra constructed from it.

In order to begin answering these questions, it is important to give a setting to this set of problems and restore the pragmatic context in which any explanatory question arises and is resolved. The more fundamental problem from which stem the above questions lies in the absence of conventions and conceptual boundaries of an established *discipline* which would permit the attenuation of the heuristic aspect of explanation: of putting something into a graspable setting. Science can well afford to abstract away the pragmatic, context-dependent setting within which a question arises since the questions are fixed by disciplinary conventions. In a young discipline like narrative semiotics seeking to establish itself, it is very important to be reflexive about the methodology and to define those arbitrary procedures which are conventions and make up a background knowledge of the field.

We cannot begin to define what these conventions actually are in semiotics and, therefore, how they could be assumed or put into practice but we can and should be reflexive about one's own mode of argumentation and try to express what Greimas had observed and abstracted from Propp's chain of functions. To make the contract and communication understandable, we need to put them in a graspable context, step outside the structural semantics and the functional analysis, and return to the prior, preformal and common-sense stage of random search. The ground which has been carefully prepared by working over the data of observation—the Proppian chain of functions—must have included a random search on communication and contract but Greimas does not make this explicit. There is a qualitative change in the final strategy and procedure which is leaps away from what must have happened in the initial stage of construction. This is not surprising since there is usually no compelling or necessary movement from observation to model-building, from the observed properties of the Proppian chain of functions to its reduction and structuration. It is, however, one of the tasks of explanation to adduce compelling reasons why this "model of narrative transformation" obtains rather than some other possible alternatives.[3]

The initial, common-sense stage of random search exhibits informal reasoning that may in part rely on reference to intuitively perceived facts or implications. To aid in a rigorous exposition of the communication component of the narrative, it will prove useful to first discuss communication in its broader context of social exchange and as the language of interaction. The purpose is not to lose precision and formality but to restore it by providing the links in the reasoning process and steps involving reliance on intuitive judgment. If part of the foundation of a model sprang from an intuitive spark, it must be capable of objective confirmation. That a discipline uses symbolic notation is an incidental rather than defining characteristic of its scientific character. While precise explanations are indeed to be preferred to vague ones, a discipline that provides explanations of a less precise character but makes them correctly and in a

---

[3]In Search of Models of Transformation" is the chapter title of the analysis of Propp's folktake. In the earlier and article version of this chapter the analysis is referred to, in the subtitle, as "Functional Analysis." In my opinion, "functional analysis" and Lévi-Strauss' term, "Boolean algebra" are more descriptive and convenient shorthand labels for the analysis of Propp's folktale functions.

systematic and reasoned way, must be regarded as a science. In rejecting formalized notation as a sign of scientific exactitude, we will be unimpeded in reconstructing the whole of the argument, the informal reasoning processes, and the intuitive guesswork and judgment which took place, owing not to slipshod formulation of otherwise precise facts but to the fundamental complexity and intractability inherent in the subject matter. We shall then be on firmer ground when we'll intermingle unformalized expertise with the more or less precise and highly abstract core of the functional analysis.

We shall concern ourselves with very general principles of contract and social exchange as developed by the legal philosophers L. Fuller and C. Fried, and the sociologists P. Blau and G. Homans. In this sphere of social sciences, formal precision is out of the question but to say this does not imply looseness of thought or method. From a pragmatic standpoint, we could not acquire a better nor a more elegant understanding of exchange through reasoned methods of exposition and explanation. What makes the expertise unformalized in Greimas is its coin usage and its total anchoring and justification in the sentence roles of the sender and the receiver. Some ideas on communication, familiar to us all, are easy to draw upon; but it is the wider set of conceptual tools, albeit simple, which will facilitate a more comprehensive and global understanding of Greimas' analysis of the Proppian chain of functions. That is, the general principles of social exchange must be substantiated in the specific folktale Test and schema with the elaboration of intervening formal principles and arguments of structural semantics.

The agreement between the subject-hero and Sender which initiates and anchors the Test is named the *contract*. In the search of understanding the nature and significance of the contract, as it arises in Greimas' functional analysis, it became apparent that the term contract must be construed more broadly and related to other forms and principles ordering the interrelations of human association. In his article on the role of contract in society Fuller begins by saying "It is a commonplace of anthropology that explicit contractual agreements are a rarity among primitive people" (Fuller, 1981:170). This comment appears obvious, immediately cognizable and clear to common sense. It would also seem to have an obvious application extending to the cultural products of primitive people, their tales of myth and folktales. To label the occurrence of an agreement in the folktale as a contract does seem to overemphasize the legal aspect of the agreement instead of indicating the mutual consent of the participants in the social exchange. However, the very use of the word 'contract' may serve and has indeed served a corrective purpose in highlighting the capital importance of the agreement in a narrative. It may be conceded that the contract, due to its explicit and formal nature, functions as the exemplar for the analysis of types of social order which are, at one pole, informal and loose, and may be enigmatic, at the other pole. In daily speech, for example, contract is sometimes used metaphorically. We speak of experiencing a new start in a relationship and we think of it *as* rewriting a *contract* with brand new terms. We say also that the sudden beginning then gives us a whole new *lease* on life. Contract is used as the paradigm for a serious agreement within a social exchange. By formalizing the agreement through a metaphor we achieve clarity but we do not mean to refer to a rigid, legal transaction. Most tales and narratives will have nothing as rigid, formal, and explicit as a contract but most everything related to agreements, loose or informal exchanges, and reciprocal expectations of what is called customary law and standard practice. This raises the key issues to be answered in the following general discussion of contract and other social exchanges, namely, what features they share together and where they differ from each other.

In any society individuals meet each other, cross each other's path, exchange goods and services. There is among them an unceasing movement of values. This provides the basic reason or the why of all social exchange. When we talk of contract, communication, and social exchange we have in mind the different ways of circulating object-values made possible by a code of exchange.

The common ground to both the contract and other forms of social exchange can be described as a *language of interaction*. To interact meaningfully individuals require a social setting in which the moves of the participants will fall within some predictable pattern offering an unwritten code of conduct. Interaction means joint social action, mutual or reciprocal influence, individuals communicating *to each other* in what they do, orienting their acts to each other. This interaction has meaning to both the giver and the receiver of the action. That is obvious when we talk to each other but it is also true of almost everything we *do* in relation to others. Interaction involves interpretation or ascertaining the meaning of the actions or remarks of the other person, and definition, or conveying indications to another person as to how he or she is to act. Human beings in interaction fit their own acts to the ongoing acts of one another and guide others in doing so. The direction taken by a participant's conduct is seen as something that is constructed in the reciprocal give and take of interdependent beings who are adjusting to one another.

Both the contract and social association deal with the exchange of rewarding goods where the goods are actions or activities. People do come together in numberless ways to their injury, exchanging costly or punishing activities and negative values. But, as G. Homans has pointed out, no exchange continues unless both parties are making a profit. From two out of the five basic propositions he formulates as governing social exchange (propositions 2 and 3), it follows that "the frequency of interaction depends on the frequency with which each rewards the activity of the other and on the value to each of the activity he receives" (Homans, 1961:55). We are, therefore, concerned with the ways individuals associate with one another because they all benefit from their association. In a rewarding social exchange individuals engage in *cooperative* action, achieving a greater total reward than either could have achieved by working alone. When individuals act in cooperation with one another, they work together for common goals or help one another achieve individual goals, or both.

In his article outlining "The Principles of Human Association" Fuller suggested that all the ways or forms of a rewarding social exchange can be grouped under two opposing principles: association of shared commitment and association by reciprocity dominated by the legal principle. While setting these two principles in a relation of polarity, Fuller was careful to point out that polarity is used as a precondition of intelligibility, a way of referring to and describing contrary distinctions often non existent in pure form. Fuller stressed that in real life human associations normally present an uneasy mixture of the two principles where they fight and reinforce each other at the same time.

Association by shared commitment is commonly found in small or intimate settings such as collaborative teams, families, neighborhood groups, or nonprofit organizations. Fuller illustrates the purest form of the principle with the association between a composer and a librettist, the collaboration of Richard Strauss and von Hofmannstal being the most famous example. Fuller sometimes suggested that common aims are a source of spontaneous ordering, typically requiring few explicit rules and little formal structure. A commitment works on a voluntary summoning of energies and a smooth fulfillment of duty and counterduty that no formal duty could instigate, inspire or even purport to command.

The opposing principle of association refers to the situation where an association is held together and enabled to function by formal rules of duty and entitlement. Although a pure type of association by reciprocity is hard to find, the nearest model being silent barter, the most common mixed type is formalized notably in a regime of contract in which social order is the cumulative product of innumerable individual agreements effecting voluntary exchanges of goods and services. The paradigm of such a regime, on a large scale, is a market economy combined with the private ownership of property. Contract plays its accustomed and often indispensable role in commercial relations where it is most at home.

In almost all human associations and all forms of cooperative social exchange both principles are in some degree present. Along the broad spectrum of exchanges, what characterizes a given association is the predominance and the explicit operation of one principle over the other.

The code of conduct, whether spontaneous or formal, which underlies the conception of exchange, can be briefly stated. Blau phrased it succinctly as follows: "An individual who supplies rewarding services to another obligates him. To discharge this obligation, the second must furnish benefits to the first in turn" (1964:89). Social exchange refers to voluntary actions of individuals that are motivated by the returns they are expected to bring and usually do bring from others. The norm of reciprocity, which we shall discuss below, provides motives for returning benefits even when power differences might invite exploitation. The need to reciprocate for benefits received in order to continue receiving them serves as a normative rule regulating social interaction and reciprocity as an exchange pattern. Exchange processes thus foster the development of a complex network of reciprocal renditions and expectations. To engage in effective social behavior individuals need the support of intermeshing anticipations that will let them know what their opposite numbers will do, should do, or might do. It is this mutual and complementary expectation about a certain type of behavior we may call a 'norm' or code, meaning a standard of judging and valuing certain acts in the light of regular or 'normal' or normally expectable conduct. The term 'norm' usually means a prescriptive rule, whether a moral or legal rule. Although this meaning is not excluded from the former one, it is important to see that *mutual* expectations are of the very essence of such a norm. It is this 'complementarity of expectations' that distinguishes such expectations from others we may have about other kinds of events. And it is also central to interaction.

When a stabilization of interactional expectancies has occurred, the parties are guiding their conduct toward one another by complementarity or by reciprocity. Complementarity and reciprocity are cognate concepts which are often used synonymously even when their distinctive meanings are not the same. Complementarity means that one's rights are another's obligations, and vice versa. It has a one-way orientation compared to the two-way one of reciprocity. Reciprocity connotes that *each* party has rights and duties so that giving and receiving are mutually contingent and mutually complementary. A. Gouldner suggests that, contrary to some cultural relativists, a norm of reciprocity is universal and makes two interrelated demands: "(a) people should help those who have helped them, and (b) people should not injure those who have helped them"; from these two, a third one may be inferred, (c) "those whom you have helped have an obligation to help you" (Gouldner in Biddle and Thomas, 1966:140,142). Whenever one individual helps another an obligation is generated such that the recipient is now *indebted* to the donor, and he remains so until he repays.

The words "rights," "duties," and "obligations" possess meaning only in the context of rules and sentences embodying them express a normative relationship, prescribing how one person shall behave in relation to another. Rules may be classified according to the activities they regulate, how they originate, or their degree of formality. Yet they all have this in common: being rules, they prescribe conduct and in so doing impose duties and obligations. Explicit or implicit rules govern every conceivable type of relationship and social exchange. Without rules and without the norm of reciprocity, an individual would not know how to make choices concerning his or her own behavior, how to do what is right rather than wrong and thus act responsibly, nor would he or she know what it means to disappoint another person. Without a normative context, it would be impossible to allocate the tasks involved in a cooperative exchange and to define the rights and duties of the interactors, that is: (1) who is to perform which task? (2) who has the right to the action of the other and when? (3) what are the rights and entitlements of each member in the group? A normative context of practical and universal rules allows each member in a social exchange to act with the foresight and awareness of the possible effects of his/her actions, including the grievances and complaints he/she might be expected to meet. Rules and prescriptions and other types of norms serve effective communication and the development of stable expectations that organize and facilitate interactions. They serve primarily to set the terms of men's relations with one another. They facilitate human interaction as traffic is facilitated by the laying out of roads and the installation of signs. Association by contract and association in other social exchanges embody these norms which underlie and maintain social order.

Let us now turn to the differences between contract and social exchange, one of which was already suggested by the polarity of the two principles of human association.

The contract differs in important ways from social exchange. The basic and most crucial distinction lies in how well-defined are the objects exchanged, O and O'. The contract stipulates precise terms of the exchange and exact obligations in the transaction, thus maximizing the possibility of rational calculation. It involves the explicit creation of verbalized rules defining the parties' rights and duties toward each other. Social exchange, in contrast, "involves the principle that one person does another a favor, and while there is a general expectation of some future return, its exact nature is definitely *not* stipulated in advance" (Blau, 1964:93). Social exchange entails either unspecified or loose obligations. It involves favors that create diffuse future obligations and the nature of the return cannot be bargained about but must be left to the discretion of the one who makes it. Moreover, as Blau mentioned, the benefits involved in social exchange do not have an exact price in terms of a single quantitative medium of exchange, in contrast to economic commodities. This is another reason why social obligations are unspecific. Furthermore, the specific benefits exchanged are sometimes primarily valued as symbols of the supportiveness and friendliness they express and it is the exchange of the underlying mutual support that is the main concern of the participants. (Cf. Blau, 1964:95.)

The rational calculation of a contractual exchange and the precise terms on which it functions do not imply that the relation is devoid of any touch of humanity or tolerance. Commercial, professional, and public dealings in which all benefits and burdens would be allocated by strict, prior arrangements and some sharply bargained quid pro quo is a grotesque misrepresentation of contracts. There are many motives, says Fried, to foster a spirit of common purpose and sharing in most contractual contexts: "from the desire to maintain goodwill so that relations will continue into the future, to a genuinely altruistic concern for one's fellow man, customer or business partner. Nothing in the liberal concept of contract, nothing in the liberal concept of humanity and law makes such altruism improbable or meaningless" (Fried, 1981:91). The legal principle dominating a contractual relation includes formalized rules of morality but the formality of these rules does not prove a strict, rigid, or literalistic interpretation of contract as a regime or doctrine. A formal but equal exchange is, after all, more welcome than an unequal but friendly exchange.

In discussing social contexts and the ordering of human relations in which a specific form of exchange is likely to be apt or appropriate, it is useful to employ Fuller's notion of a spectrum or scale of relations. This spectrum starts from intimacy, at one end, and runs to hostility, at the other, with a stopping place midway that Fuller describes as the habitat of friendly strangers, between whom interactional expectancies are largely open and unpatterned (Fuller, 1981:237). The middle ground is precisely the area where contractual law and dealings are most at home and most effective; it is also here, undoubtedly, that the very notion of explicit contracting was first conceived. As typifying the intimate relationship, Fuller takes an average family with young children at home, members who are on reasonably good terms with each other, and household chores to be apportioned. At the other end of the spectrum, we have two individuals who are enemies or two hostile groups without the presence of a third party with superior political power that might constrain their tendencies toward each other. Somewhere in the range between the intimate end of the scale and the middle ground of contract is the beneficial (rewarding) social exchange I had implicitly in mind as a contrast to contract. This is the relation of two neighbors or colleagues in a department and, in general, the members of a small, self-sufficient group who are bound by some particular cooperative endeavor. In such a human situation, says Fuller,

> Any attempt at an explicit verbalized definition of each party's performance, and the price to be paid him for it, would not produce order and might produce chaos. The ineptitude of contract as an organizing principle in this type of case becomes especially clear when we take into account the shifting contingencies affecting such a group. [...] No contractual foresight would be equal to providing in advance what should be done in these emergencies or prescribing how the contribution of each member of the group should be fitted in with that of others (1981:182).

The operational aspect of the problem makes it unlikely for the parties to think of expressing their relation in contractual terms. The self-interest of each, combined with the inescapable necessity for their collaboration provides a motivation for joint action that no contract could enhance. Moreover, if a contract were seriously insisted on by one member as a condition precedent to his/her support, it would imply a *distrust* damaging to the relationship that must obtain between members of a small well-knit group.

If we move to the opposite end of the spectrum and consider contracts between parties standing in a social relation of hostility, a contract once again, becomes useless. Fuller's way of explaining this, at the simplest level, is to say that hostile parties don't trust one another, and mutual trust is essential for both the negotiation and the administration of a contract. More specifically, the creation of a contractual relationship through explicit negotiations involves an uneasy blend of collaboration and resistance:

> Each participant must seek to understand why the other makes the demands he does even as he strives to resist or qualify those demands. Each must accept the other's right to work for a solution that will serve his own best interests. This explains why it does not fit readily into either extreme of the spectrum of human relationships running from intimacy to open hostility. Within the close-knit group, demands for a contractual spelling out of obligations will seem to imply an inappropriate distrust. Between parties openly hostile to one another, the element of cooperation for effective bargaining will be absent. Curiously enough, at the two extremes of the spectrum where men cannot bargain with words, they can often half-bargain with deeds; tacit understandings arising out of reciprocally oriented actions will take the place of verbalized commitments. (Fuller, 1981:185.)

The widest stretch of the spectrum covers relations that require *mutual trust* between the participants. Since social exchange involves unspecified or loose obligations, the fulfillment of these obligations depends solely on trust. There is no way to assure an appropriate return for a favor other than trusting others to discharge their obligations. In his eloquent book *Contract as Promise*, resplendent with a certain moral grandeur, Fried advances the thesis that contracts invoke and are invoked by promises, the latter being grounded in trust and autonomy. Promising is a convention whose function it is to give moral grounds for another to expect the promised performance. It is a device that free, moral individuals have fashioned on the premise of mutual trust and which gathers its moral force from that premise. The obligation of *contract* is the special case in which certain promises have attained legal as well as moral force. "But since a contract is first of all a promise," Fried argues, "the contract must be kept because the promise must be kept" (1981:17). In a contractual relation an appropriate return is assured since obligations can be enforced legally at any stage in the development of the relationship between exchange partners. When something goes wrong in the contract process, when people fail to reach their promises or there is a breach of trust, gains and losses can be sorted out. The injured party may claim expectation damages for the harm that has been suffered and be made to hand over the equivalent of the promised performance. Thus, contracts may be said to be a device for allocating risks with maximum rational calculation in obtaining benefits of extrinsic value. Unlike loose social exchanges, contracts are not marked by the presence of risk or uncertainty that may otherwise vitiate an agreement. The compensation of injury through reliance is an attempt to explain the force of a promise and a contract in terms of the harm and hurt befalling the promisee but the weight of these negative effects depends on the prior assumption of the force of *commitment*. By promising we transform a choice that was morally neutral into one that is morally compelled. The commitment to the other is what provides the moral force, charge, and basis to the obligation of keeping any promise, including the promise of contract. A similar commitment, I believe, underlies the norm of reciprocity.

When we focus on promises and other sources of obligations, we find there are different degrees of *bindingness* and *enforceability* matching the different degrees of formal harness the interactants put on themselves when regulating their relation with one another. As we move from the social exchange to the contract, we find there is a concordant shift in accountability of actions, based on tangible (extrinsic) harms or benefits which flow from specific acts. The "binding" effect proceeds in an ascending scale and embraces a greater reliance on rules to define members' duties and entitlements and the articulation of strict procedural requirements for distributing benefits and burdens. When the bonds holding an association together consist of such formal structural elements, members are given greater leeway and more freedom to pursue divergent aims. Social exchanges which are, by definition, less formal are vulnerable to failures in reciprocity. While penalties for these failures are enacted through group sanctions and norms, they are often difficult to enforce. One of the difficulties consists in the price paid for promoting justice which has potential political repercussions in the actional future of the mediator. In practical terms, this price is at the basis of the reluctance and perhaps the selfish fear of "getting involved" in any conflict of actional accountability.

VII

Normalization and Derivation of Contract [A] and Communication [C]: Second Approximation

In order to provide a descriptive, practical, and theoretical explanation of A, the contract, and C, communication, and to make possible a detailed second approximation of the normalization of the Proppian chain, it will prove very useful to examine in great depth the relation of the object to the contract and its relation to communication.

We distinguished between two types of communication, the factitive or manipulative and the benefactive, which correspond within the Test to A and C, respectively and in that order:

Factitive
Make-do (Sr — O'— R)   or   A (Sr, O', R)

Benefactive
Give (Sr — O — R)   or   C (Sr, O, R)

The general meaning of the Test was loosely summed up in terms of the economics of exchange: the R gives O' to the Sr and receives O in exchange.

We want to discuss first the consequence or object O in relation to the Test within which it is embedded as final position and its meaning relative to the contract and the two actants who operate therein, the Sender and the Receiver, the latter also being the virtual or actual hero and Subject. This relation is the local and immediate definition of the object either as an exchange with a Sender or as a duel or object of competition with the opponent. The discussion amounts to examining what may be called the evolution of the contract which begins as a reciprocal trust and working agreement and ends as an exchange and as fulfillment of what is retrospectively the contract and as reward for the hero. Moreover, all the stages which characterize the trajectory of the actional aim, symbolized as S ⟶ O—the possible, probable, and real degrees or moments—also operate in the exchange or communication between the Sender and Receiver. The contract is at first only a possibility or a virtuality, or "a partial contract" and it becomes real when the Sender fulfills his end of the exchange. The trade, identical to communication, happens through and with the consequence which is "thus the sanction of the contract, the proof of its realization and implies the partial re-establishment of the broken global contract" (Greimas, 1966:212).

The aspect which interests us at the outset is the tie or relation between non c, the consequence, to the other two preceding constituents of the Test, A and F. In Greimas' notation where A + F > non c the tie is symbolized by '>' and is defined only sequentially as 'is followed by.' The question we wish to raise is: how does non c *follow from* A and F?

Next, we want to relate the consequence O to the initial and final sequences of the tale which is the global interpretation marking the three springs of the tale. In relation to C, the object of communication behaves as an object-of-motion when the focus is placed solely on the circulation of the object itself.

Two general principles of social exchange given emphasis and significance in the excursus will provide some of the missing links or steps in carrying out the second approximation. First and foremost, the circulation of the object-value in a social exchange is fueled by the duties and rights of the interactors toward each other which set the terms of the agreement between them. Within the episodic unit of the Test and the final series of communication, contract and communication are exchanges of duties and rights (to have O, to do O, or to bring about O). Secondly, the components of the Test—contract, struggle, consequence—do not show nor even suggest the normative context of rules organizing and regulating the interaction. The norm of reciprocity allows for a descriptive explanation of how A, contract, and C, communication function with respect to each other and it also allows for a partial theoretical explanation as to why the consequence was chosen to be the common pivot linking A and C together. Within the Test, A and C are part and parcel of one reciprocal exchange.

1.   Relation of the object to the contract [A]

Let us consider first the consequence of the Test as an object of trade or exchange which obtains both in the Qualifying Test and the Glorifying Test, carries out the binding commitments made in the Test contract and enacts the reliable cooperation of the Sender and promisor with the Subject-hero. Next we shall look into the competitive interaction of the hero with the villain in the Main Test. The sequence of the Tests is altered from Qualifying Test, Main Test, Glorifying Test to the group of Qualifying Test and Glorifying Test first and the nested Main Test next, in last place.

1a Agreement and mutual consent

The first stage in a social interaction consists in negotiating some sort of compromise or working agreement on who is who and who is supposed to do what in the present encounter. It is both a "prise de contact" between two individuals and a situation-defining phase, which determine the minimal conditions for initiating communication. In *Identities and Interactions* McCall and Simmons point out that there are essentially two phases in this bargaining: the negotiation of social identities and the negotiation of interactive roles. That is, agreement must first be reached on the broad, relevant social categories and social positions of each person. This agreement then fades into the background as a working agreement on which the parties can stand while negotiating the specific content of their respective interactive role in the encounter.

The contract which Greimas isolates in the folktale sequence as a recurrent unit refers essentially to the negotiation of interactive roles. But when Greimas talks of the hierarchical asymmetry and non-egalitarian relation between the Sender and the Receiver, he is referring implicitly to the identity agreement and fusing it with the task agreement, naming the merger a contract. The contractual agreement, however, is neither identical nor implied by the working agreement on social identities. Many possible tasks or social activities are open to persons with given sets of identities; they must decide not only who they are but what they are doing there. In the folktale sequence of functions the would-be hero in the Qualifying Test must know he is facing the donor and not the father of the princess with whom he interacts later in the Glorifying Test. The working agreement on identities is often implicit although it constitutes a necessary and explicit "ground" in the encounter and exercises important and serious boundary rules. The fact that the Sender is identified and named by his role—dispatcher, donor, father of the princess—tends to obscure the crucial distinction between the identity agreement and the task agreement.

The Test is built on a double exchange between the Sender and the Receiver: first, an exchange of commitments followed by a reciprocity of programs of execution. The Sender *makes* or persuades the Subject-Receiver *to do* O' with the implicit promise he will give O to the Receiver or do O for him/her. The Subject-Receiver accepts the proposal and consents freely to it. The Sender *promises* O to the Subject if the Subject will *promise* O' to the Sender. The Sender wishes to be bound by a promissory obligation O, but only if the Subject-Receiver will be bound to him by promissory obligation O'. The Sender's conditional promise is called in law the offer, the Subject's the acceptance. Promises, contracts, covenants constitute a very important class of performances which we consider obliging. Promises and contracts are fundamentally relational; one person must make the promise to another and the second must accept it. The need for acceptance shows the moral relation of promising to be voluntary on both sides. It is part of the intuitive force behind the idea of exchange. And acceptance offers a point of correspondence between the moral institution of promise and the legal institution of contract. Once accepted, the consent becomes an obligation or a /must-do/ and the Sender's commitment to the Subject also becomes a future obligation:

> Le statut de A que nous avons défini comme une sorte de contrat social possède également la forme de communication: le destinateur enjoint le destinataire d'agir; le destinataire accepte l'injonction. Il s'agit d'une obligation librement consentie.
>
> (The status of A which we defined as a sort of social contract also has the form of communication: the sender charges the receiver to act; the receiver accepts the injunction. The matter is about a freely consented obligation.)   (Greimas, 1966:210)

There are two obligations, however, and not just one, as the above quote would suggest. The act of the Subject-Receiver has to be enacted first before the Sender holds up his end of the bargain and sanctions the Subject by doing something for him/her. The execution of the respective acts and the fulfillment of commitments is not simultaneous. I shall return to this topic later when discussing the consequence of the Test.

In the Proppian tale the Sender is characterized by his factitive doing and modal status which place him in a hierarchically superior position to the Subject-Receiver. This "asymmetry in the respective status between Sender and Subject" is none other than a power differential between them. In the folktale as in concrete real-life encounters the people involved seldom have altogether *equal voices* in shaping the interaction. In most cases, one actor will be in a position to drive a harder bargain for his definition of the situation. The distribution of power among actors in an encounter varies between two limits: complete equality or peerage and absolute control in tandem with abject slavery. These theoretical limits seldom if ever occur. Both the donor in the Qualifying Test and the father of the princess in the Glorifying Test dominate the interaction with the Subject-hero. The agreement is an *injunctive contract* which may be presented as a sequence of two symmetric énoncés interrelated by a relation of logical presupposition:

$$NE_1 = F : \text{prescription (Sr} \longrightarrow R)$$
$$NE_2 = F : \text{acceptance (R} \longrightarrow Sr)$$

Greimas says

> Dans le schéma de Propp le Destinateur paraît figé comme l'expression d'une certaine idéologie qui n'est qu'une variante parmi les rapports possibles entre le Destinateur et le sujet. Ainsi, la relation entre le Destinateur et le sujet, telle qu'elle paraît dans le récit proppien, est celle d'une hiérarchie établie et le rapport dominant/dominé qui le caractérise y est donné d'avance. Or il est possible, il semble même nécessaire, d'inverser les termes du problème: au lieu de considérer le *pouvoir* comme préexistant au faire-faire et comme sa source, on peut, au contraire, prétendre que le *faire-faire*, c'est-à-dire la manipulation des sujets par d'autres sujets, est un fait créateur des relations de domination et origine du pouvoir établi.

> (In Propp's schema the Sender seems congealed as the expression of a certain ideology which is only one variant among the possible relations between the Sender and subject. Thus, the relation between the Sender and the subject, such as it appears in the Proppian tale, is one of an established hierarchy and the relation *dominating/dominated* which characterizes it is given beforehand. But it is possible, it even seems necessary, to invert the terms of the problem: instead of considering *power* as pre-existing to the make-do we can, reversely, pretend that the *make-do*, that is to say, the manipulation of subjects by other subjects, is a creative fact in relations of domination and origin of established power.)   (1976a:23-24)

The identity agreement can be implicitly ascertained from the asymmetry of the respective status of the Sender and Receiver which "can only accentuate itself during the syntagmatization of the two actants" (Greimas, 1973:33). The second agreement on the task focus of the interaction is what is defined by the injunctive type of contract: the make-do by the dominating Sender and the acceptance by the dominated Receiver. The Sender's share of the contribution equalizes the exchange in terms of task performance but not in terms of status:

> La performance du sujet correspond à l'exécution des exigences contractuelles acceptées, et appelle la sanction en contrepartie. Toutefois, les relations symétriques et égalitaires qui s'établissent ainsi entre Destinateur et Destinataire—et qui permettent de les traiter dans le calcul syntaxique comme des sujets S_1 et S_2—sont en partie contredites par l'asymétrie de leurs status respectifs.
>
> (The performance of the subject corresponds to the execution of accepted contractual demands and calls forth the sanction as counterpart. However, the symmetric and egalitarian relations which are thus established between the Sender and Receiver—and which permit us to treat them in the syntactical calculus as two subjects S_1 and S_2—are in part gainsaid by the asymmetry of their respective status.) (Greimas, 1979:246-7)

In his analysis of a Maupassant short story Greimas gives an example where the Sender does not communicate his want to the Receiver *first* and where the power of the Receiver-Subject does not have its source in the Sender. In what he labels the *permissive contract* the Subject-Receiver already has a program of action and of the /want-to-do/ which organizes it. It is the Receiver who expresses first his want, then accepted by the Sender. This narrative syntagm is formulated in the following manner:

$$NE_1 = F : \text{request } (R \longrightarrow Sr)$$
$$NE_2 = F : \text{permission/prevention } (Sr \longrightarrow R)$$

The Sender, in the presence of the project of the Subject-Receiver, exercises only a secondary want by sanctioning, positively or negatively, the original want of the Subject.

Nevertheless, the standard or canonical way of representing the relation between the Sender and the Subject-Receiver is to place the Sender in a primary syntagmatic position in order to indicate the salient identifying characteristic of pre-established power:

> Plus que le pouvoir en exercice, c'est le pouvoir préétabli qui caractérise le statut hiérarchique du Destinateur: c'est par lui qu'il convient probablement de définir l'instance transcendante dans laquelle nous l'avons inscrit.
>
> (More than power in action, it is pre-established power which characterizes the hierarchical status of the Sender: it is by [pre-established power] that we should probably agree to define the transcendent instance in which we have inscribed him.) (Greimas, 1979:247)

Thus, the identity agreement prevails over the task agreement. By definition, the Sender is also more competent than the Subject-Receiver and, like a mentor or teacher, is a benevolent figure guiding the Subject-Receiver. So that the Sender's power is also the power of inner and cognitive competence. The agent who issues commands (orders, requests, or injunctions) usually enjoys some recognized position of authority over those whom he commands—such as parent or teacher or guardian. It will be noted that two of the three cases have to do with that which we call education and hence we may speak of the authority who gives such orders a *moral authority*. The paradigm of the injunctive contract in the Proppian schema is the wholly benevolent promise given by a superior agent, however authoritarian he or she is, acting in the capacity of moral authority. This is also the major reason why Greimas can say that the Sender attributes or gives modal competence to the Subject-Receiver; that is, the Sender gives the desire and the know-how to the Subject-Receiver, like a teacher would.

Until the double exchange is realized, the agreement is only a "partial contract" and depends on the mutual trust of the interactors. The balance of exchange is grounded on "a reciprocal trust, in other words, a *fiduciary contract*, implicit or explicit, between the participants of the exchange" (Greimas, 1973:32). This is even more true for the Subject-Receiver who has to do O'/ bring about O' first before the Sender fulfills his share of the contribution and honors his promise.

In Greimas' contract the promise made by the Sender can only be inferred from the consequence of the Test, after the Sender has kept his promise. The communication which stands out in the pair of functions making up the contract is the factitive doing or injunction of the Sender, the task or condition O' he specifies to be fulfilled by the Subject. No mention is made of a reward and it would seem than an offer was not made. This is, however, misleading and substantially incorrect.

Now if O' and O are objects or actions that can be transferred simultaneously there is no need for a contract or promise. As the Subject hands over O' the Sender hands over O and the exchange satisfies both of them. When the exchange is discharged on the spot, instantaneously, there is no obligation nor any juridical effect and an exchange which ends without generating obligations is not a contract. The contract is, first and foremost, an instrument of credit and trust. The discharge of the object takes place in the future, within a certain lapse of time. Here, the creditor trusts the debitor; there is credit, there is an obligation. The contract or the promise is a tool for the working out of at least two mutual wills in the world in such a way as to permit a trade over time: to allow the Subject to do O' for the Sender when he needs it or orders it, in the confident belief that the Sender will do O for the Subject when he needs it or deserves it. This is where the element of commitment enters in. Commitment is the key element which gives the promise or the contract its sharpest, most palpable form.

The mutual consent and commitment of the Sender and Receiver appear contractual only because the two objects exchanged are well-defined or can analytically be specified when the story is read in its entirety and the precise terms of the exchange are stipulated retrospectively. But the consent is almost exclusively in the nature of the social exchange involving loose terms in the transaction and diffuse obligations.

The Qualifying Test and the Glorifying Test are concerned with a cooperative exchange of rewarding activities and commitments to the other party. The fulfillment of exchange obligations depends on trust since it is essential for stable and mutually favorable social relations and bonds of fellowship. In complete contrast to the cooperation taking place between the Sender and Subject-Receiver, the Main Test is a representation of a sheer competition between the Subject and Opponent where the gain of one results in the loss of the other. There is no initial agreement or contract since that would imply the idea of an exchange and the competition, like a duel, is the expression of a will of mutual exclusion. The hero wants to take the object of the quest from the villain and give him nothing in return. And the villain does not consent to this act and wants to treat his adversary in the same way without bothering about his consent. Within the competition, as within a duel, there are two independent wills, two consents to the action which makes the hostile interaction possible. But the mutual consent is given to the risk, equal for both, of losing the object to the other. Moreover, the adversaries are hierarchically equal in status so that the hostile situation is rigorously symmetrical.

The contract which anchors the Main Test is between the subject-hero and the dispatcher who thus appears to dispatch the hero on a quest that necessarily involves a struggle with the villain. The initial agreement is between dispatcher and the subject-hero and the task is to confront the villain in order to win the key object-of-desire, or alternatively, to liquidate the lack. It seems as if the role of the dispatcher is to acknowledge the capacity of the would-be hero and to give him the chance to prove himself or herself. The offer is the fulfillment of a *heroic role* for the hero who is far from being one yet and the dispatcher's role could be phrased as a declaration to the protagonist of the nature: "I appoint you hero. I have faith in you as a potential hero. I have faith that you will be one." This actional declaration is important because at the beginning of the tale, as Greimas pointed out, "the hero is often presented as a simpleton, a sort of village idiot who lets himself be easily deceived or, in extreme cases, falls asleep while the traitor operates; in a word, we are dealing with a non revealed hero" (Greimas, 1966:200).

To illustrate the complexity of the components entering in the mutual agreement and the interpenetration of cooperative exchanges and competitive interactions in *Miss Lonelyhearts*, I would like to discuss the type of agreement struck between the protagonist Miss Lonelyhearts and Shrike, his editor, who is the syncretism of several colliding actants: Sender, anti-Sender, and villain or opponent. Although the establishment of the identity agreement is usually the first task in real life interactions, the chronological sequence of events need not and often is not fully preserved in the narrative. The sheer suspension of the temporal sequence adds an element of mystery or surprise through withheld information which is gradually dispensed like a rhythmic yet steadily building tide. The nature by which an agreement comes into being manifests the dynamics of suspense more patently. Complex and problematic in its attainment and far from stable, an agreement partakes of those conditions which constitute enigmas of knowledge and are the vehicles for suspense: delays, equivocations, deceptions, blockages, suspensions, partial answers and renegotiations. An agreement is a delicate and intricate achievement in an interaction and it does not settle the matter of identities once and for all. On the contrary, it is a precarious balance easily upset on which the interactors stand while they negotiate the finer points of their role or renegotiate a new agreement in successive rounds of bargaining and phases of interaction. The resolution of a story depends on unravelling the more stable terms of an agreement and finding out what the exchange or competition was about. In *Miss Lonelyhearts* most of the terms of the three key agreements are laid out in the first third of the novel, but its implications and its reversals only dawn pages ahead and are not fully appreciated until the end.

A few words will be necessary on the analysis of the plot structure established prior to the thumbnail sketch reviewing this particular agreement with

Shrike. In our literary analysis of *Miss Lonelyhearts* which will be presented in detail elsewhere we take the text which is, to be sure, stratified but nevertheless has a tightly knit structure, and break it up into three plot strata according to the three major communicational networks which frame and embed the action of Miss Lonelyhearts, the protagonist. To see what motivates Miss Lonelyhearts' actions, we look first at the major characters or groups of characters who are influencing him to act or against whom he acts. Taking the preliminary definition of the Sender as influencer, activator, and instigator of another's action, we arrive at three Senders and three constituent subplots, all of which will be *reconverted* to establish the articulations and the global organization of the plot and the text as a semantic universe. One subplot involves the Sender Shrike and revolves around the work situation of a newspaper columnist, Miss Lonelyhearts, and the relation of employer to editor. The second subplot, embedded yet distinct from the first, involves the Sender correspondents and concerns itself with Miss Lonelyhearts' performance in writing and advising the letter writers. Finally, the third subplot deals with the diffuse image and obsessive fixation Miss Lonelyhearts has on Christ as Sender and the pathological relation he shares with the "Christ business" and his "Christ complex."

As a lead-in to discussing the kind of agreement which exists between Shrike and Miss Lonelyhearts, let us take up the passage in which Miss Lonelyhearts describes to Betty the circumstances under which he accepted the columnist job and how serious his task is. Miss Lonelyhearts' speech summarizes some of the agreement conditions reiterated throughout the novel and since Betty must already know all this, the effect of the speech is one of a direct address to the reader. Moreover, as summary, it invites gauging the degree of truth and falsity in Miss Lonelyhearts' speech and actions, comparing it with what he said or did before and what he will say and do after. Of greater interest in the sequence of events which initiates an agreement is the following analogy between a set of Proppian functions, listed with their definition in the left column, and the *Miss Lonelyhearts* passage on the right:

f_6 **Trickery**

The villain attempts to deceive his victim in order to take possession of him or his belongings. The vil-	*A man is hired to give advice to the readers of a newspaper. The job is a circulation stunt and the whole staff*

lain, first of all, assumes a disguise.
[...] Then follows the function itself.

considers it a joke.

f_7 Complicity

The victim submits to deception
and thereby unwittingly helps his
enemy. A special form of deceitful
proposal and its corresponding
acceptance represented by the deceitful agreement. Assent in these
instances is compelled, the villain
taking advantage of some difficult
situation in which his victim is
caught: a scattered flock, extreme
poverty, etc.

*He welcomes the job, for it might lead to
a gossip column, and anyway, he's tired
of being a leg man. He too considers the
job a joke, ...*

The complicity consists in agreeing to
view the job as a joke and not in the
acceptance to the job itself.

f_8 Villainy

The villain causes harm or injury to
a member of a family.

OR

f_{8a} Lack

One member of a family either
lacks something or desires to have
something.
Either one of these functions is exceptionally important, since by
means of it the actual movement of
the tale is created.

*...but after several months at it, the joke
begins to escape him. He sees that the
majority of the letters are profoundly
humble pleas for moral and spiritual
advice, that they are inarticulate expressions of genuine suffering. He also dis-
covers that his correspondents take him
seriously. for the first time in his life, he
is forced to examine the values by which
he lives. This examination shows him
that he is the victim of the joke and not
its perpetrator.* (Ch. 8, p.32.)

The villainy and misfortune inflicted by
Shrike upon Miss Lonelyhearts is to
make Miss Lonelyhearts the victim of a
joke.

f_9 Mediation, the connective incident

Misfortune or lack is made known; the hero is approached with a request or command; he is allowed to go or he is dispatched. Example 1: A call for help is given with the resultant dispatch of the hero.

(from above) *He sees that the majority of the letters are profoundly humble pleas for moral and spiritual advice* (my underlining).

The novella itself begins its first words with a call for help; the title of the first chapter, on page 1, is *Miss Lonelyhearts, Help me, Help Me.* The story opens with Miss Lonelyhearts contemplating a venomous parody of "Anima Christi" written by Shrike which reveals Shrike's awareness of the secret, grandiose role Miss Lonelyhearts entertains of himself. The letters are for Miss Lonelyhearts prayers of salvation which have been sent to him, the tabloid priest.

f_{10} Beginning counteraction

The seeker agrees to or decides upon counteraction. This moment is characterized in such words, for instance, as the following: "permit us to go in search of your princess," etc.

The first sentence of the story contains the closing of the column which is an agreement to help: *"Are you in trouble? Do you need advice? Write to Miss Lonelyhearts and she will help you."* This could be rephrased in the Proppian characterization as 'Permit me to go in search of an answer or resolution to your problem.'

Two major contracts or agreements arise from the acceptance to the job as a joke. The pair of functions, Mediation and Beginning Counteraction, define the contract with the dispatcher which initiates the Main Test. In Miss Lonelyhearts' talk to Betty, this contract is made with the correspondents and frames the correspondent subplot. Under this agreement Miss Lonelyhearts is the *seeker hero*, to use Propp's term.

In the Shrike subplot the deceptive agreement to the job leads to victimization of Miss Lonelyhearts through jokes. Shrike as the villain causes harm or injury to Miss Lonelyhearts himself by putting him in an impossible situation. Miss Lonelyhearts is here a *victimized hero*. Propp's example of victimized heroes, under Mediation, includes "a young girl or boy [who] is seized or driven out" (Propp, 1968:36). The inducement of an agreement by the creation of lies, admission of fraud or sharp practice, or the application of any improper pressure, may be said to do harm in the victim by touching the mind, as the kidnapper does harm by laying hands on his victim's body. Assent under these conditions is not freely made and invalidates the agreement precisely through lack of free choice. Propp says that "banished, vanquished, bewitched, and substituted heroes demonstrate no volitional aspiration toward freedom, and in such cases this element [of agreement] is absent" (Propp, 1968:38). The hero may be willing but is situationally incapacitated by bondage, frustration, absurdity, or exploitation, from agreeing to or deciding upon counteraction. This, of course, simply means there never is an agreement to being victimized and the story of the victim is the sequence of actions by which he or she gains freedom. In the Shrike subplot Miss Lonelyhearts' ultimate fight is to free himself from Shrike's jokes and sardonic glove of words. Although Miss Lonelyhearts' status as the unsuccessful hero is reinforced throughout the novel, his every attempt to get himself out of his difficulty only sinking him deeper and deeper into it, he does succeed in defeating Shrike resoundingly. Miss Lonelyhearts' only triumph, as one peak of the tale, is pictorialized in a tableau scene of the folklore tradition which A. Olrik describes as a "sculptured situation" because the scene etches itself in one's memory and conveys lingering actions (A. Olrik, 1965:138):

> *Miss Lonelyhearts stood quietly in the center of the room. Shrike dashed against him, but fell back, as a wave that dashes against an ancient rock, smooth with experience, falls back. There was no second wave.*
> [. . .]
> *"Don't be a spoilsport," Shrike said with a great deal of irritation. He was a gull trying to lay an egg in the smooth flank of a rock, a screaming, clumsy gull.* (West, 51)

"There is no instance in our material," says Propp, "in which a tale follows both seeker and victimized heroes" (Propp, 1968:36). This is unequivocally the situation of Miss Lonelyhearts, paradoxically invested with the roles of both seeker hero and victimized hero. The confrontation or juxtaposition of incompatibles establishes the situational irony which sets the tone for the entire story. The situation of the protagonist and other characters are arranged in such a way as to let them expose themselves in their ironic predicament. Since the ironist does not appear in any voice, the irony is dramatized: it is pre-eminently the irony of the theater.

The job of advice columnist specifies the agreement on the task focus in the interaction between Shrike and Miss Lonelyhearts. But this agreement is recast or transformed into another type of agreement, the outer lamination or rim of the contractual frame which establishes the status in reality of the task. The outer or secondary agreement is a deceitful agreement (trickery/complicity) framing the job as a circulation stunt and as a joke:

> *When he had finished his second cup of scalding coffee, it was too late for him to go to work. But he had nothing to worry about, for Shrike would never fire him. He made too perfect a butt for Shrike's jokes. Once he had tried to get fired by recommending suicide in his column. All that Shrike had said was: "Remember, please, that your job is to increase the circulation of the paper. Suicide, it is only reasonable to think, must defeat this purpose."* (West, 18)

The deceptive agreement or assent under duress and unconscionability is mounted on an arena of sharpest conflict with the identity agreement reached between Shrike and Miss Lonelyhearts. Shrike hires him because of his priest-like demeanor:

> *He looked like the son of a Baptist minister. A beard would become him, would accent his Old-Testament look. [...] On seeing him for the first time, Shrike had smiled and said, "The Susan Chesters, the Beatrice Fairfaxes and the Miss Lonelyhearts are the priests of twentieth-century America."* (West, 4)

In the conclusion to his lecture on escapes, the brilliant evocation of the ultimate inadequacy of such escapes as the country life, the South Seas, Hedonism and art, Shrike parodies with cynical eloquence Miss Lonelyhearts' cherished role-identity in a mock imagined letter the columnist might have written to Christ, "the Miss Lonelyhearts of Miss Lonelyhearts." When Shrike points to Miss Lonelyhearts as Christ figure, he does it with jeering blasphemy and unrelenting cynicism. In the phrasing of F. Kunkel, "this articulate antievangelist, with the marvelously apt name, is so misanthropic that he salivates cyanide and spritzs with a tongue flick" (Kunkel, 1975:130).

By using the term "joke" to identify the episode of the column creation, Shrike and his staff designate it as a humorous event—a play or game not to be taken seriously: 'What is contained therein is not real.' The play cues of jokes and humor establish the situation as unreal, including itself as an integral part of the ongoing process. The 'jokes' of Shrike are to seize on that sort of pain, suffering, and deformity which is neither laughable nor acceptable. In order to sustain that sadistic humor and prolong the yield of pleasure from play, Shrike prohibits Miss Lonelyhearts from using religious talk or the "Christ business" as a way of answering the letters. Almost the first thought of Miss Lonelyhearts in reaction to the letters he is receiving is "Christ is the answer" but he blames Shrike for checkmating that avenue:

> He stopped reading. Christ was the answer, but, if he did not want to get sick, he had to stay away from the Christ business. Besides, Christ was Shrike's particular joke. (West, 3)

The advice column is a joke for Shrike and Christ is his particular joke. Acting as the pictorial pantomine of an arch cynic, Shrike finds everything a matter for joking:

> Like Shrike, the men they imitated, they were machines for making jokes. A button machine makes buttons, no matter what the power used, foot, steam, or electricity. They, no matter what the motivating force, death, love or God, made jokes. (West, 15)

But the joking effectively narrows itself down to being profane, blasphemous, cynical, and sadistic.

If Shrike is depicted as a sneering, sniveling sadist, it is because that is the way Miss Lonelyhearts' consciousness perceives him. Written in the third person, the text of *Miss Lonelyhearts* may be treated as a record of Miss Lonelyhearts' consciousness. The action from beginning to end is screened through one mind and one voice and we see all the events through the eyes of the central agent. The implicit dramatized narrator is identified throughout with the main character, and the viewpoint is like writing a first person story in third person, changing "I" to "he" or "she." We enter his mind and stay there, we know only what he tells us and we see all the other characters through his eyes. Only twice does the author, West, enter the novel, to describe Miss Lonelyhearts' appearance and to report briefly on Shrike's letter game when Miss Lonelyhearts leaves the room and is not there to witness and report the scene. Moreover, West never evaluates Miss Lonelyhearts' view of things nor does he openly state that there is anything strange or neurotic about Miss Lonelyhearts' condition. The angle of view is that of fixed center and the result is unity of focus and intensity. The psychology of Miss Lonelyhearts' obsession is dependent on a sustained inside view of great depth and has a multiplier effect on the linear momentum and the relentless acceleration of the plot. As R. Reid says:

> Obsession automatically produces unity of action—it perceives only that which is somehow relevant to the obsession. Life becomes, to the obsessive character a drama in which everything—his surroundings, his actions, his dreams—are symbolic expressions of his own compulsion (1967:57).

The main character angle is also most suitable for stories dealing with complicated psychic struggles which arise from the character's problem. In *Miss Lonelyhearts* we have a dramatized problem which is intensified by discordant elements within Miss Lonelyhearts himself: obsession, compulsion, and incipient madness.

Any inside view limited to the protagonist-narrator is especially susceptible to questions of reliability and fallibility in voice. Explicit corroboration or conflicting testimony of word to word and word to deed makes this judgment possible. It is only through an inferential matching and mismatching of speech to action that we can interpret and evaluate Miss Lonelyhearts' degree of reliability and ascertain the psychotic or schizophrenic symptoms of his disturbance. One of the main issues concerning the evaluation of Miss Lonelyhearts as character is whether he is a tragic saint, as he thinks he is, or a psychotic fool, as we think he is. West provides the ironic clues and stages the actantial situations in which to judge Miss Lonelyhearts' religious development and casts doubt on its validity all the way. The course of action is one of centering, or shifting centers in such a way that the mounting chaos within Miss Lonelyhearts, swept by turmoil, wretchedness, and angst fails to end up with the realization of a centered self and surges instead into insanity. The story is an intensely compelling, ironic and comic, cyclone of a desintegrating mind.

When the story opens with Miss Lonelyhearts contemplating Shrike's venomous parody of "Anima Christi" Shrike appears as an anti-Christ and profane satirist while Miss Lonelyhearts appears as a mock-heroic Christ figure and an existential prototype, painfully and passionately aware of the futility of the human condition:

> *Soul of Miss L, glorify me.*
> *Body of Miss L, nourish me.*
> *Blood of Miss L, intoxicate me.*
> *Tears of Miss L, wash me.*
> *Oh good Miss L, excuse my plea,*
> *And hide me in your heart,*
> *And defend me from mine enemies.*
> *Help me, Miss L, help me, help me.*
> *In saecula saeculorum. Amen.*

By the end of the story, however, when Miss Lonelyhearts has a mystical vision of being reborn as Christ, Shrike's parody rings true, revealing his clear insight into the discrepancy between the apparent idealized self of priest and humanity lover which Miss Lonelyhearts is affirming verbally and the actual grandiose image which it hides. On the plane of veridicality, the progression of the story consists in elucidating the actantial roles of the major characters which undergo abrupt reversals as Shrike's prayer is gradually actualized and its implications for the characters involved become clearer. The intertextual patterning between the parodied prayer, the alluded "Anima Christi" and the actantial situation is thus prolonged until all the information accrues in complex ways, each chapter adding some element to the prayer and altering the truth or falsity of Miss Lonelyhearts' statements. While at first, Shrike's parody seems to verbalize the vanity of the correspondents and the self-serving and self-aggrandizing purpose of religion, later, another layer of meaning is added which indicts the grandiose and secret dream of Miss Lonelyhearts himself. As the story unfolds, the reader perceives that Miss Lonelyhearts' grandiose image substitutes for a true, idealized self; a pseudoself of unlimited glory and power is secretly raised to the level of accomplished fact while healthy human strivings to achieve an idealized role are frustrated and scorned. In a second reading, Miss Lonelyhearts' relationship to the existential predicament transcends commitment; indeed it turns upon itself. Miss Lonelyhearts cannot convince Shrike that he is indeed what he claims to be. The prayer Shrike satirizes for Miss Lonelyhearts reflects Miss Lonelyhearts' own needs and Miss Lonelyhearts' religious attitude to Christ. The prayer progressively becomes one that Miss Lonelyhearts could address to Christ:

> Soul of Christ, glorify me.
> Body of Christ, nourish me.
> Blood of Christ, intoxicate me.
> Tears of Christ, wash me.
> Oh good Jesus, excuse my plea,
> And hide me in your heart,
> And defend me from mine enemies.
> Help me, Jesus, help me, help me.
> In saecula saeculorum. Amen.

A comparison with the reference text, the real "Anima Christi" or "Soul of Christ" from Loyola's *Spiritual Exercises* indicates that the most integral parts of a prayer, the adoration of God, asking for grace and the forgiveness of sins are omitted:

> Soul of Christ, sanctify me.
> Body of Christ, save me.
> Blood of Christ, inebriate me.
> Water from the side of Christ, wash me.
> Passion of Christ, strengthen me.
> O good Jesus, hear me;
> Within Your Wounds hide me;
> Separated from You let me never be;
> From the malignant enemy, defend me;
> At the hour of death, call me,
> And close to You bid me,
> That with Your saints I may be
> Praising You. Forever and ever. Amen.[4]

---

[4] The Latin version of "Anima Christi" is not easy to locate, but the English translation is found in most editions of the *Spiritual Exercises*. The edition where I found the Latin original is published by Burns & Oates in London but has no publication date: "Anima Christi sanctifica me./ Corpus Christi, salva me./ Sanguis Christi, inebria me./ Aqua lateris Christi, lava me./ Passio

The parodied prayer, addressed by Miss Lonelyhearts to Christ, is an appeal for personal power (glorify me as Christ incarnate, intoxicate me with power); the other's pity (show how sorry you feel for me through your tears and how you commiserate with my suffering and my helplessness) which is displayed for legitimating an excuse not to write his column and to wallow instead in the misery of his readers by which he lets himself and invites us to get violated; and unconditional approval, as evidenced by the thoughts Miss Lonelyhearts expresses in his mystical vision (*God approved the drafts of his column. God approved his every thought.* Ergo, *defend me from mine enemy*, Shrike, who only censors me).

1b   Task and interaction

The fulfillment of the task agreement or the actual doing of the task is named the *struggle* in all three Tests and is represented in its generalized form as a functional couple of énoncés:

$$NE_1 = F : \text{confrontation } (S_1 \longleftrightarrow S_2)$$
$$NE_2 = F : \text{success } (S_1 \longrightarrow S_2)$$

The task can assume an infinitude of forms, even in the simplest of tales. It is up to the Subject-Receiver to do O'/bring about O' first, the task specified by the Sender. In both functions, confrontation and success, it is the Subject's action that is taking place, the condition O' he has to bring about, either in union with or in opposition to another. In the folktale, the donor tests the hero: "The hero is tested, interrogated, attacked, etc., which prepares the way for his receiving either a magical agent or helper" (Propp, 1968:39). According to the folklorists Meletinsky and his team the Qualifying Test "tests traits of the hero or of his awareness of elementary norms of behavior. The hero must exhibit kindness, modesty, intelligence, politeness and, most often, the knowledge of the particular rules of the game" (Meletinsky, 1974:79). According to Greimas the interaction between the Sender and the Subject is a simulated, symbolic struggle where the Sender plays the role of Opponent.

Christi, conforta me./ O bone Jesu, exaudi me:/ Intra tua vulnera absconde me:/ Ne permittas me separari a te:/ Ab hoste maligno defende me:/ In horâ mortis meae voca me./ Et jube me venire ad te,/ Ut cum sanctis tuis laudem te/ In saecula saeculorum. Amen."

In the Glorifying Test the father of the princess assigns a difficult task to the hero which he successfully resolves. The test is given for the identification of the hero who must prove that he is indeed the hero who obtained the valuable object sought in the Main Test.

In the interaction between the hero and the villain, the two antagonists "join in direct combat" in order to obtain the object of search (Propp, 1968:51).

The progression of a narrative can be characterized as the passage from one situation to another, where by situation is meant the interaction of characters either in terms of mutual interest or of opposition, of cooperative exchange with the Sender or conflict with the anti-Subject. A cooperative and mutual exchange is delightful, as in real life, but it is fatal to a dramatic story for without the obstacles and the opponent, the protagonist would be gliding through a socially frictionless universe. The most characteristic situation of a story is a situation of conflict containing contradictory ties. "The fundamental purpose of plot," says W. Hendricks, "is to bring protagonist and antagonist together in situations where they each have an interest" in gaining the object of desire (Hendricks, 1973:179). The passage will be marked midway by a high point of conflictful situation, then away, ending in a regrouping of characters, where the conflicts are cancelled and interests reconciled.

To the extent that we survey the individual phases of the Tests analytically we gain the distinctness of a synthetic appearance of events that have already happened and which are conceptually fixed. In a dynamic apprehension when we experience the actual unfolding of events in the passage marked by the Main Test, the agonistic and polemical struggle between hero and opponent is the culminating phase at the zenith of the most intense and palpable teleological duel. "Plot is the dynamic aspect of narration, as opposed to the static nature of character opposition. [...] Plot is dynamic in that it involves a 'stretching out' or temporalization of the spatial (paradigmatic) conflict" (Hendricks, 1973:179). The polarity of dynamic vs. static has an additional feature to that considered earlier with verbs and states. The conflict is indeed a happening but its dynamic character partakes of the nature of a fight. Every struggle, inner or outer, every fight, and every battle has a pronounced dynamic character stemming from the increasingly frequent and stronger attempts to overcome the opponent which leads to the total engagement of forces on both sides. We experience the *dynamics* of a conflict through the maximal tension and the uncertainty of the outcome. In this sense, not all processes which are non-states and dynamic situations have a dynamic character. For instance, it is not present in "The door opened" which consists of a change of state in the door. The "dynamics" of a multiple phase conflict develop in the phases of tension and the variation of tempo while the agonistic process is vividly apprehended, coming into view with the process itself. One practical rule and technique in the craft of fiction writing which the novelist W. Knott formulated tells how to inject into the key antithetical opposition of the narrative the pulse of a dynamically developing process:

> Let us define plot as someone in trouble and go on from there. I repeat, people in trouble. [...] You present people with problems they will have great difficulty in solving. As you take them through their struggle, you will generate conflict. And this element is what you *must* have. [...] The point is that conflict must be an outgrowth of your character's problem. It works this way: the character's effort to resolve his or her difficulties is challenged, either by some other characters or by some natural element [and] the more menacing the challenge, the more intense the conflict. Of course, it is always best if the protagonist's problems are intensified by discordant elements within the character himself: incipient madness, compulsion, alcoholism, drug addiction, phobia, prejudice—in short, anything that makes it difficult for the protagonist to succeed (W. Knott, 1977:31,35).

To define plot as "trouble" is to define plot as desire since desires arise only when there is 'something the matter,' when there is 'trouble' in the existing situation, a lack or deficit which produces conflict in the situation as it stands. Trouble seizes upon the negative or privative factor of desire which evokes the positive aspect of desire, the formation of objectives. As the struggle between the opposing Subject-hero and the opponent reaches the degree of maximum effort and highest tension, we have come to the breaking point, the moment when the stakes will be won by one party. Every game and every fight have their stake. The protagonist and antagonist compete "for" something and the object for which they compete will be first and foremost a victory. "The situation of conflict," says Tomachevsky, "arouses a dramatic movement because the prolonged coexistence of two opposed principles is not possible and because one of them must prevail" (Tomachevsky, 1965:273). The breaking point has traditionally been called the major crisis or climax and it is the very same situation involved in the Main Test.

We have had recourse to the rising and falling curve of a graph metaphor for the narrative, as old as 1863, which is based on the rhythm and tempo marked mainly by an emotional response to the central conflict of the main characters. The point is useful insofar as it helps us seize the pulse of a struggle with the freshness, vitality and impact in which it is experienced *seriatim*, in a stream of conflictful events. Equally to the point is Tarde's suggestion that the idea of contraries and oppositions arises from our first encounters of fights and battles:

> It is probable that the recollection of fights with weapons in hand even more than the sight of symmetrically inverse objects has first aroused in the human spirit the notion of contraries; and it is still while thinking confusedly of his singular little fights with his friends that a child conceives this idea. [...] From very early, couples of irreconcilable enemies form themselves in us, historical or mythical (Christians and Turks, angels and demons). (Tarde, 1897:11)

The competitive interaction is the anthropomorphic representation of opposition where S_1 negates S_2 or inversely.

The task involved in the Glorifying Test in the Shrike subplot assumes a form amazingly similar to the one found in the Proppian tale, that of a game. In the calm just previous to Shrike's game Miss Lonelyhearts becomes a rock as West, using one of his favorite devices, starts with a simile, then allows it to take over completely. After three days of self-induced hallucination spent "aboard the bed," Miss Lonelyhearts is assuming the life of sensory deadness. He has been forcing himself into a catatonia of calm as a defense against the taunts of Shrike. The sudden reversal of Miss Lonelyhearts' whirling jumble of storm-and-stress to an equilibrium of calm is symbolized by Miss Lonelyhearts' self-image as a rock unaffected by the sea of life. Having neutralized and negated the ill effects of Shrike's jokes, Miss Lonelyhearts necessarily acquires the object-value of calmness, sureness and control whereas the antagonist, Shrike, is disjoined from it by becoming a "screaming, clumsy gull." The imagery in the Glorifying Test below institutes Miss Lonelyhearts as hero and Shrike as the antagonist or anti-subject. That Miss Lonelyhearts is aware of being the victim of irony is indicated by his acceptance to the contract and what he thinks Shrike is trying to do to him.

f_{25} Difficult task

A difficult task is proposed to the hero.	Shrike, very drunk comes to Miss Lonelyhearts' apartment and forces Miss

This is one of the tale's favorite elements. These tasks are so varied that each would need a special designation. Of the different kinds, Propp lists these groups:

Riddle guessing and similar ordeals: to pose an unsolvable riddle; tests of strength, adroitness, fortitude.

According to Greimas, this function constitutes the injunction of a third contract, A_3.

Lonelyhearts to attend a party in his home.

"Don't be a spoil-sport," Shrike said with a great of irritation. He was a gull trying to lay an egg in the smooth flank of a rock, a screaming, clumsy gull. "There's a game we want to play and we need you to play it.—'Everyman his own Miss Lonelyhearts.' I invented it, and we can't play without you."

Shrike pulled a large batch of letters out of his pockets and waved them in front of Miss Lonelyhearts. He recognized them; they were from his office file.

Acceptance to the contract, A_3

Missing function in Propp. A proposal is accepted or refused. When accepted, the contract is clinched and is followed by the struggle or task which ends in success.

The rock remained calm and solid. Although Miss Lonelyhearts did not doubt that it could withstand any test, he was willing to have it tried.

The game begins. It is the culmination of the various role playings, performances, and spectacles we have encountered. Shrike introduces Miss Lonelyhearts to the party, claiming that he will be the spiritual guide. Of course, he is taunting him, but even as he states Miss Lonelyhearts' cleansing, fiery power in ironic terms, he is yielding to the myth. Miss Lonelyhearts is already beginning to prevail.

Confrontation, F_3

(missing in Propp)

"Ladies and gentlemen," he said, imitating the voice and gestures of a circus

barker. "We have with us to-night a man whom you all know and admire. Miss Lonelyhearts, he of the singing heart—a still more swollen Mussolini of the soul.

"He has come here to-night to help you with your moral and spiritual problems, to provide you with a slogan, a cause, an absolute value and a raison *d'être.*

"Some of you, perhaps, consider yourself too far gone for help. You are afraid that even Miss Lonelyhearts, no matter how fierce his torch, will be unable to set you on fire. You are afraid that even when exposed to his bright flame, you will only smolder and give off a bad smell. Be of good heart, for I know that you will burst into flames. Miss Lonelyhearts is sure to prevail."

Shrike pulled out the batch of letters and waved them above his head.

"We will proceed systematically," he said. "First, each of you will do his best to answer one of these letters, then, from your answers, Miss Lonelyhearts will diagnose your moral ills. Afterwards he will lead you in the way of attainment."

f_{26} **Solution**

The task is resolved.

Miss Lonelyhearts stood it with the utmost serenity; he was not even interested. What goes on in the sea is of no interest to the rock.

When all the letters had been distributed, Shrike gave one to Miss Lonelyhearts.

He took it, but after holding it for a while, he dropped it to the floor without reading it.

f_{27} Recognition

The hero is recognized. He is recognized by a mark, a brand (a wound, a star marking), or by a thing given to him (a ring, towel). Tn this case, recognition serves as a function corresponding to branding and marking.

Recognition is the consequence of the Glorifying Test.

From Miss Lonelyhearts' viewpoint; he is the one who sees and through whose consciousness the event is presented. Miss lonelyhearts recognizes himself as hero:

When Miss Lonelyhearts saw Betty get up and go, he followed her out of the apartment. She too should see the rock he had become.

The unsolvable game which is posed by Shrike to Miss Lonelyhearts is couched in heavy irony. Shrike praises Miss Lonelyhearts by attributing an idealized though unfeasible role to Miss Lonelyhearts in order to undercut him and defeat him. He names Miss Lonelyhearts a spiritiual leader, a "master" but the ostensible content of this attribution asserts what is known to be false in prior segments of the text.

The confrontation or clash of incompatible and incongruous meanings is signalled in the conceit of yoking together the doings of the advice columnist with that of the religious priest, by deliberately confusing the purpose of the two, weaving the religious and moral role with the more secular and purely pragmatic role of the advice columnist. How can an advice columnist be expected to "help you with your moral and spiritual problems, to provide you with a slogan, a cause, an absolute value and a *raison d'être*" when even the priest is expected to do no more than "help you with your moral and spiritual problems"? By misrepresenting the job of the columnist, by exaggerating *ad absurdum* the duties of the priest and pretending they are interchangeable, Shrike is blatant in the ironic contradiction or incongruity. The irony becomes heaviest, joining hands with its crudest cousin, sarcasm, when Shrike says with pretended enthusiasm, that Miss Lonelyhearts ostensibly is expected to "lead you in the way of attainment." The irony and sarcasm are also stylistically placed. All references to

Miss Lonelyhearts adjoined with "fire," "flame," "torch," etc. are the exact contradictory of Miss Lonelyhearts' narrative program and semantic investment. Miss Lonelyhearts was shown to be consistently cold, dry, and dead, unable "to work [any spark] into a flame" (West, 24).

The direct conflict of information requires the reader to go beyond the surface meaning and, unlike any metaphor or simile, to retract or repudiate the surface meaning. As incompatibles are forced upon us, the open invitation we face is a need for choice. The reconstructed meaning will necessarily be in harmony with the unspoken beliefs and actional competence investing Shrike and Miss Lonelyhearts in prior sequences of the text which the reader has inferred and which have by now become attributes of the characters.

That choice, however, will not be a secure or stable one. For we cannot totally erase the surface meaning without wondering whether Miss Lonelyhearts himself has not entertained this delusion of religious grandeur himself. There is a sense in which Shrike is actually exposing and pinpointing Miss Lonelyhearts' psychotic, grandiose image and that this game could be interpreted as daring Miss Lonelyhearts to prove and legitimate this image by enacting it through a successful performance. The predominating meaning, narratively speaking, is the negation of Shrike's roles as opponent and anti-Sender. The only way Miss Lonelyhearts can triumph over Shrike's antagonistic jokes is not to respond to him at all, to ignore him. Miss Lonelyhearts interprets his own emotional non-involvement and his neutralization of Shrike's jokes through he rock he says he has become. It is noteworthy to remark that the sentence syntax alone of Miss Lonelyhearts' self-recognition as hero marks the 'rock' as a positive achievement. For one is eager to show off a victory and not a failure. To say, therefore, that Betty "should see the rock" is to say that Betty should see his victory.

1c Consequence

In the exchange between the Subject-hero and the Sender the consequence consists of the Sender's sanction, the fulfillment of his/her contractual obligation to the hero and honoring his/her promise by delivering the offer he/she made earlier. The Sender promised O to the Subject if the Subject has done O'/ brought about O'. We have here an exchange with two objects and the transaction can be loosely and globally compared to an economic trade:

The Subject-hero trades O' to the Sender for O.

The Subject-hero earned O from the Sender by doing O'.

The formula for the realized exchange may be written as a complex énoncé of junction with four actants:

$$S \cap O \cup O' \rightarrow Sr \cup O' \cap O$$

and the communicative doing between the actants is a benefactive one on the part of the Sender:

$$\text{non } c \ (Sr \longrightarrow O \longrightarrow R)$$

where non c can be interpreted as (1) consequence of the Test, (2) a reciprocated giving from the Sender and the fulfillment of his or her offer, and (3) that which is given, namely the object-of-desire and the object-of-communication. The agreement initiating the interaction and the partial contract are now fulfilled and hence real since the Sender fulfilled his or her end of the agreement. As Greimas says, the consequence is "thus the sanction of the contract, the proof of its realization" (Greimas, 1966:212). When looking at the entire contract evolution of the exchange, we may set up a contrast within the Test of the initial and manipulative Sender and the final and judicial Sender. In the result or consequence of the exchange, the Sender acts as judge and arbiter of the Subject-hero's action and rewards him or her for the successful execution of his or her action.

It is due to the reciprocity of programs of execution that the relation between the Subject and the Sender is symmetric and egalitarian. At the precise moment that the Sender carries out his end of the agreement, there is a balance of executory obligations. An obligation is characteristically *owed* to someone; agreements, promises, and contracts are all obliging practices. The subject to whom one is obliged will in most cases be the *beneficiary* of the action to which one is obliged. For the Sender to be obliged by some performance of the Subject is to be provided by that action with sufficient reason to make some return.

The transaction exhibits the keeping of promises and, more generally, the norm of reciprocity where the giving and receiving are mutually contingent and mutually complementary. In *An Anatomy of Values* Fried sees the significant and the controlling general principle of social behavior as being the principle of morality because it best expresses this reciprocity and it corresponds or lies behind a whole set of concepts of generally agreed significance and potency.

That is, in our relations and our dealings with others the most general principle applicable to rational ends and actions and which are characterized by the fair incorporation of others' ends into one's own ends is the principle of morality.

Reciprocity is the recognition of the other participants in a transaction as having their own ends and rational ends. Moreover, no participant uses the other merely as a contingent instrumentality in accomplishing his or her own ends, thus acknowledging the other person from the same perspective as that other person sees himself or herself—that is, in terms of that other person's ends. The notions of impartiality, equality and regard for all persons as ends in themselves which guide reciprocal actions are characteristic of moral principles. Morality is the general principle expressive of the recognition of human personality and it accomplishes this recognition by requiring that the most general principle of transactions place all persons in a position of parity. "Why," asks Fried, "does this equality or impartiality of the principle of morality express recognition of personality?" His answer is buttressed as a moral thesis: "All persons are alike in respect to the characteristic that they conceive of themselves as entities having ends and rational ends; and any essential preference between persons entails a violation of reciprocity in the direction of using the other person as an instrument" (1970:53).

The Sender's reciprocated action and sanction exemplify the principle of morality which is of a higher order of generality than certain other moral principles, say trust or commitment, which in turn are of a higher order of generality than some systems of conduct built upon or exemplifying trust, say reciprocity or a contractual exchange. In the schema of the Test, particularly the Qualifying Test and the Glorifying Test

   A + F > non c

the tie or relation between non c, the consequence, to the two preceding constituents A and F or *why non c follows from* A + F is by the principle of morality and the only principle completely expressing reciprocity. The tie ">" can be viewed as a rational principle guiding certain actions or as a constraint upon actions and the pursuit of ends but, in neither case, can it be said to have logical conclusiveness.

The tie is a very vulnerable point of unreliability and deception should it be broken by the Sender. The statement of intention by the Sender in a false or deceitful promise is "like a pit [the promisor] has dug in the road into which [the promisee] falls. [The promisor] has harmed [the promisee] and should make him/her whole" (Fried, 1980:10). In other words, the promisor-Sender is answerable to the promisee for the expectation caused by the promise together with the harm done by its breach. The Sender's failure to reciprocate is a breach of contract and a breach of promise which reveals the Sender to be a figure of deception and trickery. The wrong done is one of obtaining a benefit *unjustly*, which the Sender does if he deceives the Subject and at the expense of the Subject. The victimization and exploitation of the Subject by the Sender turns the latter into a villain or anti-Sender (Greimas, 1976c:63,109). When distributive justice fails of realization and the Subject-Receiver is not properly rewarded, the Sender is abusing his power position over the Subject and exploiting him/her to work in his behalf. Subjugation by coercive force and chicanery can hardly be experienced as fair and just, for it offers no compensating advantages for submission. The injury sustained by the victim is that of exploitation and oppression willfully perpetrated by the fraud and sharp practice of the more powerful contractual party. It may be said that the Sender is out of character and acts the role of villain; therefore, he never was a Sender but feigned to be one.

The tie has the same kind of conclusiveness as the conclusion of the practical inference leading to the act; that is, it is defeasible like the conclusion-act. This is the reason why logically we can say non c $\longrightarrow$ A + F but not the inverse A + F $\longrightarrow$ non c. The phenomena of breaking an obligation and cheating prevent the conclusiveness in the tie of the exchange. The tie is practical in the practical inference and both practical and moral in the exchange.

Excluded from the breach of contract is the negative sanction of the Sender following the failure of the Subject to do O'. If the promise was conditional and the condition is not fulfilled, the Sender has no obligation to the Subject.

Communication with *two objects* O and O' is typical of the Sender and Subject-hero relation. Communication with *one object* is characteristic between the hero and villain in the space of the Main Test. The hero winning O necessarily means the villain lost O. The object of value is transferred from one subject to another, both of whom are interested in gaining it:

$$S_1 \cap O \cup S_2$$

The existence of two subjects S_1 and S_2, the Subject and Anti-Subject, corresponds to two *contradictory* doings. By contrast, the relation between the Sender and the Receiver-Subject is one of *identification* or conjunction. The limiting case of a failed exchange by the *ex post facto* anti-Sender may be represented by the formula

$$(\text{Sr} \cap \text{O'} \cap \text{O}) \cup \text{S}$$

and which makes of the anti-Sender an arch villain since the equivalent object of exchange, initially promised as an offer in the agreement, is not given to the Subject-hero and, worse, the anti-Sender steals O from the Subject-hero. An unfair exchange takes place when O' ≠ O, that is, where O' and O are not objects of equivalent value and the anti-Sender (passing as Sender) pretends or foists the lie that they are. The greater the non-equivalence is between O' and O, the closer it approaches the perverse and pathological lower limit of a failed exchange and a situation of cheater and cheated.

Fried points out the third type of harm in burning an obligation or a series of obligations which leads to "infantilizing" or patronizing the promisee-victim and undercuts the possibility of maintaining complex projects over time:

> Holding people to their obligations is a way of taking them seriously and thus of giving the concept of sincerity itself serious content.[...] Others must respect our capacity as free and rational persons to choose our own good, and that respect means allowing persons to take responsibility for the good they choose. And, of course, that choosing self is not an instantaneous self but one extended in time, so that to respect those determinations of the self is to respect their persistence over time. If we decline to take seriously the assumption of an obligation because we do not take seriously the promisor's prior conception of the good that led him to assume it, to that extent we do not take him seriously as a person. We infantilize him, as we do quite properly when we release the very young from the consequences of their choices (Fried, 1981:20-1).

In this passage the "promisor" stands for our Subject-Receiver or hero and his/her capacity to determine his/her own good and the value judgment that led him/her to make a promise and enter into a contract with the Sender. By denying the other's autonomy and abusing a trust he was free to invite or not, the anti-Sender drastically shrinks the efficacy of the other and "poison(s) the source of the moral power we enjoy," that is, the trust to put into the promisee's hands the cooperative power to accomplish his or her will (Fried, 1981:18).

1d   Justice

We can also discuss the tie or the Sender's executory obligation to the

Receiver-hero in more specific principles derivable from the principle of morality: the principles of justice, which refer to the structure of institutions and practices, and the principles of fairness, which relate to the obligations of individuals involved in more or less formal institutions and in practices such as promises and contracts.

If the Subject succeeds in fulfilling the condition and task O', he has a *right* to expect O from the Sender. The right of the Subject is the duty of the Sender. Without the correlation of rights and duties and the possibility of the duty resting somewhere, the attribution of the right to O would be meaningless. Rights and duties come in pairs and the two terms are the active and passive forms of indicating the juridical power of the exercise of the act. The Subject *can* do O/ bring about O/ receive O and the Sender *cannot* oppose him/her nor refuse him/her; the Subject is *free* to do O/ take O and the Sender is *bound* to respect it. The Subject's claim to O is a juridical notion and his/her interaction with the Sender is a relationship of right. The object-goal or aim of the Subject's action, O, is an *object of right*. Thus, the consequence of the Qualifying Test and the Glorifying Test is not only an object of communication and an object of desire, it is also an object of right.

The Subject has the right to expect O, do O, bring about O from the Sender. The Sender has the negative duty to not interfere with the doing of O and, at most, has the positive duty of actively performing for the sake of the Subject. The rights indicate the source of our grievances, emanating from our desires or wants, whereas the duties specify the actions that safeguard our wants and keep them inviolate. The Subject can claim a good O and the Sender cannot inflict a harm or injury by thwarting the Subject's freedom to claim O. To say that the Sender cannot means s/he *ought not* since the Sender as power-wielder has the *can-do* to inflict avoidable harm but exercising this can-do clearly goes in the direction of abuse and exploitation. A grievance about avoidable harm presupposes one's right to be free for what could a grievance be about otherwise. In this sense the notion of liberty connects with one's (harm-less) immunity and reveals an important inner connection between the ideas of liberty and harm.

In his book on *Moral and Legal Reasoning* S. Stoljar remarks that the harm done by a breach of promise (breach of agreement, breach of contract) is in one respect quite different from the harm caused by other wrongs:

In the case of actions consisting of an interference with another's liberty or immunity, the rule broken is one relating to a prohibition formulated with a 'don't.' In a breach of promise the harm consists of the promisor's not performing an affirmative or positive act, a failure *to do*. The special obligatory element in promise-keeping then seems to enshrine just this positive duty to do rather than not to do (1980:131-2).

It is not only morally right to fulfill one's end of a promise but also one's duty or obligation—something one *positively ought* to do. The duty in promise-keeping has a coercive effect which blames for omission and approves without praising for commission. In the consequence of the Qualifying Test and the Glorifying Test the positive right of the Subject-Receiver or hero to receive O is the positive or active duty of the Sender to give O.

Moral and legal rules incorporate rights and duties to regulate reciprocal human actions for the broad moral purpose of discouraging the doing of avoidable harm. It is also this concern with *avoidable* harm which Stoljar tries to show coincides with the more familiar notion of *justice*:

> Even the word 'injustice' is closely connected with 'injury'; in fact, 'injury' did not originally mean, as it does now, actual harm done or suffered; more interestingly, it meant harm done *in jura*, 'against rights,' or more broadly, harm done by one's person superior disregard of another's integrity or immunity, thus by one person's assumption of superiority over another, what the Greeks called *hybris* (1980:72-3).

Infantilizing or patronizing someone appear to be particular cases of 'hybris,' elevating oneself in order to keep or maintain *in jura* the other in a lower or inferior position.

Justice in itself is an ideal and the ideal of justice is a juridical notion. It is an ideal which tends, like every other ideal, to realize itself, to pass onto the plane of real existence. But the *reality* of justice is the right and that of injustice, harm against a right. Justice can be attained only by becoming a right; that is, rights are nothing other than an application of the idea of justice to social interactions. Wanting to establish justice is therefore wanting to realize and actualize rights. Justice is thus primarily and even solely the principle or the source of rights but it is not yet a right. Justice becomes a right if it is applied to particular social interactions. Hence we cannot oppose justice to a right as such. We can only oppose another right, namely another application of justice or an application of another justice to given social interactions.

A situation of justice and a situation of rights can be defined at the simplest social level as an interaction involving a minimum of three people, as Kojève has brilliantly demonstrated in his *Esquisse d'une phénoménologie du droit* (1981). A situation of rights exists where there are two subjects of right, one of whom has the right to act (called the legal subject), and the other the duty not to interfere and a 'rule of right' from which stems a third person distinct from the other two who creates this rule (the legislator), or applies it (the judge) or executes it (the police). Needless to say, if the two justiciables or subjects of right are spontaneously just, they can do without the judge. But in this case the judge is virtually present in each justiciable and is thus not only an involved party but also an impartial and disinterested third. These two justiciables must place each other in a position of parity and treat each other as politically neutral even when they are at war with each other, that is, even when the political element is in force. Thus, the Sender who is later revealed to be a deceiver and anti-Sender is activating a political element with the Subject-Receiver at the end of the contract when there was none in the initial agreement.

To make justice prevail or to make it "real" is to apply a rule of right and this rule always touches at least two people in interaction. The types of justice and the rights based on them differ from each other by the rules they apply to given social interactions. What McCall and Simmons say about reality stress its intimate connection with justice:

> Reality in this distinctively human world is not a hard, immutable thing but is fragile and adjudicated—a thing to be debated, compromised and legislated (1966:42).

It is sufficient for the judge to have an idea of justice in order to apply it to specific interactions and try to make them conform to the idea or ideal of justice, or at the very least to observe their agreement or non-agreement with this ideal. The ideal of justice may be expressed under three different principles: the justice of equality; the justice of equivalence, also called distributive justice; and a synthesis of the latter two, which we may call, after Kojève, the principle of equity.

I would like to show now that the interactions in the Qualifying Test and Glorifying Test enact the justice of equivalence; the struggle with the villain or opponent in the Main Test, the justice of equality; and later I will show that the final communication series of the folktale which Greimas labels "Restoration of Order and Re-integration" reveals the justice of equity (1966:203).

Every exchange has for its basis the principle of equivalence; two objects of equivalent value are being exchanged. There is neither equality of social condition owing to the power imbalance of the identity agreement nor equality in attitude between the interactors. The contract and its evolution presuppose the inequality of conditions because if the two actants were rigorously equal, they would have nothing to exchange, to give to each other. The disadvantage or cost to the subject-hero of doing O' for the Sender is *equivalent* to the advantage or reward of receiving O from the Sender. The situation is said to attain justice because in each case the disadvantage is strictly compensated by the advantage (or inversely) so that we may speak of an equivalence of advantage and disadvantage, reward and cost, right and duty. The justice of equivalence is similar to distributive justice insofar as they share one major rule: the reward a person receives should be proportional to the costs or investments he incurs in the exchange. Or, to put this more simply, each person is rewarded according to what s/he merits or deserves, according to what is in this sense due her/him.

From start to end, the equivalence of exchange between the Sender and the Subject-hero does not radically alter the status asymmetry between them; there is a climb for the hero but the asymmetry nevertheless persists. The situation in the Main Test is the exact opposite and here is enacted the justice of equality.

The broader meaning of what Kojève defines as the 'Anthropogenic Struggle' which would encompass the competition between equals presupposes one ideal of justice, the primary justice of equality, based on the desire for recognition:

> L'idée de [la] Justice [aristocratique de l'égalité] apparaît au moment de la Lutte anthropogène et elle ne fait que révéler son aspect *égalitaire*. Dire qu'elle est juste, c'est affirmer que les adversaires l'engagent dans des conditions rigoureusement égales: objectivement et subjectivement. Et si l'homme peut réaliser la Justice dans et par ses interactions sociales, c'est parce qu'il est né d'une Lutte anthropogène *juste* par définition, puisque essentiellement égale. En naissant par et dans l'égalité et de l'égalité il ne peut se réaliser pleinement que dans l'égalité sociale. Et c'est pourquoi on dit qu'il ne peut être vraiment humain qu'en étant juste.

> (The idea of [the aristocratic] Justice [of equality] appears at the moment of the anthropogenic Struggle and does nothing but reveal its *egalitarian* aspect. To say that it is just is to assert that the adversaries begin the action in rigorously equal conditions: objectively and subjectively. And if man can realize Justice within and by his social interactions, it is because he is born from an anthropogenic Struggle [which is] *just* by definition, since essentially equal. Being born by and within

equality and from equality he cannot fulfill [realize] himself fully other than within social equality. And this is why we say that he cannot truly be human unless he is just. [Alternative translation: And this is why we say that he can be truly human only if he is just.]) (Kojève, 1981:253-4)

Between the protagonist and antagonist there is an equality of conditions, an equal balance of power (the same status in the identity agreement), a mutual agreement to the same risk in the struggle and the same goal of winning one and the same object. The interaction is said to be "fair" because it takes place in the equality of conditions. And, as Kojève says, this equality is essential for individual growth and self-realization. Note, however, that if two people are rigorously equal, they have nothing to exchange and this is the reason why the struggle between the hero and the villain, the protagonist and antagonist, becomes a competitive one. An exchange presupposes the fact that some people do not have or do not do what others have or do.

The competitive struggle in the Main Test, like the 'Anthropogenic Struggle,' is the source of the justice of equality and of equal rights and it achieves justice when it is just. But it does not actualize a right or a relation of claim to the object of right as long as there is no Arbiter, that is, the person of the Third who intervenes with the sole concern of enacting justice. In the narrative schema when the Subject-hero succeeds in obtaining the key object of desire and liquidating the lack

$$S \cap O_3 \cup \bar{S}$$

s/he cannot yet lay claim to the object as an object of right until society in its role of justice evaluates and acknowledges the success of the protagonist's goal. The presence of the Third, in its triple form of legislator, judge, and police is, in fact, the function of the Glorifying Test where a new and third Sender tests the actual hero further in order to recognize the heroic trait of the hero. The Glorifying Test is a Test to reveal justice and ends in the social acknowledgment of the hero as winner and of the villain as loser.

The Qualifying Test, the Main Test, and Glorifying Test in their sequential order achieve respectively a justice of equivalence, equality, and equivalence. The consequence in each Test is an object of right but the object of right won in the Main Test must be acknowledged through the justice of the Glorifying Test and the recognition granted to the hero is, in itself, an object of right: the credit or credentials due to the hero. Larivaille greatly underestimates the importance of "recognition" which he states is not "a concrete result: a gain" like the receipt of the magical agent and the liquidation of lack and he takes Greimas to task on this ground (Larivaille,1974:371). When we consider the fact that acknowledgement of another's competence and success can be suppressed or undermined, it follows that recognition is the greatest gain of all and its denial is experienced by the victim as a denial of claim to an object of right. To put this matter in simple terms: it would not do any good to the hero if s/he did reach the goal $S \cap O_3$ unless a just society said, "yes, you did reach $S \cap O_3$."

2. Relation of the object to communication

2a   The object-of-communication as an object-of-motion: the topological syntax of object-values

We have seen that the three Tests of the simplest tale each bear a specific consequence which is the economic, practical, and moral result of the Subject-hero's exchange with the Sender and is thus related to the anchoring contract, A, as part and parcel of one reciprocal interaction involving mutual commitments and actions. The seme-function as it manifests itself in the position of the consequence is at the same time the term of a diametrical opposition of which the contrary term is found in the initial sequence of the tale, in the paradigmatic structure $\bar{C}$ which precedes the sequence of the Tests. I want to focus now on this relationship because it is here that the object-value behaves most like an *object-of-motion*. Whereas the consequence O in its relation to the contract was a local and immediate definition, the relationship of the consequence to the initial sequence $\bar{C}$ is a global, paradigmatic correlation and interpretation of each object-consequence, The consequence is doubly defined or overdetermined on the formal level of analysis by (1) its embedding and its function within the syntagmatic unit of which it is a part, the Test, and by (2) its paradigmatic correlation to an antecedent term in the initial sequence $\bar{C}$.

The initial and final sequences of the tale are made up of units of communication which we shall designate as $\bar{C}$ in its negative form and as C in its positive form. The subscripts in C_1, C_2, C_3 represent the variable objects of communication. Moreover, let us consider the initial series of functions as the negative transformation of the terminal series, by designating these initial functions as $\bar{C}_1, \bar{C}_2, \bar{C}_3$. The category C of communication can be articulated into a pair of contrasting semes-functions c vs. non c.

Purely for the clarity of foregrounding the object-of-motion and to see its trajectory, we shall consider only the initial sequence and ignore, for the moment, its inverse relation to the final communication sequence, C.

The initial sequence $\bar{C}$, named "break-up of the order and alienation," is made up of functions which can be represented symbolically in two different notations, either as communication units $\bar{C}$ or as object-values, O. We shall also use the Proppian functions next to them.

$$\bar{C}_1 \ = \ \frac{\bar{c}_1}{\overline{non}\ \bar{c}_1} \ = \ \frac{reconnaissance}{delivery}$$

$$\bar{C}_2 \ = \ \frac{\bar{c}_2}{\overline{non}\ \bar{c}_2} \ = \ \frac{trickery}{complicity}$$

$$\bar{C}_3 \ = \ \frac{\bar{c}_3}{\overline{non}\ \bar{c}_3} \ = \ \frac{villainy}{lack}$$

The interaction is between villain and hero, respectively $\bar{c}$ and $\overline{non}\ \bar{c}$. The consequence of each Test in sequential order is

$$non\ c_2 = receipt\ of\ magical\ agent = S_1 \cap O_2$$
$$non\ c_3 = liquidation\ of\ lack \quad\ = S_1 \cap O_3$$
$$non\ c_1 = recognition \qquad\qquad = S_1 \cap O_1$$

When represented visually as a graph (figure 7.1), the sense of the consequence to the Test which stands out glaringly is that of negating the trouble, villainy, deficit or harm represented in the initial sequence of alienation. Thus, to begin with the consequence of the Main Test, the liquidation of lack appears as the positive function (non c_3) opposed to its negative transformation which is the lack ($\overline{non}\ \bar{c}_3$). The spring, rising action or dramatic tension obtained by the spread or distance of $\overline{non}\ \bar{c}_3$ vs. non c_3 is called the "Quest." The liquidation of lack corresponds to the major object-of-desire or superobjective and to the modality of "want."

The contrasted pair of functions, Lack and Liquidation of Lack, and also the

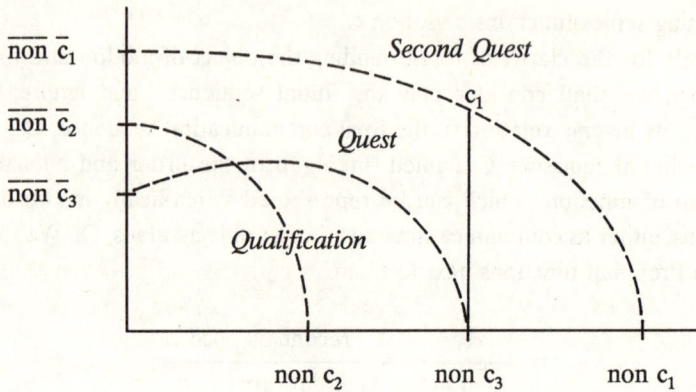

Figure 7.1

equivalent pair, Villainy and the Liquidation of Misfortune, provide genuine nodes or hinges for the course of the tale. In the folktale sequence of 31 functions these occur in 8th and 19th position. The first term of the opposed pair, Villainy or Lack, which Propp also designated as "the desire to have something" is "extremely important, since by means of it the actual movement of the tale is created," initiating the "complication" of the tale (Propp, 1968:35,30). Propp observes that all tales proceed "from a certain situation of lack or insufficiency," ready-made in one instance or created as a result of an act of villainy, in the other, both of which *provoke a quest* (Propp, 1968:34,35). The second term of the contrary pair, Liquidation of Misfortune or Lack is important because "the narrative reaches its *peak* in this function" (Propp, 1968:53, my emphasis).

The receipt of the magical agent which is the consequence of the Qualifying Test (non c_2) is opposed to submission ($\overline{\text{non}}\ \overline{c}_2$) which represents the privation of heroic energy.

The opposition of the terms is not obvious here. It is only by comparing the first Test the hero undergoes and of which the result is the receipt of the magical agent that we can see that the transfer taking place during the *deception*, what is taken away by the traitor is, so to speak, the heroic nature of the hero which creates a hiatus between appearance and reality. The magical agent is the mythical equivalent of the modal "can-do," know-how, means or power. By submitting to the traitor's deception, the hero appears to be a fool or simpleton when, in reality, he is not. The spring obtained by the distance between ñōñ $\bar{c}_2$ and non c_2 is called "Qualification" insofar as it qualifies the hero to become a hero later.

As to the third dramatic spring of the tale, recognition (non c_1) appears as the receipt of a message which is opposed to the "mark" (c_1) and to "delivery" (extorted communication, $\overline{\text{non}}$ $\bar{c}_1$). The hero is recognized by a mark, a brand, a wound which he receives during the main struggle with the villain. In this case, as Propp says, "recognition serves as a function corresponding to branding and marking" (Propp, 1968:62). The third spring may be called "Request" or "second Quest," that is to say, demand of recognition due to the hero. The object of communication does not correspond to the modality of "know what/how" as clearly as it does to the modalized verb "make know," namely the social acknowledgement, sanction, and reward of the hero's deeds which are made known (Greimas, 1966:209; 1976c:233).

The object-value, non c or O, behaves as an *object-of-motion* only if the actants are considered as places where the object-value is located and their operative or causative role is suspended or not taken into consideration. In the orientational schema

MOVE (SOURCE, OBJECT-OF-MOTION, TERMINAL)

we can think of the object-value as moved or transferred from $\bar{C}$ to non c. The object-value was taken away from the hero in $\bar{C}$ by the villain and retrieved by the hero in non c. The object-value "moved" from the villain to the hero. It is impossible to use the benefactive schema of communication

GIVE (SENDER, OBJECT, RECEIVER)

or what Greimas calls a translational énoncé F : transfer (Sr ⟶ O ⟶ R) since the villain who, by definition cannot be a Sender, does not give or transfer the object to the subject-hero. What happens when we reactivate the actantial role of the Sender is to make him/her appear as the instigator of the transfer or movement, which is incorrect.

If we keep in mind that the object, O, refers to a valued goal-object and is often not as tangible as the meaning of the word 'object' would indicate, interpreting that object as an object-of-motion is to stress its behavior as a *reified* object, i.e. something that is acquired rather than achieved or brought about. The entire trajectory of the subject's aim toward O is lost and the object-value can be seized and read as an object-of-motion in the terminal position only, retrospectively from the completed act or outcome, symbolized as $S \cap O$, in the consequence of the Test. The aim of the act and the subjective features with which it is invested is lost due to the flexible and shifting nature of the goal-object as an end-in-view which is arbitrarily fixed only by an outcome. The aim of the act is also lost or thrown out of focus in the acquisition or movement towards subjective values which point to broad, ongoing concerns that influence one's actions often unconsciously and, unlike external values, cannot be acquired or lost abruptly. The subjective features of an object-value such as, for example, goodness, integrity, and gentleness are often difficult to name as components of a goal-object since they are not readily thinkable as "reified" objects-of-motion. We tend to think of all moral, ideational, and affective values which create our inner and subjective experience as internal states inhering in some nuclear substance of ourselves, a soul or ego. Although we *are* a certain mood and *are* merged with our inner values, when we seek to analyze subjective values in a goal-object, it is necessary to disjoin the subjective affect and value from the object in its terminal position and to externalize those values as if they were articles of furniture which the actor or character wanted to *own* or *have* in some interior living room of his or her psyche.

In the circulation of the object-value, of which the trajectory is traced by the three springs of the tale, the transfer may be interpreted simultaneously as a privation or a disjunction and as an attribution or a conjunction. The topological interpretation of the consequence to the Test is a transfer and not just a gain of an object-value. If the object-value is *attributed* to the dominating subject S_1, it is because the dominated subject S_2 is *deprived* of it. The double chaining of two narrative programs, characteristic of the simplest tale, is assured by the concomitance of two opposed functions, defining the two subjects. (See figure 7.2.)

	syntagmatic junction
paradigmatic junction	$(S_1 \cup O) \longrightarrow (S_1 \cap O) \longrightarrow$ $(S_2 \cap O) \longrightarrow (S_2 \cup O) \longrightarrow$

Figure 7.2

(The matrix of junctions in this figure is in Greimas, 1973:25.) This functioning also represents each spring of the tale and the arrow represents the "movement." The consequence non c, identically the same as the object-value O, when viewed as an object-of-motion oscillates all through the story between hero and villain, S_1 and S_2.

Both on a theoretical and practical level of analysis the object-of-motion is clearly defined in the position $S_1 \cap O$ and all other junctions are derivative. Or, to put this differently, $S_1 \cap O$ is fixed and the other junctions are dependent on it. Although the object value and the object-of-motion are exceptionally obvious to recognize and identify in Propp's sequence of 31 functions, the framework of the simplest tale, the object is rarely explicitly manifested in more complex tales. The analysis of literary narratives consists precisely of attempts to determine where that position $S_1 \cap O$ is and is reconstructing the network of relations to the object which lies behind the pivot to the spring of the story and tracing it backward to its source. In his article on "Eléments pour une théorie de l'interprétation du récit mythique" which was published in the same year as *Sémantique structurale* Greimas uses a Bororo myth to set forth a descriptive methodology of myth analysis. It becomes obvious by the end of the article that determining what or who the object of the quest is demands so many bold and strategic choices for the textual analyst that a detailed and separate treatment of the object actant is given in the last third of the article, the section on "le message structurel." Since the central section of the tale corresponding to the Main Test manifests the basic contents or the basic semantic structure, the object obtained as a consequence of the Main Test, $S_1 \cap O_3$, will be the fundamental or primary object of the quest. The structural, semantic reading of the myth as a whole starts from this object and the general economy of the narrative, goes backward, forward, and, so to speak, on top, to establish the fundamental and unique isotopy of the mythical tale, re-converting all narrative syntagms and semantic contents to cohere with the semantics of the object.

The limiting poles of each narrative spring or "movement" are contraries. Now, all change, transition, process or movement takes place between the terms of an antithesis such as lack and liquidation of lack, reconnaissance and recognition; or, between an intermediate member of a pair of opposites and its extreme, such as mark and recognition. The Test sequence which defines the story syntagmatically receives its semantic investment, its meaning from the sequences which precede and follow the Test. Neither the reasons nor the consequences of the Test are readable in the Test sequence alone, taken by itself. The first term of the contrasted pair in the initial sequence $\bar{C}$ answers *why the Subject-protagonist wanted the object.* The Subject wanted non c or O *because* non c was inflicted on him by the anti-Subject or villain and this trouble or privation forms the content of a specific end-in-view, that which later becomes non c. The interaction $\bar{C}$ gives the reasons why the Subject interacts with the Sender or the anti-Subject in all three Tests. And, it emphasizes the negative aspect of desire which arises as trouble, misfortune, deficit, or privation in the initial sequence $\bar{C}$. Generalizing, we may symbolize the pair of opposites as $\bar{O} \longrightarrow O$, the negative aspect of the object of desire or its absence, followed by its presence. Thus, to explain the object-consequence is to see the negative factor of the object in its emergence. The Test and particularly the constituent F, struggle, accounts for the change between $\bar{O}$ and O:

> C'est par conséquent, la lutte (F)—seul couple fonctionnel non analysable en structure achronique, et qui précède immédiatement l'apparition, sous sa forme positive, du terme appartenant à la structure que l'on cherche à transformer—qui doit rendre compte de la transformation elle-même.
>
> (It is consequently the struggle (F)—the only functional couple non analyzable into an achronic structure, and which immediately precedes the appearance, in its positive form, of the term belonging to the structure we seek to transform—which must account for the transformation itself.)   (Greimas, 1966:211-12)

By way of gathering the discussion let us give prominence to the negative factor of the emerging object of desire. The conditions under which desires take shape and consequences are projected as ends to be reached are those of deficit, lack, and conflict. The lack or privation is something lacking or absent *in the situation,* in the network of interrelations and interactions with others. In each situation of the alienation sequence, the villain harms or causes trouble to the hero. The villain does something *to* the hero so that the type of evental or dynamic situation taking place is on the order of the action-process verb. The Subject-hero is the patient and the trouble and lack stand for the terminal point of an action-process inflicted by the villain. In its terminal position the lack is a state but it can also form the starting premise in a practical inference and hence bridges the process undergone by the Subject to the foreseeable action of the Subject by being the common ground. The object of desire is the contrary of the trouble, which might be symbolized as a double negation

$$-(\bar{O}) = O$$

where O is the object of desire and $\bar{O}$ is the shortage of it. Or rather, $\bar{O}$ may be seen as the desire and O as the fulfillment of desire. Existentially, dialectically, and from the viewpoint of the character-in-situation, $\bar{O}$ is actually the desire as it springs from the trouble and as the formation of an end-in-view and O would then be the fulfillment of desire. The object-value is framed with reference to a negative factor but it is positive insofar as it marks the doing away of the negative factor.

2b   The recognition of the hero and his acceptance by society

The tale does not end abruptly with recognition, the terminal of the last dramatic spring. It is followed by a positive sequence of communication which Greimas refers to as re-integra-tion into society and restoration of order. The final communication units are these:

$$C_2 = \frac{c_2}{\text{non } c_2} = \frac{\text{exposure of the false hero}}{\text{transformation of the hero}}$$

$$C_3 = \frac{c_3}{\text{non } c_3} = \frac{\text{punishment of false hero}}{\text{marriage}}$$

The final sequence consists in the positive social sanction of the hero and a corresponding negative sanction of the false hero or villain. The trickery of the villain ($\bar{C}_2$) is exposed (c_2) and the villainy ($\bar{c}_3$) is punished (c_3). The communication units non c_2 and non c_3 appear to be conceptually and symbolically redundant since each unit marks the overlapping of two events associated with the hero: non c_2 is the receipt of the magical agent and the transfiguration of the hero; non c_3 is the liquidation of lack and marriage. The two uses of non c_2 are explained by Propp who tells us that the hero's transfiguration "is directly effected by means of the magical action of a helper" (Propp, 1968:62). The last function in the folktale, marriage, is a reward of the hero for having liquidated the lack by recovering the stolen object-value—the paradigm being the princess—and returning that object to her father and to the original society where she belonged. Since the father gives his daughter back to the hero, the marriage is a counter-gift and a contract '"consolidated' by the communication of the object of desire" (Greimas, 1966:196). The marriage is symbolized as a contract and a communication: $A(non\ c_3)$.

The object-value continues to behave as an object-of-motion in the closed topological structure of the tale. But the movement or spring between the acquisition of the object-values toward their social sanction at the end of the tale is no longer bouncing between the villain and the hero. It shifts instead to the polarity of the private and individual possession of the object-values won by the hero and to its social evaluation, acceptance, and sanction. The relationship established is between the Subject-protagonist, the object, and the Sender of a wider social whole. Greimas' structural, semantic symbolism of the communication units in the final sequence does not reflect this change as clearly as it does the opposition between hero and villain but this gap can easily be remedied. The development of the individual as a member of a social nexus may be indicated by the two "movements" of the social sanction of the hero's values (see figure 7.3).

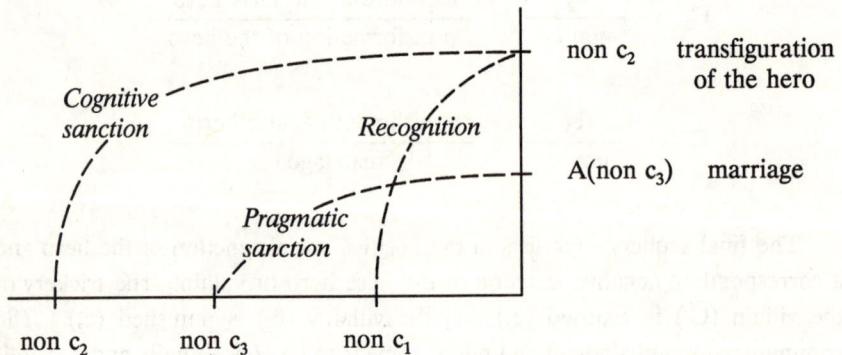

Figure 7.3

The communication units on the horizontal line represent the individual aspect of the hero's acquisition of object-values, $S \cap O$. Those same units on the vertical line represent the social evaluation, justice, and reward. The two poles between which the movement takes place is between the individual and society, the Subject-hero and a global Sender. The integration of the hero takes place through society rewarding him/her. Thus, we may call these movements *reward springs* which signal a reconciliation that is the genuine closure of a happy story.

The dual movement which obtains by the distance of the hero's acquisition of power (non c_2) and the recognition of his/her heroic self (non c_1) to the revelation of the hero or his/her transfiguration may be called a *cognitive sanction*. This is a public recognition of the hero's acts which is expressed as support to the subject-hero for his/her implicit or explicit claims concerning his/her role-identity. The support is a set of reactions and performances by others, the expressive implications of which tend to confirm his/her detailed and imaginative view of himself/herself as an occupant of a position. *Role* is thus a social object determined jointly through the interaction of performer and audience.

The movement which obtains by the distance between the hero's liquidation of lack or the major "heroic" deed (non c_3) to marriage is first and foremost a *pragmatic sanction* although it necessarily presupposes a cognitive sanction. There is a direct link between the heroic deed and the pragmatic sanction and this link is that of an exchange. The pragmatic sanction is the ultimate reward since it consists of a solid gain in occupying the higher social position and winning the opportunity-structure to fulfill oneself in the social nexus. The marriage can be thought of as the perfect union and harmony between the individual and his/her community. The hero not only marries the princess but ascends the throne and the former union might well be totally insignificant without the latter gain in social status and power; that is, the situational power to fulfill oneself. This pragmatic sanction involves the Sender's "promotion" of the Subject-hero which is rooted in the exercise of his/her benevolent power. The Sender or society not only acknowledges the heroic deed of the hero but also rewards him/her politically. And this reward may be seen as the only acknowledgement that counts or means anything because it actively supports the hero in his/her deeds and it does so by welcoming similar future deeds. By contrast, a cognitive sanction without the pragmatic one does not welcome nor integrate the hero socially. A certain distance and rift is maintained between the individual and society because the individual values are asserted to belong uniquely to the individual or to be idiosyncratic and not to be valued on a larger social scale. The pragmatic sanction falls in the category of the contract, A, which is a union whereas the cognitive sanction by itself falls in an intermediate position between $\bar{A}$, breach or conflict, and A, union, but closer to $\bar{A}$.

2c   Progression of the hero's role-identities and his/her individuation

The Self and identity arise in interaction and change or remain stable due to interaction. The concrete actions or performances which the folktale hero enacts in his/her encounters with others are represented in such a way as to suggest a sequence of growth in his/her individual and social role-identities. In particular, the situational Self in the consequence of the Test where the hero gains an object-value also means a new role-identity acquired by the Subject-hero in the exchange with the Sender or in competition with the villain. Defining Self, like all the other actions the Subject takes, is carried out in interaction with others and identity becomes the *social location* of where one "is situated" in relation to others, what one announces actionally to others that one is and others bestow on you.

In the initial sequence of the tale, $\bar{A} + \bar{C}$, the Subject-protagonist undergoes "a redundant series of privations" which make him appear as "a simpleton, a kind of village idiot" whose heroic nature is hidden (Greimas, 1966:200,201). The evolution of the ideal and heroic Self begins with the individual experiencing conflict with others, a time of crisis, trouble, and harm inflicted by an antagonist and an anti-Sender. In psychological novels and stories of the creative process, in a religious experience, or any profound transformation and regeneration of the Self, the conflict is experienced as a fracture in consciousness, a personal chaos and disorder, an alienation from self and a ferment of 'storm and stress.' The conflict may be characterized as an inner division resulting from a discrepancy between what is and what might be, between our actual, real Self and our ideal Self. The folktale, of course, does not dwell on serious psychological issues but it does indicate the growth change in an actional pathway. One well-known and memorable children's adventure story, *Pinocchio*, which provided Genot the topic for a lengthy structural analysis shows the transformation of a wooden puppet (actual self) to a little boy (real self). In the global summary Genot says that "Pinocchio, the hero, appears as the Subject of the global sequence, but also as the Object of it. This double function is born from the fact that there is in reality two complementary actions entering in a hypotactical relation: the transformation of the puppet into a little boy (main action), the adventures of the hero" (Genot, 1970:89). The simplest tales do indeed represent a transformation of the main character but without the welling-up of pain, baffled struggle, and all the psychological processes involved in the breaking of the Self and its recreation. In *Pinocchio* one aspect of the conflict is suggested by the meaningful and visual metaphor of a wooden and stiff self changing to a live self, acting with ease. The acquisition of the ideal role-identity, that of becoming a little boy, is the main object of Pinocchio. Narrativity, in general, seems to exact a protagonist that is both the Subject and Object of the story.

In the Qualifying Test, the overall process is the acquisition of competence, know-how, and power, and the new role-identity is that of the Qualified or Competent Self. Similar but non-fantastic processes of personal creativity encompassed by competence include inner growth, incubation, and self-surrender. Actualizing one's possibilities, one's competence, always involves negative as well as positive aspects. It always involves destroying the status quo, destroying old patterns within oneself and creating new and original ways of doing as well as something new in human relations. Thus, every experience of creativity or competence has its potentiality of aggression or denial toward established patterns within one's self or other persons in one's environment.

The Main Test and the Quest deal with the acquisition of the object of desire and the heroic deed. The struggle between two equal competitors, the hero and the villain, and the hero's victory enact and make real the heroic self which is also the idealized and masterful self. In psychological narratives the struggle between Subject and anti-Subject can take place in one actor. The picture of the mental state at the turning point is as if two lives, the present, imperfect, aspiring one and the wished-for righteous one which is to blossom out, were pressed together in intense opposition, and were both struggling for possession of consciousness. Paralleling the hero's victory is the release of illumination, a glimpse of a new self-image, or the blazing light of a new vision, all of which transcend old ways of thinking and being. In this stage, the victory is the birth of new powers, the individual transformation enabling one to tap one's own highest center of energy, on the basis of an ideal social self which takes center stage.

The heroic deed and heroic self are not readily acknowledged nor accepted by society. Following the Main Test and before the Glorifying Test takes place, there is a sequence of functions which Larivaille calls "confirmation or salvation of the hero" (1974:376). They consist of function 21, Pursuit of the Hero; 22, Rescue of the Hero; and 23, Unrecognized Arrival. The aggression against the hero indicates the possibility of losing the object of quest and the heroic role-identity to an opponent who attempts to steal it or wrench it from the hero.

The hero is challenged to protect the ownership of his/her object-value by fighting his/her situational opposition, the opponent or traitor, strongly and with intensity, after his/her victory which is rejected and not forgiven by the bad sportsmanship of the opponent. Analogous to the pursuit, we may speak of a potential relapse or doubt in a psychological narrative in which the Subject is torn between contending forces of success and failure. The unrecognized arrival of the hero indicates that he is no longer the simpleton and village idiot and that his actual heroic self meets with dismay and disbelief. The would-be hero has changed and the fact that s/he is *now* a hero surprises if only because s/he was not before.

In the Glorifying Test and the terminal series of communication, C + A, the new self-image and heroic role-identity are expressed and tested in a social environment. The successful presentation of the idealized self is essentially the object sought in an existential quest or any story of conversion which brings its central figure to 'salvation' or wholeness. It will communicate the achievement of a new, exalted identity and improved social functioning. On the receiving end, the social reward of the hero allows him/her to interact more positively with a wider range of people or social situations. The "village idiot" who becomes the hero or the imperfect self who becomes the idealized self is like the slave who has liberated himself/herself and become the "citizen," that is, both master and slave, recognized as master by the right to own the property of his/her work and to assert his/her freedom and autonomy. The aim to become a citizen combines the principle of equality (excellence and mastery in and through the work or performance) with the principle of equivalence (exchange for rewards, justice, and fulfillment). The folktale hero gets both the extrinsic rewards via the justice of equivalence (the pragmatic sanction) and the status and role-support via the justice of equality (the cognitive sanction). The fusion of the two types of justice into the *justice of equity* blends varying proportions of mastery and servitude, of equality and equivalence. The passage to equity makes the hero-citizen both equal and equivalent not only judicially, "by the law," but also politically and "socially," that is, in fact. The normal evolution of the character, the bursting of the self into a larger life of new powers and freedom, dying to the "old" person and rising to the "new," all solicit a conscious hold on one's ideals and a willful claim to back one of our nascent selves as our "real" self. The self-image, the new way of seeing ourselves in our own world, which provides a foundation for building a new reality seems to come from within the self and radiate outwards through the striving of a fragile and vulnerable aim of self-transformation. In the folktale sequence and in the terminal series which is the condition of coming into harmonious relationship with the social order, the hero does not manifest a self-awareness or an illumination from within. The new, exalted self does not become the point of reference for the larger world of experience inasmuch as it is recognized only from the outside, as if through a foil and the glance of the other—the Test of the other. There is, in other words, something automatic, effortless, and external in the rapid success of the transformation of the non-hero to the hero which is unlike the normal evolution of character. In any case, the final role-identity of the hero is the recognized hero or idealized self and the integrated hero or citizen.

It is the norm of reciprocity, the justice of equality, and the reward springs of the tale which allow the narrative to be, in P. Madsen's succinct and fine wording "a kind of individuation-tale, a narrative about the [subject's] growing acquisition of 'self' and growth into his social role, [...] a model for integrated or integrating individuation" (1971:199).

VIII
Global Interpretation of the Tale

The pairing of the second and third functions in the Proppian schema

interdiction vs. violation

articulate the two contrary semes of a larger meaning-unit which is the negative transformation of the contract, $\bar{A}$:

$$\frac{\text{interdiction}}{\text{violation}} = \text{breach of contract} = \bar{A}$$

whereas the positive form is

$$\frac{\text{proposal}}{\text{acceptance}} = \text{establishment of contract} = A$$

As we have seen, the proposal or Greimas' "injunction" are but two modal operators of persuasion or manipulation. The folktale begins with a breach of contract and ends with the establishment of a contract in the form of marriage.

The category of communication C was designated to stand for three pairs of functions and similarly for $\bar{C}$. Due to their iteration and despite the notable variations in the content of the object the events of communication lend themselves to a much greater reduction and generalization than the unit of contract.

The paradigmatic and achronic reduction and interpretation of the Proppian sequence of functions has yielded two functional categories:

A vs. $\bar{A}$ establishment of contract vs. breach of contract
C vs. $\bar{C}$ positive communication vs. negative communication
(integration vs. alienation).

The two outer sequences of the tale, initial and final, are made up of two functional categories, in its positive or negative form

Initial sequence   Final sequence
$$\bar{A} + \bar{C}$$ $$C + A$$

We see that the two sequences show similarities and differences:

a) they are similar because they are made up of the same semantic categories A and C;

b) they are different because the first sequence is a transformation of the second and the order of succession in the second is inverse relative to the first;

c) neither sequence represents stative verbs or static situations and only the final sequence shows an "equilibrium" that is, however, enacted through dynamic, evental situations.

The narrative as a sequential whole is a process of change which overlaps with the reversal of a situation. The changes that take place in the narrative are determined by some antithesis between opposing or contrasted situations and these are $\bar{A} + \bar{C}$ at one end and $C + A$ at the other end. The change is not only in the contrast of two polar situations but also in the inverse *order* in which the events occur. So that the simplest tale gives us two polar situations which cannot be subsumed under the simplest antithesis, i.e. from $\bar{A}$ to A, or from $\bar{C}$ to C, even when it includes these changes. The two poles between which the narrative change takes place are not the isolated relations but bundles of such relations.

The four terms which make up the two sequences can be related and formulated in two different ways which leads to two different global definitions of the tale and gives rise to two possible interpretations of the tale. The first formulation consists in an achronic grasp of the terms in the form of categories and in the establishment of a *correlation* between the categories:

$$\frac{\bar{A}}{A} \sim \frac{\bar{C}}{C}$$

The second formulation takes into account the syntagmatic and diachronic order of the terms and defines the connection to be *implications*:

$$(\bar{A} > \bar{C}) \sim (C > A)$$

Because the contract is broken, alienation ensues; *because* positive values are reacquired, contract or social order is re-established. This is an approximate and rough meaning which we shall refine in a moment.

1. The achronic and paradigmatic structure of the tale

The paradigmatic structure of the tale is the final apprehension of the narrative whole in a single sweep. It is obvious that every story, in order to be grasped as a coherent whole, must first be capable of being seized in its simultaneity, as a whole that is relatively simple and which, therefore, provides a simple semantic structure: a relation of relations. The literary text can be brought to appearance only in a multiplicity of successive aspects but this succession is absorbed by a paradigmatic ordering which links similarities and differences among those elements that may appear syntagmatically at remote intervals. To use L. Mink's pictorial imagery:

> Experiences come to us *seriatim* in a stream of transience and yet must be capable of being held together in a single image of the manifold of events in order to be aware of transience at all. [...] To comprehend temporal succession means to think of it in both directions at once—forward and backward—and then time is no longer the river which bears us along but the river in aerial view, upstream and downstream, seen in a single survey (1970:547, 554-5).

The "aerial view" of the narrative can be seen only in condensed form, losing the details while gaining the purely schematic structure and limiting the point of view to the vantage point (we have) at the end of the work. The paradigmatic reduction of the Proppian functions to the functional categories, A vs. $\bar{A}$ and C vs. $\bar{C}$, does, in fact, presuppose the entire sequence of the Proppian schema, and was carried out only in this internally closed whole. Thus, a paradigmatic interpretation and analysis of the narrative assumes at least one reading from beginning to end and views the text in an aerial survey.

The correlation established through the achronic grasp of the tale allows the tale to be understood as a simple semantic structure which can be represented by the elementary structure of meaning, that is, the semiotic square (see figure 8.1). This basic model accounts for the simplest representation of the achronic meaning of the tale in its totality. The *correlation* is the relation between the two *schemas* ($\bar{A}$ vs. A and $\bar{C}$ vs. C) and it is precisely this correlation which Greimas calls *semiosis* (1970:140). By setting the four-term homology in this form, we obtain the complete network of relations among the terms that are now mutually interdefined.[5]

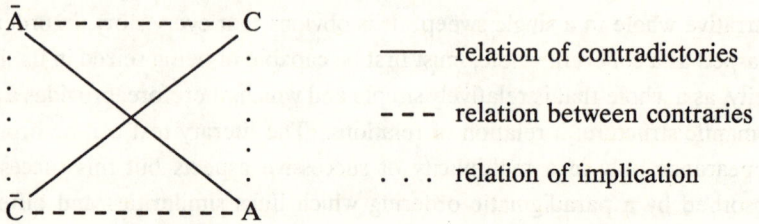

Ā - - - - - - - - - - C
  \   /
   \   /   —— relation of contradictories
    \   /
     \   /   - - - relation between contraries
      \   /
       \   /   . . . relation of implication
C̄ - - - - - - - - - - A

Figure 8.1

The correlation itself can be verbalized by the conjunction *as* or *like* and establishes the *conjunctive* relation between the terms of the homology. For the two schemas to be seized together, they must have something in common, i.e. they must be *like* each other. This is the relation of resemblance, identity, or conjunction. For the two schemas to be distinguished they must in some way be different, i.e. they must be *unlike* each other. This is the relation of non-identity, difference, position, or disjunction. We see that a semantic relation is simultaneously a conjunction and a disjunction. The achronic structure of the tale establishes a similarity between two changes, two types of disjunction, the disjunction of contradictories, the one from Ā to A and the one from C̄ to C. The breach of contract corresponds to the re-establishment of the contract like alienation and negative communication correspond to reintegration and positive communication.

The paradigmatic formulation of the tale correlates two kinds of events which belong to two different domains:

---

[5]Minor correction. The homology Ā : A :: C̄ : C does not map correctly on the square, with the first term of the second schema in its formal position at the upper right hand corner. Ā and C̄ are not contraries; neither are C and A. Ā does not imply C and C̄ does not imply A. Since we know that Ā implies C̄ and C implies A, the correction is a simple matter of permuting the positions of C and C̄. Of course, contraries and contradictories do not have order: they are said to be commutative, C̄ * C = C * C̄. But this one positional switch within the square as given above in the text, corrects four relations depicted on the four sides and restores internal consistency and well-formedness. The correct form of the homology should then be Ā : A :: C : C̄.

1. The *social* domain: the area of mutual agreement or consensus, the element of promise, trust and morality, the contractual ordering of associations and the attendant cooperation, the normative and legal code of conduct regulating interaction.

2. The *individual* or *interindividual* domain: the acquisition and ownership of personal value-objects thanks to social exchange and the acceptance by society of these value-objects as objects of right which belong to the individual.

The correlation between the two domains says that the fate of the individual is tied to that of society and inversely. The polarity of the two domains is defined only at a theoretical level and manifests itself, on a practical level, in situations of serious conflict and disagreement. More often, a dialectical interpenetration characterizes the relation of the individual and society.

Let us now consider the two changes of the correlation more closely. We have already covered the second change of the proportion, $\bar{C}$ to C, as the circulation of the object-value traced by the dramatic springs and the reward springs of the tale. The remaining analysis will consist of the first change in the proportion, $\bar{A}$ to A.

Greimas sees a positive meaning in the broken contract, $\bar{A}$, which is the affirmation of individual freedom. Since the opposition A vs. $\bar{A}$ is between an established contract and its breach, the breach of contract deprives the individual of the possibility of action but this deprivation is social such that we may assert

$$\frac{A}{\bar{A}} = \frac{\text{team action}}{\text{individual action}}$$

to be another acceptable meaning of the contract and its breach. In A the freedom to act is social whereas in $\bar{A}$ the freedom is individual and in conflict with society or the Sender. Broadly speaking, in A the freedom is under law (contract and norm) and in $\bar{A}$ the freedom is from law (contract and norm). When there is no mutual agreement nor free mutual consent between the Sender and Subject-Receiver, there is no positive communication. So $\bar{A}$ may mean failure to reach agreement or inability of the Subject-Receiver to stop negative manipulation of the Sender as higher-up, and it is negative in the sense of being irresponsible or abusive to the Subject-Receiver.

In the Proppian schema, the passage from $\bar{A}$, the violation of the prohibition, to the other end of the tale, A, marriage, takes place through three Tests which can be abbreviated as $A \Longrightarrow C$. Let us abbreviate the full narrative schema as follows:

$\bar{A} \Longrightarrow \bar{C}$ initial alienation sequence

$3(A \Longrightarrow C)$ the 3 Tests

$\quad\quad C$ the consequence of the Tests and acquisition of the object-value

$\quad C \Longrightarrow A$ final reintegration sequence

In other words, the passage from $\bar{A}$ to A takes place through three contracts which we shall label A_1, A_2, A_3 and hence the complete contractual sequence is this one

$\bar{A}$, A_1, A_2, A_3, A.

Greimas also speaks of A as social order and of $\bar{A}$ as break-up of the social order. In order to remedy any breach in communication or contract *three* Senders have to interact positively with the hero. Three Senders agree to help and deliver the rewards O_2, O_3, and O_1 before there is *harmony* between the hero and society, or (and this is the same) before the social contract gets re-established and the political and "social order" is restored. It is as if the hero rebels against some law or norm of society and three Senders hear him/her out, agree to help, deliver the goods and then, with the hero ascending social space, there is *union* again between the individual and society.

The most remarkable feature in the contractual sequence of the folktale is the way it discloses the disruptive and dehumanizing effect of a breach of trust or contract. The harm in human interaction is so enormous that it takes three *kept* promises by one Sender or another before re-establishing the trust and security of interaction and ultimately before reintegration and two-way communication can take place. The negative power to harm the promisee through a breach of promise is as great as the power of stabilization inherent in the faculty of making mutual promises. "The great variety of contract theories since the Romans," says H. Arendt, "attests to the fact that the power of making promises has occupied the center of political thought over the centuries" (1958:244). We may also trace it to the folktale in a pattern beginning with a breach of contract which is amazingly similar to the biblical story of the Fall, where an original prohibition by God was violated by Adam and Eve. At any rate, the events of the contractual sequence in the folktale appear to function along these political, diplomatic, and ultimately moral, lines of interaction:

$\bar{A}$: disagreement with Sr_1, breach of contract;

A_1 : conciliatory gesture by Sr_2 who calls on the hero to confront the villain;

A_2 : conciliatory gesture by Sr_3: contract and exchange;

A_3 : conciliatory gesture by Sr_4: contract and exchange;

A : union and harmony with the final Sr_5; the social order is perceived as a mutual agreement between the individual or hero and society.

Crucial is the fact that the hero does not acquire the object-value alone. Both sides contribute and the hero is never, so to speak, free. Thus, in the Proppian schema $\bar{A}$ does not mean freedom of the individual; it means disagreement, conflict, breach of trust and it clamors for a social remedy which the three Test Senders provide. It is therefore somewhat misleading to say, as Greimas does, that "reintegration of values has to be paid for by giving up liberty" or what we symbolized above as $C \implies A$ (1966:210). We may conclude, that is, we are authorized to conclude the contrary assertion since the final reintegration takes place only after three positive exchanges with a Sender or a graduating scale of mutual trust, cooperation, and integration. The hero never acted on his/her individual freedom, always benefiting from team action; he/she did not go from $\bar{A}$ to A in a straight line, on his/her own individual liberty.

2. The diachronic and syntagmatic structure of the tale

The second interpretation of the narrative is on the syntagmatic order which takes into account the temporal arrangement of the terms and the relation of implication between them: $(\bar{A} > \bar{C}) \sim (C > A)$. The two implications form the deixes on the square (see figure 8.2); $\bar{A} > \bar{C}$ defines the negative and dysphoric deixis which makes up the initial situation and $C > A$ defines the positive and euphoric deixis which makes up the final situation. We define the sign $>$ to mean both temporal succession and implication. Thus $\bar{A} > \bar{C}$ means: $\bar{A}$ is followed by $\bar{C}$ and is implied by it. Whereas its logical expression would be $\bar{C} \implies \bar{A}$ ($\bar{C}$ implies $\bar{A}$). We can establish a relation between the syntagmatic structure and the paradigmatic structure only by introducing "historicity" and "historical causation," that is, by transforming the correlation into a double

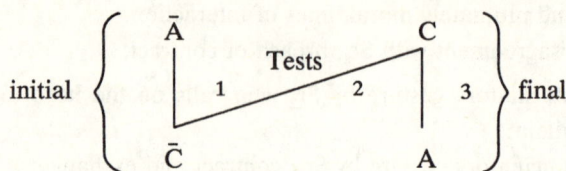

Figure 8.2

relation of implications, which form the two deixes. We read the diachronic order as a "then" and "because" relation: because $\bar{A}$, $\bar{C}$ happens; and then, because C, A happens.

However, we know that the object-value O, as a consequence of the Test, changes $\bar{C}$ to C. Consequently, between the two deixes is nested the formula defining the Test

$$\frac{\bar{A}}{\bar{C}} \ldots (\, A + F > \text{non c} \,) \ldots \frac{C}{A}$$

Since $C = S_1 \cap O \cup S_2$ where S_1 is the Subject-hero and S_2 the villain antagonist, the above is identical to

$$\frac{\bar{A}}{S_1 \cup O} \ldots (\, A + F \,) > \text{non c} \ldots \frac{S_1 \cap O}{A}$$

The role of the Test is to take in charge a given structure of contents and transform it into its opposite by negating the negative terms on which it operates, leading to an assertion. The Test itself defines the minimal tale in its diachronic order. The Test is that intervening dynamic situation and crucial 'middle' which accounts for the transformation of initial to final situation. Furthermore, since desire and action can be related only to an agent or anthropomorphic being, the protagonist appears as the efficient agent thanks to whom the reversal of the situation takes place; in other words, the protagonist is the personalized mediator between the situation before and the situation after.

It is one of the greatest values of the syntagmatic summary formula that the unity which it establishes as the organization of successive events *does* stand in a clearly definable relationship to the kind of unity that is set up by human action itself. It assigns a central place to the role of the protagonist's action and shows what the relationship of the actantial situation—the underlying interactional conditions—was to the act itself. Although it avoids reference to the protagonist's purpose or intention in taking the action s/he did it reintroduces the very notion of purposiveness by describing the change as an *action* and *interaction*. It does not "pass through" voluntary human actions in search of an explanation of events which is an *alternative* to the teleological type of explanation that gives focal attention to them.

In this alternative explanation of narrative involving subsumption under general laws, the role of action evaporates or disintegrates. As the philosopher of history, F. Olafson, pointed out "in this analysis we find references to states of affairs that impinge upon human beings, and to dispositions in those human beings which are actualized in what happens to them. [...] No one *does* anything at all in [these] versions. [...] The subject is simply the logical container of its initial and terminal states, and, of course, of its own dispositions as well. It is never active in the sense of doing something for some purpose" (1970:268-9). But even other kinds of explanation avoid describing narrative change as an action. While reviewing and summarily analyzing the actantial model, R. Scholes perceived the Subject-hero as a patient who undergoes someone else's action, including the position he/she contracts with the Sender, and deduces that the hero "in a very real sense is not an actant at all" and "actantial deficiency" is characteristic of the Subject (1974:110). The comment is too glib to merit attention but together with other non-intentional ways of schematizing events, point to an abhorrence of the central role of action and agency and of a purposeful or teleological explanation of a sequence of events.

In the syntagmatic structure of the tale the organization of events as temporal wholes is assimilated and integrated to the "social behavior" of anthropomorphic beings linked through interactional patterns. This fusion has never been shown in any other narrative theory as clearly, or even at all. The basic narrative statement defined as a network of roles—Event ($role_1$, $role_2$, ...)—is not filtered out nor abstracted away by the global generalization of the tale and semantic operations of universalization. The one 'through action' spanning S $\cup$ O to S $\cap$ O is the change which the protagonist produces, in his or her own action through the reversal of the situation. What happens is made to happen by the protagonist and it is his/her actions that keep "moving" the narrative along the course it takes.

3. Colligation: narrativity, human agency, and authority

One of the ways to integrate the account of the two global interpretations of the tale is to "colligate" them judiciously in a general description of narrativity nd the logic of explanation and representation used to show that certain events display the formal coherency of a story. As a contrast and counterpart to the folktale schema which achieves full narrativity, we shall also use the brief and magnificent example of an "imperfect" history or story which H. White gives in his article on "the Value of Narrativity" where he considers non-narrative and imperfect forms of history to shed light on problems of narration. From our perspective, the most illuminating aspect of the text which White selects, a passage from the *Annals of Saint Gall* during the period of 709-734 A.D., is the extreme brevity of the entries which are comparable to the Proppian functions or to the short definition which follows each function in the *Morphology*. The entries of the annals and the Proppian functions are either one or two-word events or a kernel sentence like our simple narrative statement. The segment is radical and perhaps therein lies "the theoretically most interesting" feature to his author and to us because, as he says, "there is no necessary connection between one event and another" among the 11 entries of this 24-year period (H. White, 1980:7):

709.	*Hard winter. Duke Gottfried died.*
710.	*Hard year and deficient in crops.*
711.	
712.	*Flood everywhere.*
713.	
714.	*Pippin, Mayor of the Palace, died.*
715.	716. 717.
718.	*Charles devastated the Saxon with great destruction.*
719.	
720.	*Charles fought against the Saxons.*
721.	*Theudo drove the Saracens out of Aquitaine.*
722.	*Great crops.*
723.	
724.	
725.	*Saracens came for the first time.*

726.
727.
728.
729.
730.
731.   *Blessed Bede, the presbyter, died.*
732.   *Charles fought against the Saracens at Poitiers on Saturday.*
733.
734.

The list of events in the annals is recorded in a chronological sequence but lacks completely that structure or order of meaning which is *other* than that of a mere sequence and this *other* is the narrative component attained by the folktale. It possesses none of the attributes that we normally attribute to a story; no central subject or protagonist *about which* a story could be told and the absence of which undercuts the impulse to work up the discourse into the form of a narrative; secondly, the events which make up the temporal progression are not organized to form a continuous, successive or unified sequence of change in such a way as to mark the beginning, the middle, and the end of a coherent whole; thirdly, there is no reversal and no recognition; fourthly, there is no identifiable narrative voice.

The narrative, like the folktale and the folktale schema, but unlike the annals, gives us two terminal situations that both involve some character, the Subject or protagonist, which in some sense remains the same throughout the acquisition or loss of some goal-object and object of desire. The narratologist has to explain what this change consists of and why it happened. But the selection of this intervening dynamic situation is possible only through the application of general laws or quasi-laws, regularities or recurrences, and limited generalizations. One reason why we go on reading a narrative is to see what happens next but the more captivating reason is to see how one thing leads to another or *why things happen*. For we aim at understanding the pattern of causality and the pattern of relationships and since we never think we understand something until we can give an account of its *how and why*, it is clear that the general concepts must look into the how and why of narrative change. The mere fact that a narrative is constructed from the verbal representation of events or dynamic situations shows that it involves change. Any decision one makes about what is to constitute the 'crucial middle' must be selected by asking whether there is a middle or what the middle is, for the middle is precisely the how and why we seek in all our enquiries. In the folktale schema the change to account for is the how and why of $\bar{A} + \bar{C}$ to $C + A$ and this account will be syntagmatic and diachronic in nature.

The crucial middle in a narrative *cannot* be "the event H, that which happens to x and causes x to change" as the philosopher A. Danto, representing one viewpoint, claims it to be (Danto quoted by Olafson, 1970:267). That which happens to the Subject and causes the Subject to change is the initial situation $\bar{A} + \bar{C}$ and it specifies the circumstances *from which* the change arises, and C + A, *into which* it is completed. In the folktale the initial sequence of alienation, $\bar{A} + \bar{C}$, appears as an extended sequence of privations and trouble undergone by the hero. In the given segment of the annals, it would seem that *all* of the events are endless deprivations and hardships and, in fact, White brings this feature first to our attention:

> This list immediately locates us in a culture hovering on the brink of dissolution, a society of radical scarcity, a world of human groups threatened by death, devastation, flood, and famine. All of the events are extreme, and the implicit criterion for their selection is their liminal nature. Basic needs—food, security from external enemies, political and military leadership—and the threat of their failing to be provided are the subjects of concern (1980:7-8).

In the folktale the hero *does* certain things: by interacting with others, s/he gains the means and know-how to liquidate the lack and s/he earns social recognition for it. The Subject makes things happen or brings them about but in the annals things *happen to* helpless patients:

> The account deals in *qualities* rather than *agents*, figuring forth a world in which things *happen to* people rather than one in which people *do* things. It is the hardness of the winter of 709, the hardness of the year 710 and the deficiency of the crops of that year, the flooding of the waters in 712, and the imminent presence of death which recur with a frequency and regularity that are lacking in the representation of acts of human agency (White, 1980:10).

According to Danto's way of conceptualizing narrative change we would have to ask "what happened to" the Subject-hero between the initial situation $\bar{A} + \bar{C}$ and the final situation $C + A$. It is, however, transparently clear that nothing happened *to* the Subject during this transition but inversely, the Subject *made* things *happen*. That which happens happens *to the story* and it is the essence of narrative as a reversal of a situation. If it happens to the protagonist, it happens in the initial situation $\bar{A}$ + $\bar{C}$; as interim obstacles to the protagonist's superobjective; or in unhappy stories of frustration, failure, degradation, and tragic 'hamartia,' whereby the protagonist fails to attain his/her objective. Thus, asking Danto's question is likely to prove puzzling and, needless to say, inapplicable in a monotonous repetition of devastating events.

The hypothesis which White advances as to what is lacking in the events of the annals is the notion of a political-social order by which the events can be located with respect to one another and charged with ethical or moral significance. Without such a social center, Charles' struggles with the Saxons remain simply "fights" and the *why* of these interactions will remain unexplained and incomprehensible. The folktale, by contrast, does attain a fullness of narrativity, by displaying a social content through the agreement or contract, A, which also symbolizes social order and a legal system. Propp's folktale schema is marked by a breach of contract which initiates it and which indicates an inherent normative or legal conflict between the first Sender and the Subject-hero, between the Sender's proposal or injunction and the Subject's desire. All this suggests to me that White is right when he proposed that a genuine narrative originates from the conflict between the Subject's desire (S ⟶ O) and the Sender's law or social norms (A), a point that is "empirically verified" in Greimas' analysis of the folktale schema:

> The reality which lends itself to narrative representation is the *conflict* between desire, on the one hand, and the law, on the other. Where there is no rule of law, there can be neither a subject nor the kind of event which lends itself to narrative representation. This proposition could not be empirically verified or falsified, to be sure; it rather enables a presupposition or hypothesis which permits us to imagine how both "historicity" and "narrativity" are possible. It also authorizes us to consider the proposition that neither is possible without some notion of the legal subject which can serve as the agent, agency, and subject of historical narrative, in all of its manifestations (White, 1980:12).

Now, the syntagmatic summary of the tale, $(\bar{A} > \bar{C}) \sim (C > A)$, can be interpreted as a legal interaction where the Subject's role is that of the legal Subject. Because law is destroyed, the circumstancial freedom of self-realization and the coeval pursuit of an object-value and object-of-desire is possible. The Subject's freedom to actualize desirable values is a freedom from law. Because this freedom is enacted and it happens to coincide with the acquired freedom of self-perfection (to live as one ought), the hero is sanctioned (made legal) and his/her deed becomes a freedom under law.

Alerted to the close relationship between law, social order, and narrativity, we are put one in mind with White's remark that

> We cannot but be struck by the frequency with which narrativity, whether of the fictional or factual sort, presupposes the existence of a legal system against or on behalf of which the typical agents of a narrative account militate. And this raises the suspicion that narrative, in general, from the folktale to the novel, from the annals to the fully realized "history" has to do with topics of law, legality, legitimacy, or, more generally, *authority* (1980:13).

This is true because the topics of law, legality, legitimacy, and authority are at the basis of any exchange or communication.

In sum, the two global and schematic definitions of the tale tell us that the crucial middle does not consist only of the action of the protagonist. They highlight the fact that there are two changes to account for: from $S \cup O$ to $S \cap O$, the action of the protagonist and from $\bar{A}$ to A and, furthermore, that the Test causes both changes. The second change is in the political-social order since it deals with the agreements the protagonist reaches with others and which anchor his/her actions and those of his/her interactors and ultimately affect the reward he/she will receive in the exchange. The one 'through action' of the protagonist has social consequences in terms of sanction/integration or punishment/alienation of the Subject-hero and thus the closure of the story is in terms of A, or more precisely in terms of $C + A$, the cognitive and pragmatic sanctions. The final reward springs of the tale lead to a resolution which consists of the Justice of the Situation or a demand for moral meaning that White describes as a demand that "sequences be assessed as to their significance as elements of a *moral* drama" (1980:20). The moral and judicial element of the narrative ending can be shown, i.e. represented in an actantial situation as it is in the folktale schema, rather than told by the author. In either case, the moral and judicial element of a narrative closure requires knowing the moral principle in light of which the narrator and the reader may judge the resolution to be just or unjust.

4. The actantial model

To the two global interpretations of the tale must be added another derivative and achronic interpretation of the narrative as a cohesive unit. This is the
atemporal matrix of actants with which we started our investigation. It will be
appropriate to remind ourselves of an important statement by Greimas:

> A semantic micro-universe cannot be defined as universe, that is to say, as a whole
> of meaning, unless it can surge forth at any moment before us as a simple spectacle,
> as an actantial structure (1966:173).

The semiotic interpretation of the tale in terms of two schemas and the actantial
model are both achronic, paradigmatic models which grasp the story as a whole
of meaning and thus, both are tools for discovering *the simple semantic structure.*

These two models are interlocked due to the fact they are made up of the
same actants, S ⟶ O and Sr ⟶ O ⟶ R. Hence they are permutations of
the same constituents of the narrative and a transformation of the same underlying structure. The analysis of the communication component of the narrative
and the complete narrative schema enabled us to define more precisely what the
actantial model is all about. It is a simple matter of gathering the pertinent
threads of the discussion in order to understand the positional meaning of the
object as an intersection of relationships lying on two relational axes:

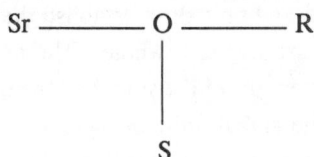

$$Sr \text{————} O \text{————} R$$
$$|$$
$$S$$

The actantial model is a "staggered" system of relations that telescopes the
passage of all actantial situations into one spatial summation. Within this
passage two situations, in particular, stand out as representing the most important meanings of the model and they both start from the decisive culminating
point, one looking backward to the initial situation and the other forward to the
final situation. (The model can, of course, be a spatial regrouping of the Test,
any one of the three Tests but especially the Main test. See chapter IV.3.)

When looking backward, the object refers uniquely to the consequence of
the Main Test which is the terminal of the main dramatic movement of the tale,
the Quest, and the peak of the narrative. Since the central section of the tale

corresponding to the Main Test is assigned to handle the topical contents of the tale, the consequence of the Main Test will manifest the contents at the most fundamental level. The object is just about the major contents which are postulated to correspond to the functional sequences and that which allows the semantic reading of the tale. Determining what or who the object of the quest is demands many interpretative and strategic choices for the textual analyst because the Object is rarely explicitly manifested. In *Miss Lonelyhearts* the goal-object is diffuse and vague but the relationship to the goal-object, aimed through action and affirmed by word, is intensely charged and invested with value: vague purposes are pursued passionately. In the Bororo myth Greimas analyzes the hero is made to do so many things in the tale that it becomes crucial for the analyst to find exactly what is the key object or superobjective of the quest. In any case, the object cannot be identified solely through desire or teleology nor as an object of communication. The only useful heuristic device is to keep in mind the entire narrative schema and locate the object-value as a consequence of the Main Test. As Calloud correctly emphasized, "in practice, the distinction among 'qualifying,' 'main,' and 'glorifying' tests is relative. We are not dealing with static and frozen states but with 'effects of relations.' What is a qualifying test at one level may be a main test at another level, etc." (1976:28). Viewing the text as a whole, the object is a specific *position* within the narrative syntagmatic chain. A structural, semantic reading of a narrative starts from this object and goes backward, forward, and on top, to establish the fundamental, general, and unique isotopy of the narrative as a whole. The net result is the approximate reconstruction of the meaning of the story and the object served as the one instrument for generating the global unity of the story.

By virtue of being the consequence of the Main Test, the object is an object of conflict and competition between protagonist and antagonist. At this point, if we think of the Sender in his/her factitive doing, as the activator and motivator for the Subject's quest, the only characters in the Proppian schema who fit the role are the dispatcher and the donor. There is no single global Sender assigned to that role although we may take the final contract to be the global, retrospective contract which was operating implicitly from the start, in its negative aspect like $\bar{O}$ to the object-of-desire. More important is the fact that the folktale begins with a serious disagreement between the Subject and the Sender and with the Subject's active denial through the violation of a prohibition. The tale begins with what we may call an anti-Sender, $\bar{S}$, and this fact is not reflected in the actantial model.

All the events which follow the consequence of the Main Test, in the latter third of the tale, indicate the other important meaning of the object and it is the sense of an object of exchange. The Subject-hero trades O to the Sender for O', as evidenced by the reward springs of the tale. The Sender here acts as Arbiter and Rewarder. The exchange simultaneously acknowledges the idealized self of the hero so that the ultimate object of any story is the achievement of the ideal role-identity and, most important of all, gaining social recognition for it. In a global and summary reading of the tale, the final reward and the social recognition of the new, exalted self would seem to be what the protagonist really wants and the object of the quest is then only the means of getting it.

Appendix:
The "Boolean Algebra" of Narrative Events[*]

BREAK-UP OF THE ORDER AND ALIENATION $\bar{A} + \bar{C}$		Hero designated	QUALIFYING TEST	MAIN TEST
$\bar{A}$ { ℓ_2 = interdiction / ℓ_3 = violation }		A_1 { ℓ_9 = mediation / ℓ_{10} = beginning counter-action }	A_2 { ℓ_{12} = first function of the donor / ℓ_{13} = hero's reaction }	A_1 { ℓ_9 / ℓ_{10} }
$\bar{C_1}$ { $\bar{c_1}$ = ℓ_4 = reconnaissance / non $\bar{c_1}$ = ℓ_5 = delivery } $\bar{C_2}$ { $\bar{c_2}$ = ℓ_6 = trickery / non $\bar{c_2}$ = ℓ_7 = complicity }			Simulated and symbolic struggle where the Sender plays the role of Opponent F_2	ℓ_{16} = struggle / ℓ_{17} = the hero is branded = c_1 / ℓ_{18} = victory $F_1 + c_1$
$\bar{C_3}$ { $\bar{c_3}$ = ℓ_8 = villainy / non $\bar{c_3}$ = $\ell_8 a$ = lack }			ℓ_{14} = receipt of magical agent non c_2	ℓ_{19} = liquidation of lack or misfortune non c_3
ℓ_1 = absentation		ℓ_{11} = departure	ℓ_{15} = transference between two kingdoms	ℓ_{20} = the hero returns
$\bar{p}$	p	$\bar{p_1}$	d non $\bar{p_1}$	non p_1

ℓ = Propp's function
A = contract (injunction vs. acceptance)
$\bar{A}$ = breach of contract
C = communication

F = struggle (confrontation vs. victory)
p = presence
d = rapid displacement

[*]Expanded and adapted from V. Propp, *Morphology of the Folktale*, and A. J. Greimas, *Sémantique structurale*, p.203. We may also refer to this table as a "functional analysis" of Propp's folktale chain of events or the "structural semantics" of a full narrative.

Hero saved	GLORIFYING TEST	REINTEGRATION AND RESTORATION OF ORDER $C + A$		
. . . .	$A_3 \begin{cases} \ell_{25} = \text{difficult task} \\ \;\; \ldots \ldots \end{cases}$			$A(\text{non } c_3) = \text{marriage}$
$\ell_{21} = \text{pursuit of the hero}$ . . . . . $\ell_{22} = \text{rescue of the hero}$ dF_1	. . . . $\ell_{26} = \text{solution of task}$ F_3	$C_2 \begin{cases} c_2 \;\; = \ell_{28} = \text{exposure of false hero} \\ \text{non } c_2 = \ell_{29} = \text{revelation of hero; transfiguration} \end{cases}$		
	$\ell_{27} = \text{recognition}$ non c_1	$C_3 \begin{cases} c_3 \;\; = \ell_{30} = \text{punishment of false hero} \\ \text{non } c_3 = \ell_{31} = \text{marriage} \end{cases}$		
$\ell_{23} = \text{unrecognized arrival}$ P_1				
$\ell_{24} = \text{a false hero presents unfounded claims}$				

Bibliography

Adler, Mortimer J. 1973. *The Idea of Freedom*, 2 vols., Reprint of the 1958-61 editions, Westport, CT, Greenwood Press.

Arendt, Hannah. 1958. *The Human Condition*, Chicago-London, The Univ. of Chicago Press.

Barthes, Roland. 1970. *S/Z*. Paris, Seuil. Engl. trans. *S/Z*, New York, Hill and Wang, 1974.

——. 1971. "Action Sequences," in: Strelka, Joseph, ed., *Patterns of Literary Style*, University Park-London, The Pennsylvania State Univ. Press, 5-14.

Biddle, Bruce J. and Edwin J. Thomas. 1966. *Role Theory: Concepts and Research*, New York-London, John Wiley & Sons.

Binkley, Robert, R. Bronaugh, and A. Marras (eds.). 1971. *Agent, Action, and Reason*, Toronto, Univ. of Toronto Press/Oxford, Basil Blackwell.

Blanché, Robert. 1966. *Structures intellectuelles*, Paris, J. Vrin.

Blau, Peter M. 1964. *Exchange and Power in Social Life*, New York-London, John Wiley & Sons.

Brand, Myles (ed.). 1970. *The Nature of Human Action*, Glenview, IL, Scott, Foresman, and Company.

Broden, Thomas F. 1990. "Paris Semiotics and the Development of A. J. Greimas: History and Structures," to appear in *The American Journal of Semiotics* (accepted Spring 1990). The page numbers currently refer to the typed manuscript.

Budniakiewicz, Therese. 1978. "Conceptual Survey of Narrative Semiotics," *Dispositio* III:7-8, 189-217.

Calloud, Jean. 1973. *L'Analyse structurale du récit*, Lyon, Profac. Engl. trans. *Structural Analysis of the Narrative*, Philadelphia, Fortress Press, 1976.

Chafe, Wallace. 1970. *Meaning and the Structure of Language*, Chicago-London, The Univ. of Chicago Press.

Cole, Peter, and Jerrold M. Sadock (eds.). 1977. *Syntax and Semantics, Volume*

8 : *Grammatical Relations*, New York-San Francisco-London, Academic Press.

Collingwood, R. G. 1940. *An Essay on Metaphysics*, Oxford, The Clarendon Press.

Coquet, Jean-Claude. 1973. "La relation sémantique sujet-objet," *Langages* 31, 80-89.

Davis, Lawrence. 1979. *Theory of Action*. Englewood Cliffs, New Jersey, Prentice-Hall.

Dewey, John. 1938. *Human Nature and Conduct*, New York, Henry Holt.

Doležel, Lubomir. 1972. "From Motifemes to Motifs," *Poetics* 4, 55-90.

——. 1976. "Narrative Semantics," *PTL* 1:1, 129-51.

Ehrman, Madeline. 1966. *The Meaning of the Modals in Present-Day American English*, The Hague-Paris, Mouton.

Fabbri, Paolo and Paul Perron. 1990. "Foreword" to Greimas, vi-xii.

Fillmore, Charles J. 1968. "The Case for Case," in: Bach, Emmon, and Robert T. Harms, eds., *Universals in Linguistic Theory*, New York-Chicago, Holt, Rinehart and Winston, 1-88.

——. 1971. "Some Problems for Case Grammar," in: C. J. Fillmore, ed., *Working Papers in Linguistics No.10*, Columbus, The Ohio State Univ., 245-65.

——. 1977. "The Case for Case Reopened," in Cole and Sadock, 59-81.

Fowler, Roger. 1977. *Linguistics and the Novel*, London, Methuen.

Fried, Charles. 1970. *An Anatomy of Values*, Cambridge, Harvard Univ. Press.

——. 1981. *Contract as Promise*, Cambridge-London, Harvard Univ. Press.

Fuller, Lon L. 1964. *The Morality of Law*, New Haven-London, Yale Univ. Press.

——. 1981. *The Principles of Social Order*, Durham, N.C., Duke Univ. Press.

Gauthier, David P. 1963. *Practical Reasoning*, London, Oxford Univ. Press.

Genot, Gérard. 1970. *Analyse structurelle de "Pinocchio"*, Florence, Italie, Quaderni della Fondazione Nazionale "Carlo Collodi".

——. 1979. *Elements of Narrativics*, Hamburg, Helmut Buske Verlag.

Greimas, Algirdas J. 1965."Le conte populaire russe. Analyse fonctionnelle," *International Journal of Slavic Linguistics and Poetics* 9, 152-75. Revised as the unnumbered chapter "A la recherche des modèles de transformation" of Greimas 1966.

——. 1966. *Sémantique structurale*, Paris, Larousse. Engl. trans. *Structural Semantics* by D. McDowell, R. Schleifer and A. Velie, Lincoln, Univ. of

Nebraska Press, 1983.

——. 1966a. "Eléments pour une théorie de l'interprétation mythique," *Communications* 8, 28-59. Rpt. in Greimas 1970. Engl. trans. "The Interpretation of Myth: Theory and Practice," in : Maranda, Pierre, and Elli Köngäs Maranda, eds., *Structural Analysis of Oral Tradition*, Philadelphia, Univ. of Pennsylvania Press, 1971, 81-121.

——. 1969. "Eléments d'une grammaire narrative," *L'Homme* 9:3. Rpt. in Greimas 1970, 157-83. Engl. trans. "Elements of a Narrative Grammar," *Diacritics*, March 1977, 23-40, and in Greimas 1987, 63-83.

——. 1970. *Du Sens*, Paris, Seuil.

——. 1971. "Narrative Grammar: Units and Levels," *Modern Language Notes* 86, 793-806.

——. 1973. "Un problème de sémiotique narrative: Les objets de valeur," *Langages* 31, 13-35. Engl. trans. "A Problem of Narrative Grammar: Objects of Value" in Greimas 1987, 84-105.

——. 1973a. "Les actants, les acteurs et les figures," in: Chabrol, Claude, ed., *Sémiotique narrative et textuelle*. Paris, Larousse, 161-76. Engl. trans. "Actants, Actors, and Figures" in Greimas 1987, 106-120.

——. 1976. "Pour une théorie des modalités," *Langages* 43, 90-107. Engl. trans. "Toward a Theory of Modalities" in Greimas 1987, 121-139.

——. 1976a. "Les acquis et les projets," in Courtés, Joseph, *Introduction à la sémiotique narrative et discursive*, Paris, Hachette, préface: 5-25.

——. 1976b. "The Cognitive Dimension of Narrative Discourse," with J. Courtés, *New Literary History* 8:3, 433-47. Rpt. in *New Literary History*, 1989, 20:3, 563-79.

——. 1976c. *Maupassant. La Sémiotique du texte: exercices pratiques*, Paris, Seuil. Engl. trans. *Maupassant. The Semiotics of Text: Practical Exercises* by P. Perron, Amsterdam-Philadelphia, J. Benjamins, 1988.

——. 1977. "Postface," in: Groupe d'Entrevernes (Jean Calloud et al.), *Signes et paraboles*, Paris, Seuil, 227-37. Engl. trans. "Postface," in: The Entrevernes Group, *Signs and Parables*, Pittsburgh, PA, The Pickwick Press, 1978, 297-310.

——. 1983. *Du Sens II*, Paris, Seuil.

——. 1987. *On Meaning: Selected Writings in Semiotic Theory*, trans. by P. Perron and F. Collins, Minneapolis, Univ. of Minnesota Press.

——. 1989. "On Meaning," *New Literary History*, 20:3, 539-50.

——. 1990. *The Social Sciences: A Semiotic View*, Minneapolis, Univ. of Minnesota Press.

Greimas, Algirdas J. and Joseph Courtés. 1979. *Sémiotique. Dictionnaire raisonné de la théorie du langage*, Paris, Hachette. Engl. trans. *Semiotics and Language: An Analytical Dictionary*, Bloomington, Indiana Univ. Press, 1982.

——. (Eds.) 1986. *Sémiotique. Dictionnaire raisonné de la théorie du langage II. Compléments, débats, propositions*, Paris, Hachette.

Greimas, Algirdas J. and Jacques Fontanille. 1991. *Sémiotique des passions. Des états de choses aux états d'âme*, Paris, Seuil.

Grimes, Joseph E. 1975. *The Thread of Discourse*, The Hague-Paris, Mouton.

Guillaume, Gustave. 1965. *Temps et verbe*, Paris, Champion.

——. 1974. *Leçons de linguistique*, Tome 4, Québec, Les Presses de l'univ. Laval.

Harré, Rom and Paul F. Secord. 1973. *The Explanation of Social Behavior*, Oxford, Basil Blackwell.

Hendricks, William O. 1973. *Essays on Semiolinguistics and Verbal Art*, The Hague-Paris, Mouton.

——. 1975. "The Work and Play Structures of Narrative," *Semiotica* 13:3, 281-328.

——. 1977. "'A Rose for Emily': A Syntagmatic Analysis," *PTL* 2:2, 257-95.

Homans, George Caspar. 1961. *Social Behavior. Its Elementary Forms*, New York-Chicago, Harcourt, Brace, & World.

Jackendoff, Ray S. 1972. *Semantic Interpretation in Generative Grammar*, Cambridge-London, The MIT Press.

Jackson, Bernard S. 1985. *Semiotics and Legal Theory*, London-Boston, Routledge & Kegan Paul.

Jameson, Fredric. 1987. "Foreword" to Greimas, vi-xxii.

Jespersen, Otto. 1963. *The Philosophy of Grammar*, London, George Allen & Unwin (First published in 1924).

Jules-Rosette, Bennetta. 1990. "Semiotics and Cultural Diversity: Entering the 1990s," *The American Journal of Semiotics* 7:1/2, 5-26.

Kenny, Anthony. 1963. *Action, Emotion, and Will*, New York, Humanities Press, London, Routledge & Kegan Paul.

——. 1975. *Will, Freedom, and Power*, New York, Harper and Row.

——. 1979. *Aristotle's Theory of the Will*, New York, Yale Univ. Press.

Knott, William C. 1977. *The Craft of Fiction*, revised ed., Reston, VA, Reston Publishing Company.

Kojève, Alexandre. 1947. *Introduction à la lecture de Hegel*, Paris, Gallimard.

The Engl. trans. by J. H. Nichols covers slightly less than half of the original work, *Introduction to the Reading of Hegel*, New York-London, Basic Books, 1969.

——. 1981. *Esquisse d'une phénoménologie du droit*, Paris, Gallimard.

Kunkel, Francis L. 1975. *Passion and the Passion*, Philadelphia, The Westminster Press.

Landowski, Eric. 1979. "Introduction," *Sémiotique des passions, Actes Sémiotiques–Bulletin* II:9, 3-8.

——. 1988. "Towards a Semiotic and Narrative Approach to Law," *International Journal for the Semiotics of Law / Revue Internationale de Sémiotique Juridique*, I:1, 79-111.

——. 1989 *La société réfléchie. Essais de socio-sémiotique*, Paris, Seuil.

Larivaille, Paul. 1974. "L'analyse (morpho)logique du récit," *Poétique* 19, 368-88.

Lévi-Strauss, Claude. 1960. "La Structure et la Forme: Réflexions sur un ouvrage de Vladimir Propp," Paris, *Cahiers de l'Institut de Science Economique Appliquée*, série M, no.7, mars, 3-36. Rpt. in Lévi-Strauss 1973, 139-73.

——. 1973. *Anthropologie structurale deux*, Paris, Plon.

Lyons, John. 1968. *Introduction to Theoretical Linguistics*, Cambridge-London-New York, Cambridge Univ. Press.

——. 1977. *Semantics*, 2 vols., Cambridge-London-New York, Cambridge Univ. Press.

Mabley, Edward. 1972. *Dramatic Construction. An Outline of Basic Principles*, Philadelphia-New York, Chilton.

McCall, George J. and J. L. Simmons. 1966. *Identities and Interactions*, New York, The Free Press.

Madsen, Peter. 1971. "Integrated Norm-Breaking. A Narratological Analysis," *Orbis Litterarum* 26:3, 185-210.

Marin, Louis. 1976. "Concerning Interpretation: A Parable of Pascal," in: Patte, Daniel, (ed.), *Semiology and Parables*, Pittsburgh, PA, The Pickwick Press, 189-220.

Martin, Wallace. 1986. *Recent Theories of Narrative*, Ithaca-London, Cornell University Press.

Meletinsky, E. et al. 1974. "Problems of the Structural Analysis of Fairy Tales," in: Maranda, P. (ed.), *Soviet Structural Folkloristics*, The Hague-Paris, Mouton, 73-139.

Mink, Louis O. 1970. "History and Fiction as Modes of Comprehension," *New Literary History* 1:3, 541-58.

Nef, Frédéric. 1979. "Case Grammar vs. Actantial Grammar," in: Petöfi, Janos, (ed.), *Text vs. Sentence*, Hamburg, Helmut Buske Verlag, vol.2, 634-53.

New Literary History. 1989. Special journal issue devoted to *Greimassian Semiotics*, 20:3, with an introduction by Paul Perron.

Nilsen, Don L. F., and Alleen Pace Nilsen. 1975. *Semantic Theory*, Rowley, MA, Newbury House Publishers, Inc.

Olafson, Frederick A. 1970. "Narrative History and the Concept of Action," *History and Theory* 9:3, 265-89.

Olrik, Axel. 1965. "Epic Laws of Narrative," in: Dundes, Alan, (ed.), *The Study of Folklore*, Englewood Cliffs, NJ, Prentice-Hall, 129-41.

Parisi, Domenico, and Francesco Antinucci. 1973. *Elementi di grammatica*, Turin, Italy, Boringhieri. Engl. trans. *Essentials of Grammar*, New York-San Francisco-London, Academic Press, 1976.

Parret, Herman. 1986. *Les Passions. Essai sur la mise en discours de la subjectivité*, Bruxelles, P. Mardaga.

———. 1989. "Introduction," *Paris School Semiotics*, vol. 1, vii-xxvi, ed. by P. Perron and F. Collins.

Parsons, Talcott, and Edward Shils (eds.). 1962. *Toward a General Theory of Action*, Cambridge, Harvard Univ. Press (Fifth printing, c. 1951).

Pavel, Thomas. 1986. "L'Avenir de la sémio-linguistique: à propos d'une polémique récente," *Canadian Journal of Comparative Literature*, 13:4, Dec., 618-35.

———. 1988. "Formalisms in Narrative Semiotics," *Poetics Today* 9:3, 593-606

Perron, Paul. 1987. "Introduction" to Greimas, xxiv-xiv.

———. 1989. "Introduction," *New Literary History* 20:3, 523-38

Perron, Paul, and Frank Collins (eds.). 1989. *Paris School Semiotics*, 2 vols., Amsterdam-Philadelphia, John Benjamins.

Prince, Gerald. 1973. *A Grammar of Stories*, The Hague-Paris, Mouton.

Propp, Vladimir. 1968. *Morphology of the Folktale*, Austin-London, Univ. of Texas Press, second ed.

Reid, Randall. 1967. *The Fiction of Nathanael West. No Redeemer, No Promised Land*, Chicago-London, Univ. of Chicago Press.

Sandmann, Manfred. 1979. *Subject and Predicate. A Contribution to the Theory of Syntax*, second, rev. and enl. ed., Heidelberg, Carl Winter.

Schank, Roger C., and Kenneth M. Colby (eds.). 1973. *Computer Models of Thought and Language*, San Fransisco, W. H. Freeman.

Schleifer, Ronald. 1987. *A. J. Greimas and the Nature of Meaning: Linguistics, Semiotics and Discourse Theory*, Lincoln, University of Nebraska Press.

Scholes, Robert. 1974. *Structuralism in Literature*, New Haven-London, Yale University Press.

——. 1982. *Semiotics and Interpretation*, New Haven-London, Yale University Press.

Segre, Cesare. 1989. "The Style of Greimas and Its Transformations," *New Literary History* 20:3, 679-92

Souriau, Etienne. 1950. *Les Deux cent mille situations dramatiques*, Paris, Flammarion.

Stanislavski, Constantin. 1961. *Creating a Role*, New York, Theatre Arts Books.

Stoljar, Samuel. 1980. *Moral and Legal Reasoning*, New York, Barnes & Noble.

Tarde, Gabriel. 1897. *L'Opposition universelle. Essai d'une théorie des contraires*, Paris, Félix Alcan (451 pp.)

——. 1898. *La Logique sociale*, Paris, Félix Alcan (466 pp.)

——. 1973. *Ecrits de psychologie sociale*, choisis et présentés par A. M. Rocheblave-Spenlé et J. Milet, Toulouse, Privat.

Tesnière, Lucien. 1965. *Eléments de syntaxe structurale*, Paris, Klincksieck (first published in 1959).

Thalberg, Irving. 1972. *Enigmas of Agency*, New York, Humanities Press.

Thérien, Gilles. 1987. "Semiotic Studies at the Université du Québec à Montréal," *The Semiotic Web 1986*, ed. by T. Sebeok and J. Umiker-Sebeok, Berlin-New York-Amsterdam, Mouton de Gruyter, 619-21

——. 1990. "Sémiotique et études littéraires," *RS/SI (Recherches Sémiotiques/ Semiotic Inquiry)* 10:1-2-3, 9-26.

Tomachevski, Boris. 1965. "Thématique," in: Todorov, Tzvetan, (ed.) *Théorie de la littérature*, Paris, Seuil, 263-307. Engl. trans. "Thematics," in: Lemon, Lee T. and Marion J. Reis, *Russian Formalist Criticism: Four Essays*, Lincoln, Univ. of Nebraska Press, 1965, 61-95.

Von Wright, Georg H. 1963. *Norm and Action*, New York, Humanities Press.

——. 1971. *Explanation and Understanding*, Ithaca, NY, Cornell Univ. Press.

West, Nathanael. 1962. *Miss Lonelyhearts & The Day of the Locust*, New York,

New Directions (first published in 1933).

White, Alan R. (ed.). 1968. *The Philosophy of Action*, London, Oxford Univ. Press.

———. 1975. *Modal Thinking*, Ithaca, NY, Cornell Univ. Press.

White, Hayden. 1980. "The Value of Narrativity," in: Mitchell, W. J. T., (ed.), *On Narrative*. Chicago-London, The Univ. of Chicago Press, 1980, 1981, 1-23. (Rpt. of *Critical Inquiry* 7:1 (Autumn 1980) and 7:4 (Summer 1981)).

Withalm, Gloria. 1987. "The International Association for Semiotic Studies: A View of its Past, Present, and Future," *The Semiotic Web 1986*, ed. by T. Sebeok and J. Umiker-Sebeok, Berlin-New York-Amsterdam, Mouton de Gruyter, 627-70.

In the series SEMIOTIC CROSSROADS (SC) the following titles have been published and will be published during 1993:

1. GREIMAS, Algirdas Julien: *Maupassant. The Semiotics of Text: Practical Exercises*. Amsterdam/Philadelphia, 1988.
2. PERRON, Paul and Frank COLLINS (eds): *Paris School Semiotics: Theory*. Amsterdam/Philadelphia, 1989.
3. PERRON, Paul and Frank COLLINS (eds): *Paris School Semiotics: Practice*. Amsterdam/Philadelphia, 1989.
4. ARRIVÉ, Michel: *Linguistics and Psychoanalysis*. Amsterdam/Philadelphia, 1992.
5. BUDNIAKIEWICZ, Therese: *Fundamentals of Story Logic. Introduction to Greimassian Semiotics*. Amsterdam/Philadelphia, 1992.
6. PARRET, Herman (ed.): *Peirce and Value Theory: On Peircean Ethics and Aesthetics*. Amsterdam/Philadelphia, n.y.p.